'The recent pandemic and resultant lockdown h₂ publications in the Leadership Consultancy and C the contributions are from professionals with ne hands. This book is different! It is not one to pick up and read from cover to cover. Instead it is a Cornucopia of ideas and skills that encourages the reader to reflect on their personal style and practice and for that to be done in the widest peripheral context as presented by the contributors to this excellent volume.'

Anton Obholzer, former Chief Executive, Tavistock Clinic, London

'We can imagine the leader-follower relationship as a two-way street. The conscious and unconscious fears and wishes of followers and the nature of the leader's personality organization may cause traffic jams and shared problems. In this book authors from different academic backgrounds such as psychoanalysis, history and anthropology examine these issues and the differences between a male and a female leader. Thinking of worldwide societal and political divisions I consider this book very important and timely.'

Vamık D. Volkan, MD, Emeritus Professor of Psychiatry, University of Virginia and the author of Blind Trust: Large Groups and Their Leaders in Times of Crises and Terror

'This is an exciting exploration of different styles and motivations of leadership, some more effective than others, and the psychodynamics of Presidential leaders, including Donald Trump and Joseph Biden. This volume is essential for every modern historian and biographer.'

Peter Loewenberg, Professor of History, Emeritus, UCLA; New Center for Psychoanalysis, Los Angeles

'What makes for a great leader—or a dangerous one? What's common among Gandhi, Churchill, Hitler and Donald Trump? This book provides the psychoanalytic insights that helps explain these critical differences. How has leadership changed from prehistoric times to the present? This book provides deep insights into the clinical underpinnings of leadership and helps explain why the leaders we need for today are different from those in the past.'

Charles O'Reilly, Frank E. Buck Professor of Management at the Graduate School of Business at Stanford University, California

'There is widespread acknowledgment that new forms of leadership and change are essential for business and society today. Combining their knowledge from practice and research with historical insight, the practitioners and scholars in Leadership, Psychoanalysis, and Society highlight lessons from diverse forms of leadership for new and varied contexts. This is required reading in the era of stakeholder capitalism.'

Sherri Douville, CEO, Medigram and Editor of Mobile Medicine: Overcoming People, Culture, & Governance

'I was delighted to read Leadership, Psychoanalysis, and Society, edited by Maccoby and Cortina. They gather essays by a group of fluent, careful and experienced professionals who have worked hard—through diverse perspectives and field practices—to understand the process of leadership and its relationship to followers. By doing this, they point to alternative ways the future of the United States can become a more just and mutually supporting society.'

Sonia Gojman de Millán, Former Secretary General of the International Federation of Psychoanalytic Societies IFPS

'Michael Maccoby and Mauricio Cortina have concocted an array of star scholars to examine leadership from a variety of directions at precisely the time we need such a book. It's an excellent addition to the leadership literature.'

Keith Grint, Professor Emeritus, Warwick University, Coventry

LEADERSHIP, PSYCHOANALYSIS, AND SOCIETY

Leadership, Psychoanalysis, and Society describes leadership as a relationship between leaders and followers in a particular context and challenges theories of leadership now being taught.

This book includes essays that view leadership from psychoanalytic, social psychological, sociological, evolutionary, developmental anthropological, and historical points of view to fully describe the complexity of leadership relationships and personalities. These essays analyze the different kinds of leadership needed in organizations; the development of Black Leadership that provides hope for people who have been oppressed; the difference between charismatic and inspirational leadership; and the kind of training needed to develop leaders from diverse backgrounds who inspire followers and collaborate with them to further the common good.

This book offers a guide to understanding the different types of leadership and will be of interest to business, government, health care, universities, and other organizations.

Michael Maccoby, PhD, is a psychoanalyst and anthropologist who is a globally recognized expert on leadership. He has taught or consulted to leaders in 36 countries and has taught leadership at Oxford's Saïd Business School, Sciences Po, and Harvard's Kennedy School. He is also the author/co-author of 16 books.

Mauricio Cortina, MD, is a psychiatrist psychoanalyst who is recognized as a leading figure in attachment theory having received the 2019 Bowlby Ainsworth Award and has written many chapters and books on attachment and human evolution. He is the author and editor of four books.

PSYCHOANALYTIC INQUIRY BOOK SERIES

Series Editor: Joseph D. Lichtenberg

Like its counterpart, *Psychoanalytic Inquiry: A Topical Journal for Mental Health Professionals*, the Psychoanalytic Inquiry Book Series presents a diversity of subjects within a diversity of approaches to those subjects. Under the editorship of Joseph Lichtenberg, in collaboration with Melvin Bornstein and the editorial board of *Psychoanalytic Inquiry*, the volumes in this series strike a balance between research, theory, and clinical application. We are honored to have published the works of various innovators in psychoanalysis, including Frank Lachmann, James Fosshage, Robert Stolorow, Donna Orange, Louis Sander, Léon Wurmser, James Grotstein, Joseph Jones, Doris Brothers, Fredric Busch, and Joseph Lichtenberg, among others.

The series includes books and monographs on mainline psychoanalytic topics, such as sexuality, narcissism, trauma, homosexuality, jealousy, envy, and varied aspects of the analytic process and technique. In our efforts to broaden the field of analytic interest, the series has incorporated and embraced innovative discoveries in infant research, self-psychology, intersubjectivity, motivational systems, affects as process, responses to cancer, borderline states, contextualism, postmodernism, attachment research and theory, medication, and mentalization. As further investigations in psychoanalysis come to fruition, we seek to present them in readable, easily comprehensible writing.

After more than 25 years, the core vision of this series remains the investigation, analysis, and discussion of developments on the cutting edge of the psychoanalytic field, inspired by a boundless spirit of inquiry. A full list of all the titles available in the *Psychoanalytic Inquiry Book Series* is available at https://www.routledge.com/Psychoanalytic-Inquiry-Book-Series/book-series/LEAPIBS.

Recent Books in the Series:

The Self-Restorative Power of Music: A Psychological Perspective
by Frank M. Lachmann

Psychoanalysis and Society's Neglect of the Sexual Abuse of Children, Youth and Adults: Re-addressing Freud's Original Theory of Sexual Abuse and Trauma
by Arnold Wm. Rachman

Leadership, Psychoanalysis, and Society
by Edited Michael Maccoby and Mauricio Cortina

LEADERSHIP, PSYCHOANALYSIS, AND SOCIETY

Edited by
Michael Maccoby and Mauricio Cortina

Routledge
Taylor & Francis Group
LONDON AND NEW YORK

Cover image: © Getty Images

First published 2022
by Routledge
4 Park Square, Milton Park, Abingdon, Oxon OX14 4RN

and by Routledge
605 Third Avenue, New York, NY 10158

Routledge is an imprint of the Taylor & Francis Group, an informa business

© 2022 selection and editorial matter, Michael Maccoby and Mauricio Cortina; individual chapters, the contributors

British Library Cataloguing-in-Publication Data
A catalogue record for this book is available from the British Library

Library of Congress Cataloging-in-Publication Data
A catalog record has been requested for this book

ISBN: 978-1-032-20764-3 (hbk)
ISBN: 978-1-032-20765-0 (pbk)
ISBN: 978-1-003-26512-2 (ebk)

DOI: 10.4324/9781003265122

Typeset in Joanna
by MPS Limited, Dehradun

CONTENTS

TABLES

ACKNOWLEDGEMENTS

The editors very much appreciate Maria Stroffolino's editing and work in preparing this manuscript.

CONTRIBUTORS

Mauricio Cortina, MD, is a psychiatrist psychoanalyst who is recognized as a leading figure in attachment theory having received the 2019 Bowlby Ainsworth Award and has written many chapters and books on attachment and human evolution. He is the author and editor of four books with Mario Marrone in Spanish and English; *Attachment and the Psychoanalytic Process*; *La Teoria de Apego, Un Paradigma Revolucionario* and with Michael Maccoby, *A Prophetic Analysts; The Contributions of Erich Fromm to Psychoanalysis*.

Robert Cosby, PhD, MSW, is Assistant Dean of Administration, an Associate Professor, and Director of the Howard University School of Social Work Multidisciplinary Gerontology Center. The Center serves in three areas, research, community service, and training. Dr. Cosby is a gerontologist and a policy specialist.

Bob Duckles, PhD, retired from a career working with organizations seeking to improve their effectiveness through employee involvement. He personally seeks deeper understanding of how organizations and their employees bring out the best in each other. He currently leads two writers' workshops, meeting on ZOOM since the pandemic.

Janice B. Edwards, PhD, PhD, LICSW, LCSW, BCD, is an Associate Professor in the School of Social Work at Howard University. She maintains a private practice where she provides clinical social work psychodynamic and psychoanalytic-oriented treatment. Her research is in clinical social work practice and social work education.

Paul H. Elovitz, PhD, is a research psychoanalyst, presidential psychobiographer, historian, editor-in-chief of *Clio's Psyche* (1994–), professor (1963–), and founder/director of the Psychohistory Forum (1982–). After teaching at Fairleigh Dickinson, Rutgers, and Temple universities he became a founding faculty member of Ramapo College. His most recent book among his 390 publications is *The Making of Psychohistory: Origins, Controversies, and Pioneering Contributors* (Routledge, 2018). Currently, he is editing *The Many Roads to Insight of the Builders of Psychohistory*. Dr. Elovitz may be contacted at cliospsycheeditor@gmail.com.

Charles Heckscher, PhD, is a Distinguished Professor at Rutgers University and co-Director of the Center for the Study of Collaboration. His research interests include societal trust, organization change, and the changing nature of employee representation. Before coming to Rutgers he worked for the Communications Workers' union and taught Human Resources Management at the Harvard Business School.

Michael Maccoby, PhD, is a psychoanalyst and anthropologist who is a globally recognized expert on leadership. He has taught or consulted to leaders in 36 countries and has taught leadership at Oxford's Saïd Business School, Sciences Po, and Harvard's Kennedy School. He is the author or co-author of sixteen books including *The Gamesman; Narcissistic Leaders; The Leaders We Need, and What Makes Us Follow; Transforming Health Care Leadership* and *Strategic Intelligence*.

Jeffrey Pfeffer, PhD, is the Thomas D. Dee II Professor of Organizational Behavior at the Graduate School of Business at Stanford. He has authored or co-authored 15 books and more than 160 articles and chapters. His current research focuses on the effects of management practices on health and well-being as well as power and leadership.

Rafael Ramirez, PhD, is the University of Oxford's first Professor of Practice and directs the Oxford Scenarios Programme. His PhD dissertation at the Wharton School was on an aesthetic theory of organisation, and he has since then deployed aesthetics to enhance strategy and scenario planning theory and practice.

Tim Scudder, PhD, is a Principal at Core Strengths, an organization dedicated to improving working relationships through personality assessment, training, and online collaboration tools. He is the world's leading authority on the application of the Strength Deployment Inventory and the author of several books, training programs, and articles.

Jon Stokes, MA, Dip.Clin.Psych., is a clinical and business psychologist and a former Senior Fellow in Management Practice at the Said Business School, University of Oxford. He is a Clinical Associate of the British Psychoanalytical Society and a director of the leadership consulting firm Stokes & Jolly Ltd.

PROLOGUE, LEADERSHIP, PSYCHOANALYSIS, AND SOCIETY

Michael Maccoby and Mauricio Cortina

In a time like the present of rapid change in cultures and economies, a time of extreme threats and promising opportunities, leadership will determine the future of countries, organizations, the environment, and our lives. To increase our ability to find and follow good leadership, it is essential to understand the leader–follower relationship and the personality of would-be leaders.

Eleven students of leadership present their views in these chapters. They view leadership through different lenses. What they have in common is the view that, as Michael Maccoby puts it, leadership is a relationship in a context. Although the personality of leaders determines their behavior, they only become leaders if they have followers. And people follow someone for different reasons. These reasons depend on the needs and values of followers as well as the qualities of leaders. Cultural values and historical challenges also shape leader–follower relationships.

The complexity of leadership relationships and personalities requires analysis by different academic disciplines, and we have included chapters that view leadership from psychoanalytic, social psychological, sociological, evolutionary, developmental, anthropological, and historical points of view. Some of the chapters include personal observations and experiences of leadership.

The material in these chapters can be grouped in two main themes. One is the leader–follower relationship and how it is formed in different contexts. The other focuses on the personalities of leaders and how their motivation and philosophies are expressed in their leadership behavior.

The Leader–Follower Relationship

Leadership is a relationship in a context.

Mauricio Cortina describes egalitarian and antiauthoritarian leader–follower relations in pre-history reporting that leadership among illiterate prehistorical nomadic hunter-gatherers was unobtrusive and antiauthoritarian as it is with contemporary nomadic foragers around the world. Social hierarchies and authoritarian leadership emerged starting with large agricultural societies. In a psychological–anthropological study of a Mexican village, Fromm and Maccoby found that peasants only accept leadership when they are threatened or for promising projects, attitudes toward leadership common in peasant societies similar to Cortina's description of the nomadic forager societies studied by anthropologists during the last 100 years.

Why do people follow a leader? There are different reasons. Sigmund Freud viewed that the masses follow leaders either because they are coerced or because they share the illusion that the leader loves them, and they make him their ego ideal. Erich Fromm added that they identify with the leader and with each other.

The description of Black leadership in the USA by Robert Cosby and Janice Edwards illustrates how people who have been oppressed and threatened for many years have followed leaders who have protected them and provided hope for a better future.

Jon Stokes writes that leadership relationships can result in either the development or regressive behavior of followers. He proposes that charismatic leaders cause regression as followers substitute the ego ideal of the leader for their own while inspiring leaders provide an example of a progressive ego ideal to which followers can aspire more progressively.

This description of the charismatic leader–follower relationship fits the relationship between Adolf Hitler and his Nazi followers as well as that of

Donald Trump and his base that believes his lies and delusions and accepts his ethics in place of their own. The image of the inspiring leader fits less toxic relationships such as Franklin Delano Roosevelt, Mohandas Gandhi, Martin Luther King, and their followers.

In another context, Charles Heckscher describes a change from bureaucratic to more collaborative relationships as standardized work roles are replaced by teams, especially with knowledge workers. He argues that the ability to lead wide-ranging public conversations is increasingly important in a highly polarized context. Bob Duckles reports that even factory jobs are made more productive when managers take account of workers' feelings and thinking. Heckscher reports a case where a leader engages knowledge workers in developing values to adapt a company to a changing business environment. Maccoby cites Gallup surveys indicating that only a minority of employees in the USA and other highly industrialized societies are engaged by their work. He lists the kinds of behavior and actions by leaders that result in motivated employees. These leadership actions are effective in different national cultures, but the type of leadership-follower relationship varies. For example, Maccoby observed that in China, the cultural revolution abolished the traditional Confucian, paternalistic relationships, but with the ethnic Chinese of Taiwan and Singapore, this relationship still exists.

The Personality of Leaders

Freud's view of a patriarchal leader is a narcissist, someone strong and independent with no need for reinforcement from others, who loves no one but himself or others only so far as they serve his needs. Jeffrey Pfeffer reports studies that show that many narcissists reach the top of organizations. He agrees with Maccoby's differentiation of productive narcissists who have a progressive philosophy from unproductive and malignant narcissists, but he is concerned that there are few of these, and leadership training is not preparing non-narcissists to gain top leadership positions.

Freud contrasted normal narcissists from erotic and obsessive personality types. Fromm added the marketing orientation as a fourth type. Both Freud and Fromm observed that people are a mixture of types. Maccoby has proposed leadership versions of these types and has shown that different types fit different leadership roles. Tim Scudder, building on Elias Porter's interpretation of Fromm's types, has employed psychometrics to develop an instrument that is used to enlighten both leaders and followers about their motivation, strengths, overuse of strengths, and management of conflict. Scudder has also statistically validated Freud's types.

Most theories of personality focus on motives (as in Freud's types) and temperament (as in the Big Five). Maccoby suggests that these factors are incomplete. People with the same psychoanalytic type behave differently according to their personal philosophies, their purpose, and values.

Rafael Ramirez adds another important element to leadership personality: the aesthetics of leaders, how they organize the perceptions of those they seek to lead. He describes how populist leaders like Donald Trump capture the minds of followers with images and slogans.

Freud and Fromm wrote only about male leaders. Maccoby reports studies on differences between men and women leaders and suggests that women as national leaders have been more effective than men in dealing with the coronavirus epidemic. Cosby and Edwards report an increase in effective Black women leaders.

How do people become leaders? How does the personality of leaders develop? As an example, Paul Elovitz, a psychohistorian, describes how he became a leader in his field and a student of the personality of American presidents. He traces the development of Donald Trump and Joe Biden from their childhoods to the presidency, describing the formation of both their motivations and personal philosophies.

These analyses provide a basis for understanding variations in leader–follower relationships and the impact of the personalities of leaders. To build on this understanding we can improve our ability to develop leaders from diverse backgrounds who inspire followers and collaborate with them to further the common good.

1

LEADERSHIP IN CONTEXT

Michael Maccoby

Introduction

My understanding of leadership grew first from a study of engineers and managers in companies creating new technology (Maccoby, 1976), then from directing projects to improve the quality of working life (Maccoby, 1981) and subsequently from advising leaders in companies, unions, universities, government agencies in 36 countries in North America, Latin America, Europe, the Middle East, Africa, and Asia, and an organization with homes and schools for orphans and at-risk children in nine Latin American and Caribbean countries. In these studies and practice, I have built my view of leadership on the theories and writings of three great psychoanalytic thinkers: Sigmund Freud, Erich Fromm, and Erik H. Erikson.

DOI: 10.4324/9781003265122-1

Sigmund Freud

Freud viewed leaders in the context of a patriarchal society where he believed they were needed to control the passions of lazy and ignorant masses and force them to work. He wrote, "All is well if these leaders are persons who possess superior insight into the necessities of life and who have risen to the heights of mastering their own instinctual wishes" (Freud, 1927, 7).

According to Freud, leaders are most effective when they create the illusion that they love all their followers equally. Members of the group make the leader their ego ideal and consequently identify themselves with one another; "but the leader himself," wrote Freud, "need love no one else, he may be of a masterful nature, absolutely narcissistic, self-confident and independent" (Freud, 1921, 123–4). I found that this description fits some but not all leadership relationships.

In his brief paper on Libidinal Types (Freud, 1931), Freud described three basic or normal personality types that I found useful for understanding leadership behavior. These are: the erotic whose main interest is loving and being loved, the obsessional who is self-reliant and dominated by a strict conscience, and the narcissistic, who is Freud's natural leader. According to Freud, narcissists have weak superegos and large amounts of aggression. They are independent and not open to intimidation. He wrote that "People belonging to this type impress others as being personalities; they are especially suited to act as support for others, to take on the role of leaders and to give a fresh stimulus to cultural development or to damage the established state of affairs" (Freud, 1931, 218).

Freud also described mixed types and proposed that the narcissistic-obsessional type was the most valuable for society. This type describes some of the most successful entrepreneurs who I have termed productive narcissists (Maccoby, 2000, 2003, 2007a). It also described Freud who combined the visionary leadership of a movement with careful attention to writing his theories and documenting clinical cases. I found a pattern in the histories of male productive narcissists. Typically, they do not identify with a father who is either absent or not admired. Supported by strong supportive mothers, they develop their own ego ideals. The lack of identification with a father explains their weak superegos, but their demanding ego ideals drive their ambition. Their narcissism gives innovative leaders confidence and protects them from inevitable attacks.

Erich Fromm

In *Escape from Freedom*, Fromm (1941) analyzes Adolph Hitler's authoritarian and sadistic personality as expressed in his ideology and behavior. Fromm proposes that in a time of extreme cultural change and economic depression and inflation, Hitler appealed to many Germans, especially those with an authoritarian-obsessive social character who had been humiliated by defeat in World War I, had lost their savings, and saw him as a savior. This analysis is consistent with Freud's view of the masses identifying with the narcissistic leader and with each other. Although Fromm did not use the term narcissist in this work, he did so twenty-two years later in *The Heart of Man* (Fromm, 1964) where he described Hitler's personality in terms of malignant narcissism, regressive feelings of omnipotence, and necrophilia, attraction to death and destruction. Fromm writes that Hitler thrived on violence, hate, and racism rationalized as the love of country, duty, and honor.

Consistent with Freud's analysis of the relationship between the leader and the group, Fromm writes that a narcissistic group wants a leader they can identify with. The greater the leader, the greater become the followers. Narcissists are most likely to fulfill this function. The narcissism of the leader who has no doubts attracts the narcissism of followers.

Fromm renamed Freud's personality types in terms of their modes of assimilation and relationships. The erotic became receptive, the obsessive became hoarding, and the narcissistic became exploitative. Fromm described both positive and negative behaviors of each type (Fromm, 1947). He added a fourth type, the marketing orientation, describing someone who lacks an inner identity and is driven to shape behavior to gain acceptance and approval from significant others. I found the marketing type increasingly describes both leaders and followers in the post-industrial service economy. Donald J. Trump expresses the marketing orientation combined with narcissistic grandiosity that serves as a defense against his emptiness and neediness (Maccoby, 2020). This combination results in an extreme need for praise and affirmation of the grandiose insecure persona he has constructed.

In some ways like Hitler, Trump appealed to Americans who distrusted elites and who felt anxious, forgotten, disrespected, and threatened by progressive movements that attacked their traditional culture. Hitler

Table 1.1 Personality Types

Freud	Fromm	Maccoby
Erotic	Receptive	Caring
Obsessive	Hoarding	Exacting
Narcissistic	Exploitative	Visionary
—	Marketing	Adaptive

blamed Jews, Communists, and the countries that had defeated Germany for the disastrous economic state of these Germans, and he promised to make Germany great again. Trump blamed immigrants and other countries for stealing American jobs. He promised to make America great again by stopping immigration and bringing back jobs by imposing tariffs on foreign products. He created the illusion that he loved his followers, and many of his followers loved him. Populist leaders like Hitler and Trump amplify and focus the anger and resentment of people who have been left behind by cultural and economic change. They create the kind of narcissistic group Freud and Fromm described.

In contrast to Trump, Joseph Biden has a caring personality. He does not fit Freud's model of a narcissistic leader. He does not have cultish followers. He has supporters and collaborators. He is a problem solver who attempts to create cooperation for the common good. A challenge for him will be dealing with conflict, between political parties and within his own party.[1]

When applying the types Freud discovered and Fromm modified to leaders I studied, I named the more productive versions of these types caring, exacting, visionary, and adaptive. I developed a questionnaire based on Freud's and Fromm's types. The results support their view that people express mixtures of these types (Table 1.1).[2]

Erik H. Erikson

In *Gandhi's Truth*, Erikson (1969) analyzes the development of Mohandas Gandhi, his identifications with his mother and father, his struggles to become pure by wrestling with his sexual and aggressive instincts, and how he developed his leadership philosophy of *satyagraha*, truth force.

Erikson describes how Gandhi's personality was expressed in his leadership during a labor conflict. Erikson focuses on the obsessive aspects of Gandhi's personality, his moralism, and controlling behavior. Erikson describes Gandhi's relationship to his followers and the historical context from which he emerged as a national leader. He describes Gandhi's narcissistic behavior without using the term. Rather than offering generalizations about the leadership relationship, Erikson, like Fromm, provides a powerful case history of a leader who does not coerce but inspires followers to transform society. Of course, once Hitler inspired enough Germans to gain political power, he coerced the others to follow his disastrous leadership.

My Studies of Leadership

As the examples of Hitler and Gandhi show, leadership is a relationship between leaders and those they lead within a particular context. The context might be a culture in a historical time or an organizational role. Someone can gain followers and be a leader in one context but not in another. For example, Winston Churchill was the indispensable leader for Great Britain during World War II, but he was rejected by the British public both before and after the war. Before the war, he warned the public that Britain should prepare for war against Hitler's Germany, but the public saw him as an alarmist and warmonger. During the war, his courage and indomitable spirit inspired Britain during its darkest time, but after the war, the public rejected his Tory imperialist ambition in favor of a more egalitarian socialist vision.

Churchill had the same personality when he was an effective leader and when he was not. His narcissistic self-confidence and image of invulnerability gave hope to the beleaguered wartime public but did not connect to a war-weary post-war public.

In the private sector, visionary entrepreneurs may effectively start a company but once it is up and running, they prove unable to lead it, because they lack the ability to relate to employees. In starting the company, they are able to inspire investors and a small team with their vision, but once a company grows, effective leaders need the ability to collaborate with others, to respect different viewpoints, and manage conflict creatively. A good example is described by Ed Catmull (2014), president of

Pixar and Disney Animation. With a few exceptions, narcissistic visionaries have a hard time listening to others. The most effective narcissistic leaders partner with someone who has these skills.

The lesson is that personality traits alone don't explain effective leadership. Leadership is a relationship between leader and led in a particular context and if the context changes, the relationship may also change.

But different personality types do fit particular contexts. And personality determines, in large part, how leaders practice leadership and their relation to followers.

Types of Leaders

Theories of leadership like Freud's assume one type of leadership, but there are different types of leaders. Different roles are best filled by different personality types. Leadership behavior may also be shaped by national cultures. In 1982, I was engaged by a Swedish think tank funded by the Employers Confederation to study Swedish leaders and recommend the kind of leadership needed for Sweden (Edstrom et al., 1985; Maccoby, 1991). The board of the think tank proposed the study because they were concerned that Sweden, a country that had prospered after World War II because of its neutrality, had become complacent and was falling behind in international competition, losing industries to Asian companies. Swedish leaders were proposing old solutions for new challenges. They were not visionaries. I found a few exceptions, innovators in companies and public administration who were models for a more dynamic society. Three of the most inspirational and successful business leaders led their companies to exceptional success for more than a decade, but all of them eventually were failures. Why did they fail?

Their narcissistic personalities caused their failure. They over expanded their businesses and ignored warnings from their subordinates. From being seen by the public and press as charismatic superstars, they were reviled as losers. Like Pericles of Athens and Napoleon Bonaparte, many successful narcissistic leaders lose touch with reality and believe that they have become invincible. The ones that avoid this downfall typically have advisers who bring them down to earth. Napoleon was successful until he fired Talleyrand, his foreign minister who warned him against invading Russia, an invasion that became a disaster that led to Napoleon's downfall.

In contrast to these examples is the case of Steve Jobs the visionary narcissistic CEO of Apple. Jobs was known for his exploitativeness, lying, and contemptuous disregard for others in his first stint running Apple leading to his firing, but he learned to partner with Tim Cook in operations and Jony Ives, the product designer, in his return to running Apple, partnering that resulted in his fabulous success.

As Freud indicated, narcissistic visionaries typically lead to change. Narcissistic business leaders exploit new technologies. Narcissistic political leaders promise to solve social problems and lead societies to greatness. To succeed, these leaders need subordinate leaders to execute their visions. I found that large technology-based companies need three types of leaders who work interactively: strategic, operational, and network (Maccoby, 2015).

Strategic leaders set the direction of organizations, their vision, and values. In contrast to administrators and managers who carry out set policies, strategic leaders focus on future threats and opportunities and develop strategies for organizational success. The best strategic leaders I've studied and worked with were productive narcissists who were able to partner with the other types of leaders.

To implement strategies, operational leaders are needed to develop processes and human resources. They need to create the conditions and relationships necessary for a motivated workforce. Typically, they have balanced personalities with a strong exacting-obsessive mode of relationship.

In the most advanced technology-based companies, employees with different skills and those working in different locations have to work interactively. To develop teamwork, companies need network leaders who are able to build understanding and trust among employees. The most effective of these leaders have caring and adaptive personalities. They show empathy and understanding and create a culture of respect, trust, and collaboration.

Why People Follow Leaders

According to Freud, people follow a leader either because they are forced to or they want to because they feel loved by the leader and make him their ego ideal. Curiously, Freud doesn't describe this loving relationship in terms of transference, but he might have done so. I've observed employees viewing leaders as parental figures and often being disappointed when the leader doesn't treat them as they hoped and expected (Maccoby 2004). A CEO told me that she had to tell some employees that she was not their mother. Some national leaders like Abraham Lincoln, called father Abraham by Blacks, Franklin D. Roosevelt, and Ronald Reagan have been seen as father figures by their followers. Germans have called Angela Merkel *Mutter*. When there is a positive transference people see their leaders like an idealized image of protective parents. They will follow the leader even when they are unsure of where the leader is taking them. There can also be a negative transference when leaders have disappointed their followers. A number of voters viewed Hilary Clinton as a bad mother.

Another type of transference takes place when people project magical qualities on a leader, seeing the leader as super human. This was the case for many followers of Barack Obama who expected him to change the American culture and somehow end racism. Obama writes that when he has running for president, he realized that "people were no longer seeing me…with all my quirks and shortcomings. Instead, they had taken possession of my likeness and made it a vessel for a million different dreams" (Obama, 2020, p. 136).

The concepts of transference and projection help to explain the phenomenon of charisma, when a leader has a magnetic quality that inspires people. While some people seem to have an innate charism, we can observe that a narcissistic leader can become suddenly charismatic to followers who identify with the leader and decide he or she can do no wrong. The leader then feels omnipotent and projects total certainty. But only this charisma lasts so long as the leader is successful. With failure, leaders lose their charisma.

Consider why people feel love for leaders, why transference takes place. This may happen when people feel threatened as in war or competitive sports and a leader gives them confidence. It may happen when leaders give people hope for a better future. But people can have different views of a better future, and they may follow the same leader for different reasons. Some people, especially Whites, voted for Trump because they identified with his grandiose image and his support for their cultural interests. They hoped for a future that would turn back progressive advances that empowered minorities. Others voted for Trump in the hope he would favor their economic interests by lowering taxes and reversing regulations ordered by President Obama that put constraints on businesses.

In factories and offices, the question is not only why employees follow leaders but also how they follow them. In bureaucracies where jobs are individualized and standardized, it may be enough for workers to meet a set quota. Factory workers may only do their repetitive work for a paycheck and this may be enough to meet productivity standards. Industrial bureaucracies are typically designed so that individual work can be coordinated and controlled by administrators. Leaders are not needed. But the productivity of advanced knowledge workers depends not only on their engagement with the work, but also their willingness to collaborate, share ideas, and keep learning. Surveys by the Gallup organization show that only a third of American employees are engaged or fully motivated at work, and the percentage is even lower in many other countries. What makes the difference is leadership. Coercive leadership in the workplace only gains compliance, not engagement. Effective leaders employ a combination of tools I have termed the five Rs: Reasons, Responsibilities, Relationships, Recognition, and Rewards (Maccoby, 2015).

Reasons have to do with the purpose of work. People are motivated when the work fits their values, when it is meaningful for them. Leaders who understand this communicate a philosophy that includes the purpose of the organization and the practical values essential to achieve it. I have interviewed leaders at some of the most admired health-care organizations in America (Maccoby et al., 2013). Health-care providers at these organizations were most engaged when leaders articulated and practiced a philosophy including the organization's purpose, the practical values essential to achieve the purpose, and how results would be determined. A prime example is Mayo Clinic where the philosophy stated by its founder William Mayo is still practiced. The purpose Mayo emphasized was serving the patient and to do that well he required physicians and other health-care providers to cooperate in their diagnosis and treatments. He also valued continual learning and personally traveled to different states and countries to learn new surgical techniques. He required that all physicians do clinically focused research to keep learning and improving care. Mayo leaders periodically measure patient evaluations and compliance with the values which they've expanded to include environmental sustainability.

Responsibilities refer to the work people do. Effective leaders place people in roles where they can exercise their skills. People are motivated by meaningful work that challenges them to demonstrate their abilities. A craftsman is motivated to build an excellent product, an ethical salesman is motivated to satisfy a customer's needs, just as a physician is motivated by the challenge of curing a patient.

Freud wrote that people are motivated to follow a leader either because they are coerced or because they identify with the leader. I have added to this the motivating effects of transference, shared meaning, and a hopeful future promised by a leader. These tend to be relationships from afar, shared by a group that follows a leader. In organizations, lower-level leaders, middle managers, and supervisors have a more direct personal relationship with their subordinates, and this relationship can be crucial in determining a person's motivation to work and willingness to follow the leader. People want to follow managers who respect them, listen to their ideas, help them to develop their skills, and recognize their contributions. They are turned off by managers who are autocratic, don't listen, and take credit for their ideas and contributions. Studies show that the main reason why talented people leave organizations is a bad relationship with their manager (Goler et al., 2019).

Economists assume that people are most motivated by rewards or in-centives. This may be so when people feel their work is meaningless, but when I have asked professionals to rank the five Rs for themselves, rewards are typically ranked last. People are demotivated when they consider they are being underpaid, but the promise of more money does not make good professionals do their job better. Good teachers don't teach better when there is a monetary incentive, nor do good physicians treat patients better in order to be paid more. Rewards for exceptional work are always ap-preciated and may strengthen a positive transference to a leader. Some younger employees I've interviewed value opportunities for learning that improves their marketability, including courses and conferences, even more than monetary rewards.

Culture and Leadership

Variations of the five Rs explain motivation in all the different cultures I have experienced, but I've observed that people seek different kinds of leadership relationships in some of the 36 countries where I have taught, studied, and coached leaders. I interviewed and consulted leaders in the offices of a technology company in twelve countries in Europe, Asia, and

North America. Even though their work was similar, I found different models of leadership in some of these countries. In Sweden, the ideal leader was collaborative and managers were encouraged to get to know each other. They called each other by the informal *du* and sometimes brought their families to offsite events. But decision-making often took a long time. Typically, Swedes tried to avoid conflict and sometimes the decisions made by consensus were not clear and were interpreted in different ways by the managers.

In contrast, the Germans in this company avoided socializing with colleagues because they believed that intimacy eroded objectivity. They used the formal mode of address, even with colleagues they had worked with for years. Leaders encouraged managers to challenge each other as long as their arguments were supported by facts. But once the leader made a decision, everyone marched in step. The Germans thought their Swedish colleagues lacked integrity because they avoided creative conflict. The Swedes thought the German leaders were authoritarian because they didn't seek consensus.

The managers I interviewed in Beijing and Taipei were all Chinese, but their cultures and leadership models were different. Taiwan had a more traditional culture than mainland China that had gone through Mao's cultural revolution that had attacked the Confucian model of leadership. When I asked Taiwanese managers to describe an ideal leader, I was presented with the Confucian image of a benevolent father figure who demands obedience and loyalty but in turn is a caring teacher. In Beijing, the model of a good leader was a basketball coach who knew the strengths of each player, put them in the right roles, developed a winning strategy and was able to adapt quickly to change.

I've lectured on leadership to groups of Chinese university students who were in the USA on study tours, and I've asked them which kind of leader they would most want to follow. They all choose the basketball coach over the benevolent Confucian leader.

Leadership in Mexico

For eight years, I lived in Mexico, graduating from the Mexican Institute of Psychoanalysis, becoming a training analyst and with Erich Fromm studying the social character of Mexican villagers (Fromm & Maccoby, 1970).

In this village and other villages I studied (Maccoby & Foster, 1970), there were no established leaders. Independent peasant farmers see no need for leaders except for particular projects. Otherwise, decisions are made by consensus in town meetings. During the Revolution of 1910–20, villagers in the State of Morelos hired Emiliano Zapata Salazar, a tough gunman, to defend them. One can imagine that feudalism began when peasants hired strong men for defense, and these warriors made themselves feudal lords, forcing the peasants to be their vassals in return for protection. Zapata didn't survive the Revolution.

From my psychoanalytic practice and interactions with Mexican colleagues, I learned that the dominant model of leadership in Mexico is the semi-feudal *patrón* who is like a commanding but benevolent father figure.

Fromm accepted this model of leadership as founder and director of the Mexican Institute of Psychoanalysis. He analyzed the twelve psychiatrists who became the first members of the institute. They followed Fromm because of his theories, but there was also a strong psychocultural transference. I followed Fromm not only because of his psychoanalytic theories but also because I shared his engagement in the anti-nuclear peace movement (Fromm & Maccoby, 1962). I also experienced a positive transference. I have written elsewhere (Maccoby, 2017) that Fromm didn't analyze the transference.

Both Freud and Fromm were productive narcissists with cultish followers. A difference was that Freud demanded that his followers stick to his theories while Fromm tolerated differences from his followers. Although the analysis of the transference is central to psychoanalysis, it is questionable whether analysts practice what they preach in training analyses.

While in Mexico, I met Father William Wasson who founded a home for orphaned and abandoned children. Father Wasson asked me to advise him on questions of leadership, and after his death, I continued to advise the leaders of the organization he founded *Nuestros Pequeños Hermanos* (NPH), with homes in nine countries of Latin America and the Caribbean.

Father Wasson became the father of hundreds of children (Now, 65 years after he founded the organization, over 20,000 children have been raised in the homes he established.) His leadership success was based in large part on the organizational philosophy he practiced, including a purpose and the practical values essential to achieve that purpose.

Father Wasson's purpose was to develop his children to be productive and caring citizens of their countries, what he termed "good Christians." To do this he needed to provide the children with a sense of security, an understanding that they would be cared for and educated until they were able to live independent lives. To balance security, he required that every child contributes to the homes by their work. Everyone had a job, in the kitchens, farms, dormitories, and schools. Even small children were given tasks such as sweeping the walkways. When the children graduated from secondary school, they were expected to contribute a year of service to their home before going off either to a university or a job. To nurture caring attitudes, he urged the children to share with each other, and he took them on visits to hospitals and prisons so they could learn about people in need of help. He also lectured them to take responsibility for themselves and the well-being of others. He didn't want to lead a rules-based organization, but rather a family where members took responsibility for doing the right thing.

Some of the children brought up with these values have graduated from universities, had jobs and then returned to leadership at NPH. They continue to preach and practice father Wasson's philosophy. I've asked some of them why they wanted to become leaders at NPH. One answer was to care for the children. Another was to overcome injustices, in particular the injustice of children threatened with poverty and lack of care.

Clearly, some people become leaders to gain money or personal power. Others want to change the world for the common good, to improve the quality of life with their products or services. The purpose of leaders depends on their philosophy. It can be either conscious or unconscious, serving self or the common good. How leaders carry out that purpose depends on their motivational type and their culture?

Leadership and Gender

Neither Freud, Fromm, nor Erikson wrote about women leaders. When they were writing about leadership, there were few women in leadership roles in either business or government although women in psychoanalysis—Anna Freud, Melanie Klein, Karen Horney—were leaders. But since Freud wrote about leadership, the number of women leaders has been increasing as women have challenged traditional patriarchy and cultures have evolved.

How are women leaders viewed? Do they act differently from male leaders? Alice H. Eagly, a social psychologist known for her work on gender, stereotyping, and leadership writes,

> Worldwide, people expect women to be the more communal sex—warm, supportive, and kind—and men to be the more agentic sex—assertive, dominant, and authoritative (Williams & Best, 1990). To the surprise of some observers, these gender stereotypes have not disappeared in the United States as women's roles have changed. Representative U.S. public opinion polls show that the expectation that women are the more communal sex has increased since the mid-20th century, while the expectation that men are the more agentic sex has held steady (Eagly et al., 2019). People also ascribe mainly agentic qualities to leaders, with the result that beliefs about leaders are more similar to beliefs about men than women (Koenig et al., 2011). Therein lies the cultural incongruity between women and leadership.
>
> (Eagly, 2020)

Eagly goes on to report that

> Pressures on women leaders, especially White women, to conform to expectations to be communal but not especially agentic likely contribute to their reliance on more democratic and participative leadership styles. Meta-analyses on leadership styles thus found that female leaders tended to be more democratic, collaborative, and participative than male leaders—that is, they more often invited input from others and attempted to build consensus (Eagly & Johnson, 1990; van Engen & Willemsen, 2004). Male leaders, in contrast, were more likely to have a more autocratic and directive approach. Women thus did more of what is sometimes called "leading from behind," that is, working with others to reach collective decisions.
>
> (Eagly, 2020).

According to a report on Women and Foreign Policy by the Council on Foreign Relations, "In the aggregate, women's leadership promotes bipartisanship, equality and stability."

(Vogelstein & Bro, 2020)

As heads of state, some notable women fit this stereotype, but others do not. Jacinda Ardern of New Zealand, Angela Merkel of Germany, Sanna Marin of Finland, Erma Solberg of Norway, and Tsai Ing-wen of Taiwan were able to lead their countries to address the coronavirus pandemic in a way that gained greater collaboration and better results than were achieved by male heads of state.

But some women leaders have not fit this stereotype. Examples are Margaret Thatcher, Golda Meir, and Indira Gandhi, all known as tough and dominating. I have worked with both types of women leaders and also with both communal and agentic male leaders.

Some men and women have changed their styles of leadership to fit different contexts. Gail McGovern reports that when she was a manager at AT&T, she led with her head, but as president of the Red Cross, she leads from her heart, because "people need to know, and understand, how their actions are going to impact the mission" (Gelles, 2020). McGovern leaves open the question of whether her subordinates at AT&T might have become more engaged with their work if she had led from the heart there.

In conclusion, psychoanalysts and social psychologists offer theories about leadership, but we should be wary of over generalizations. Although personality influences leadership behavior, there are different types of leaders in terms of personality. Although gender is a factor in predicting leadership behavior, there are exceptions to the stereotypes. There are different reasons why people want to become leaders, and there are different reasons why people follow leaders. Different types of leaders fit different historical, cultural, and organizational contexts. What we can gain from the studies and theories presented in this and other chapters are conceptual tools to understand particular leaders and their relationships with their followers.

Notes

1 See Paul Elovitz's article in this issue where he analyzes the development of Trump's and Biden's personalities.
2 That questionnaire and description of the types can be found in my book, *Narcissistic Leaders* (Maccoby, 2007b). A factor analysis showed that the types are statistically valid (Maccoby, 2007b). Tim Scudder's chapter also reports on the validity of Freud's types and their variations.

References

Catmull, E. (2014). *Creativity, Inc: Overcoming the unseen forces that stand in the way of true inspiration*. Random House.

Eagly, A. H. (2020). *Once more: The rise of female leaders-How gender and ethnicity affects the electability and success of women as political leaders*. American Psychological Association. https://www.apa.org/research/action/female-leaders.

Eagly, A. H. & Johnson, B. T. (1990). Gender and leadership style: A meta-analysis. *Psychological Bulletin, 108*(2), 233–256. doi: 10.1037/0033-2909.108.2.233.

Eagly, A. H., Nater, C., Miller, D. I., Kaufmann, M. & Sczesny, S. (2019). Gender stereotypes have changed: A cross-temporal meta-analysis of U.S. public opinion polls from 1946 to 2018. *American Psychologist, 75*, 301–315. doi:10.1037/amp0000494.

Edstrom, A., Michael M., Lennart S., & Jan E. R. (1985). *Leadership for Sweden*. Liber.

Erikson, E. H. (1969). *Gandhi's Truth*. W.W. Norton & Company.

Freud, S. (1921). 'Group psychology and the analysis of the ego', in *The standard edition of the complete psychological works of Sigmund Freud, vol. XVIII*. The Hogarth Press, 1955, pp. 65–144.

Freud, S. (1927). 'The future of an illusion', in *The standard edition of the complete psychological works of Sigmund, Freud. Vol. XXI*. The Hogarth Press, 1961, pp. 5–56.

Freud, S. (1931). 'Libidinal types', in *The standard edition of the complete psychological works of Sigmund Freud, vol. XXI*. The Hogarth Press, 1961, pp. 215–220.

Fromm, E. (1941). *Escape from freedom*. Rinehart.

Fromm, E. (1947). *Man for himself: An inquiry into the psychology of ethics*. Rinehart.

Fromm, E. (1964). *The heart of man*. Harper & Row.

Fromm, E. & Maccoby, M. (1962). 'The question of civil defense: A reply to Herman Kahn'. In Merton, T. (Ed.), *Breakthrough to peace: Twelve views on the threat of thermonuclear extermination*. (pp. 59–81). New Directions.

Fromm, E. & Maccoby, M. (1970). *Social character in a Mexican village*. Prentice-Hall.

Gelles, D. (2020). Facing disaster after disaster, the American Red Cross C.E.O. stays optimistic. *The New York Times*, https://www.nytimes.com/2020/10/10/business/gail-mcgovern-red-cross-corner-office.html.

Goler, L., Gale, J., Harrington, B., & Grant, A. (2019). Why people really quit their jobs. *Harvard Business Review*. https://hbr.org/2018/01/why-people-really-quit-their-jobs.

Koenig, A. M., Eagly, A. H., Mitchell, A. A. and Ristikari, T. (2011). Are leader stereotypes masculine? A meta-analysis of three research paradigms. *Psychological Bulletin*, 137(4), 616–642. doi:10.1037/a0023557.

Maccoby, M. (1976). *The gamesman*. Simon & Schuster.

Maccoby, M. (1981). *The leader, a new face for American management*. Simon & Schuster.

Maccoby, M. (2000, January-February). Narcissistic leaders: The incredible pros, the inevitable cons. *Harvard Business Review*, 78(1), 68–77. https://hbr.org/2004/09/why-people-follow-the-leader-the-power-of-transference.

Maccoby, M. (2003). *The productive narcissist: The promise and peril of visionary leadership*. Broadway Books.

Maccoby, M. (2004, September). Why people follow the leader: The power of transference. *Harvard Business Review*, 82(9), 76–85, 136.

Maccoby, M. (2007a). *Narcissistic leaders: Who succeeds and who fails*. Harvard Business School Press.

Maccoby, M. (2007b). *The leaders we need, and what makes us follow*. Harvard Business School Press.

Maccoby, M. (2015). Strategic intelligence: Conceptual tools for leading change. Oxford University Press.

Maccoby, M. (2017). Learning and doing. *Psychoanalytic Review*, 104 (4), 523–537. 10.1521/prev.2017.104.4.523.

Maccoby, M. (2020). 'Trump's marketing narcissistic leadership in an age of anxiety.' In M. Maccoby & K. Fuchsman (Eds.), *Psychoanalytic and historical perspective on Donald Trump's leadership, narcissism, and marketing in an age of anxiety and distrust*. (pp. 11–23). Routledge.

Maccoby, M. & Foster, G. (1970). Methods of studying Mexican peasant personality: Rorschach, TAT and dreams. *Anthropological Quarterly*, 43(4), 224–242. 10.2307/3316914.

Maccoby, M., Norman, C. L., Norman, C. J., & Margolies, R. (2013). *Transforming health care leadership: A systems guide to improve patient care, decrease costs, and improve population health*. Jossey-Bass.

Maccoby, M. Ed. (1991). *Sweden At the Edge: Lessons for American and Swedish Managers*. University of Pennsylvania Press.

Obama, B. (2020). *A promised land*. Crown.

van Engen, M. L. & Willemsen, T. M. (2004). Sex and leadership styles: A meta analysis of research published in the 1990s. *Psychological Reports*, 94(1), 3–18. 10.2466/pro.94.1.3-18.

Vogelstein, R. B. & Bro, A (2020). Women and foreign policy, council on foreign relations. https://www.cfr.org/article/womens-power-index.

Williams, J. E. & Best, D. L. (1990). *Measuring sex stereotypes: A multination study*. Sage.

2

OUR PREHISTORY AS EGALITARIAN NOMADIC FORAGERS WITH ANTIAUTHORITARIAN LEADERSHIP: WHAT THESE NOMADS CAN TEACH US TODAY

Mauricio Cortina

Introduction

Most of what we know about human leadership from the beginning of human history dates to the first civilizations that appear 4000–5000 years Before Common Era (BCE) in the Fertile Crescent in Mesopotamia, often referred to as the cradle of civilization. These first civilizations were hierarchical and often had despotic leaders that oppressed or enslaved their people. The emergence of these civilizations was preceded by two major events: (1) The end of the ice ages 11,700 years ago that put an end to severe climate oscillations and brought the beginning of a period of climate stabilization and (2) The invention of agriculture and domestication of animals 10,000 years ago[1] (the Neolithic revolution) that produced a rapid increase of sedentary populations.

DOI: 10.4324/9781003265122-2

What we know about *prehistoric* leadership is based on evidence gathered from the fossil record and from the ethnographies of the few hundred remaining illiterate nomadic hunter-gatherers studied in the past 100 years all over the world. These nomadic foragers all live in small groups of about 30 individuals who are highly cooperative and egalitarian. Leadership is antiauthoritarian, unobtrusive, and functional based on competencies such as hunting and gathering skills (Boehm, 1999, 2012; Hill et al., 2009, 2011; Kelly, 2013; Lee, 1979; Woodburn, 1982). The prehistorical evidence is confined to nomadic foragers that lived in Africa during the Middle Palaeolithic 100,000 years ago and in Europe during the Upper Palaeolithic 45,000 years ago. There is a scientific consensus that by the Middle and Upper Palaeolithic our nomadic ancestors had achieved emotional, cognitive, symbolic, and behavioral capacities that are comparable, if not identical to contemporary humans.

To put this in perspective, what we know about leadership in egalitarian nomadic societies represents 95% of the prehistory and history of our species. Our recorded history, beginning with the first civilizations in Mesopotamia 5000 years ago, represents just 5%. This is a very conservative estimate because many students of human evolution believe we began the transformation toward more cooperative nomadic foragers 2 million years ago with the appearance of *Homo erectus*. That means a staggering 99.98% of the total timespan of our species.

A Roadmap for the Chapter

To begin to tell the story of this 95% plus of our human timespan I will describe two recorded cases of encounters of Europeans—coming from societies that have designated leaders—when they come into contact with illiterate and "primitive" nomadic foragers in which headmen do not exist. Following these telling anecdotes I divide the chapter into four parts:

- In Part I, I review the evidence that supports the view that contemporary nomadic foragers and their prehistoric ancestors have had an egalitarian social organization that has resisted being dominated by bullies.
- In Part II, I explain that our human ancestors diverged from a common ancestor we had with contemporary chimpanzees six to seven million

years ago. Chimpanzees live in dominant-submissive hierarchies controlled by alpha males. This means that this common ancestor also had a social organization based on dominance-submission. Humans are the only great ape[2] that made a transformation from this hierarchical type of social organization to a new egalitarian social organization in which dominance by alpha males was suppressed. I review current explanations of how this major transformation might have taken place.

• In Part III, I show that soon after we began abandoning our nomadic existence new forms of hierarchical and despotic leaders emerge in the form of complex agricultural societies. These social hierarchies were not just a return to dominance hierarchies of our great ape relatives, but a new form of social organization.

• In Part IV, I sketch historic milestones in the development of new republican and democratic institutions that constrain tyrants from gaining control and attempt to create more equal and just societies.

I conclude by summarizing what we can learn from this brief sweeping dive into the *prehistory* of human egalitarianism and leadership and the *historic* evolution that followed.

Nineteenth-century Europeans First Encounters with Nomadic Foragers

Europeans often wanted something from "primitive natives" when they came in contact with them and would ask for their headman. Christopher Boehm, a cultural anthropologist, and primatologist that has studied the history of egalitarianism from evolutionary and cultural perspectives, recounts two of these encounters (Boehm, 1999). Boehm tells us about an English missionary who had been living for some time among the Ona, nomadic foragers who lived in Tierra del Fuego in the southern tip of South America. The English missionary was introducing a "certain scientist visitor" to the Ona who was inquiring about who was their headman:

> [...] In answer to inquiries about this matter, I told him that the Ona had no chieftains, as we understand the word. Seeing that he did not

understand me I summoned Kankoat, who by that time spoke some Spanish. When the visitor repeated the question, Kankoat, too polite to answer in the negative, said: "yes, señor, we, the Ona have many chiefs. The men are all captains, and the women are all sailors."

(Boehm, 1999, p.62)

This clever and polite answer is similar to one reported by Richard Lee who wrote a classic ethnography of the !Kung, the nomadic foragers living in the Kalahari desert (Lee, 1979). When asked who their headman was, and sensing the puzzlement of his interlocutor, a member of the !Kung responded: "Of course we have headmen...each one is a headman over himself" (Boehm, 1999, p. 61).

This principle of equality is one of the defining characteristics of leadership among modern nomadic foragers living in disparate geographic regions. Autonomy is highly valued among them, and upstarts are not allowed to dominate the group. Any attempt by a member of the group to become dominant is fiercely resisted through a combination of social pressures and sanctions such as ostracism, and through the power that social reputations have in keeping bullies in check.

Rather than describing qualities of leadership in positive terms, nomadic hunter-gatherers tend to describe humility and lack of arrogance as desirable qualities. Boehm quotes Richard Lee, whose informant explained the kind of attitude that the !Kung expects from exceptional hunters:

Say a man has been hunting. He must not come home and announce like a braggart, "I have killed a big one on the bush!" He must first sit down in silence until I or someone else comes up to his fire and asks. 'What did you see today'?" He replies quietly, "Ah I am not good for hunting. I saw nothing at all...maybe just a tiny one." Then I smile to myself because I know he has killed something big (Boehm, 1999, p. 49).

Polly Wiessner who did fieldwork over several decades with the !Kung Bushman reports that one of the main themes of social gossip that she recorded involved several dozen instances where critical comments were made about "big-shot" behavior (Boehm, 1999, p. 70). Criticisms of braggarts and active suppression of any member of the group who tries to exert dominance over the group can only be understood by looking at nomadic foragers holistically as egalitarian societies that shape individual behaviors and personality types.

Part I: The Shared Traits of Egalitarian Nomadic Foragers

These stories of first encounters with Europeans capture essential qualities about leadership among nomadic egalitarian societies, and are summarized by the anthropologist Richard Lee:

> Egalitarianism is not simply the *absence* of a headman and authority figures, but a positive insistence on the essential equality of all people and the refusal to bow to the authority of others.
>
> (Richard B. Lee The !Kung San: Men, Women, and
> Work in a Foraging Society 1979, p. 457)

This principle of equality among all members of nomadic bands is one of their defining characteristics of leadership. What is remarkable is that this principle is present among nomadic foragers living in as disparate geographic regions as the !Kung in the Kalahari desert, the Inuit in the Arctic tundra, or the Yanomamo in the Amazon jungle (Boehm, 1999).

Christopher Boehm embarked on a systematic review of all the 339 ethnographies of illiterate nomadic hunter-gatherers scattered all over the world (Boehm, 1999, 2012). To find the "right kinds of modern hunter-gatherers" that might resemble our prehistoric foragers, Boehm selected illiterate nomadic bands based on their maintaining their nomadic existence with minimal or no contact with the outside world. This meant excluding bands that had been interacting with Europeans for a long time, had become dependent on evangelizing missions, bands that traded with surrounding horticulturalists, or that had begun to cultivate their own food. Boehm also excluded nomadic bands such as the Apache and the Comanche that had domesticated horses. That left 150 nomadic groups. In his 2012 book on the Evolution of Morals, Boehm looked more carefully at 50 of these nomadic groups and selected ten of them for systematic coding of common traits (Boehm, 2012). These 10 selected nomadic groups live in completely different geographic areas around the world and are good representatives of nomadic bands' ecological diversity. These strict selection criteria provide a basis to believe that whatever similarities in leadership and social organization emerge are due to a nomadic hunter-gathering mode of existence, and not to adaptations to living in radically diverse geographic and climatic conditions. The common denominator of all the 10 nomadic bands is their mode of subsistence based on hunting and gathering activities.

But even before this exhaustive analysis, in his 1999 book on the *Evolution of Egalitarianism*, Boehm had already concluded: "Extant foragers seem to be invariably egalitarian, as long as *they remain basically nomadic*" (my italics, Boehm, 1999, p. 88). This general conclusion is consistent with many other anthropologists that have done extensive fieldwork and lived for many years among illiterate nomadic hunter-gatherers (Kelly, 2013; Lee, 1979).

Even after having domesticated plants and animals, the majority of nomadic groups became organized into larger tribes that maintained an egalitarian social organization. According to Service (1962) and Fried (1967), tribesmen are *by definition* an egalitarian stage in political organization between pre-Neolithic nomadic foragers and post-Neolithic hierarchical chiefdoms dominated by strong men. This shows that an egalitarian social organization continued to have a significant pull even after we developed into agricultural and pastoral societies.

The Social Character of Nomadic Bands

Within the psychoanalytic literature, Erich Fromm's *social character* theory explains how the way humans make a living exerts a strong influence, sometimes determining their social values, behaviors, and personalities. As opposed to an *individual* character that is the result of genetic, parental, and cultural factors interacting with each other through development, *social* character refers to *shared* character traits and social norms that are internalized by group members as adaptations to prevailing socioeconomic conditions in which they live (Fromm, 1941, 1962; Fromm & Maccoby, 1970). As Fromm put it, social character functions so people "will want to do what they have to do to survive within society" (Fromm & Maccoby, 1970, p. 19). According to Fromm, parents act as the psychic agents of society in the process of socializing and internalizing values, attitudes, and behaviors, and this socialization is reinforced later through social institutions.

In their Mexican study, Fromm and Maccoby advance the concept of social selection to explain how certain traits in people are selected to fit in the culture and class in which they live. As I will show, the concept of social selection is starting to be used in evolutionary theory to explain how some costly behaviors can nevertheless remain in the gene pool. This is an interesting convergence of concepts coming from a sociological and psychologically informed analysis of society and evolutionary theory. Using Fromm's social character theory we can examine Boehm's systematic coding of frequently mentioned personality traits and values to obtain a social character profile of these nomadic foragers.

In all these nomadic groups generosity toward kin is unanimously mentioned. But what is remarkable and rare about nomadic foragers is that generosity toward members is not only limited to family members but is expressed toward all members of the band that are not family members that become "as if " adopted family members living in neighboring bands (Wiessner, 2002). This pattern is consistent with a large study of nomadic foragers, comprised of over 5000 individuals that found that most members of these bands were not genetically related (Hill et al., 2011).

Polly Wiessner was able to observe first-hand how this form of altruism or generosity toward neighboring bands worked—some who were kin and some who were not but are considered "as if" or adopted family members that lived as far as 200 km away from each other (Wiessner, 2002). The San people in the Kalahari Desert were able to mitigate starvation during a severe and prolonged drought through a system of gift-giving called Hxaro that designates gift exchanges to genetically related and nonrelated "as if" group members. This form of extended altruism toward nonkin is very rare and usually is only found in ultrasocial and hyper-cooperative species, technically referred to as eusocial species

Aside from generosity, the other social character traits mentioned in Boehm's ten nomadic foraging groups were:

- Sharing, particularly sharing of meat.
- Humility.
- Even temperedness.
- A strong condemnation against antisocial behaviors. Most frequently mentioned were selfishness, bullying, cheating, stealing, and lying (Boehm, 2012, pp. 191–199).

These attitudes of humility, even temperedness, and generosity are inculcated in childhood while arrogance and lack of emotional control are seen as highly undesirable (Boehm, 1999, 2012; Bonta, 1997; Lee, 1979).

The Archeological and Fossil Evidence

Despite Boehm's careful attempt to select modern nomadic foragers that might have resembled their prehistoric ancestors, his evidence for continuity is indirect. Does the archeologically evidence provide any support? Behavior does not fossilize, so archeological excavations and fossil records have to be explored carefully to infer behaviors. The strongest and most remarkable archeological evidence showing cultural and cognitive continuity between prehistoric and *some* historic hunter-gatherers comes from the Border Cave in southern Africa. The cave gets its name because it is situated on the border between the Lambobo Mountains in Mozambique and Swaziland. Using a variety of methods the artifacts and ornaments in the cave were dated to be 44,000 years old (d'Errico et al., 2012). All these artifacts and ornaments are nearly identical to those used by contemporary San hunter-gatherers that live in southern Africa—also known as the Bushmen. The artifacts include "digging sticks" used to dig out tubers, bone points used as arrowheads bearing traces of a poisonous compound found in the castor bean, four bones with notches that the team interprets as "tally sticks" used for counting, personal ornaments made of ostrich eggs possibly used as necklaces (also seen in contemporary San people), and traces of organic material used as resins for gluing. The main investigator, Francesco d'Errico concludes that the artifacts "strongly point to a continuity in material culture and lifestyle" with the San People living today (Balter, 2012, p. 512). Yet, d'Errico points out, this is not a proof of continuity in other cultural expressions such as language abilities, religious beliefs, and social organization over 44,000 years, but it does make this a viable hypothesis. Polly Wiessner who lived among the San People for several years believes the evidence is convincing, but cautions that similar artifacts might not have had the same meaning in the past. Erella Hovers, a distinguished archeologist from Hebrew University thinks that the Border cave evidence "is probably as strong as prehistory can offer" (Balter, 2012, p. 512).

Developmental Studies

Present day research supports the view of a natural inclination toward prosocial tendencies. In one study, three- and nine-month-old infants are shown animated movies with a round red geometric figure with eyes (to help them look more human-like) trying to climb up a hill. In one clip, a square yellow figure comes from behind and gently nudges the red figure up the hill (the helper). In another clip, a green triangular figure goes in front of the red figure and pushes him down (the hinderer). When infants are exposed to a clip with the helper or hinderer characters approaching the red round figure, they look longer at the hinderer because it violates their expectations that caregivers will behave as helpers (Bloom, 2013; Hamlin & Wynn, 2011; Hamlin et al., 2010). The research team designed another experiment using puppets to recreate a similar helper/hinderer story instead of movie clips with older infants. After the mini-show, the helper and hinderer figures were placed in a tray in front of the infants. Invariably, the infants reached for the helper puppet. According to Bloom, "These experiments show that infants have what philosophers of the Scottish Enlightenment call a moral sense. This is not the same as the impulse to do good or evil. Rather ... it is the capacity to distinguish good and bad, kindness and cruelty" (Bloom, 2013, p. 31).

Another indication of the prosociality of our species is shown in older infants that will spontaneously help others. Tomasello and colleagues have documented spontaneous prosocial motivations in 14–18-month-olds (Warneken & Tomasello, 2006, 2007). In a typical example, an adult experimenter, who is a stranger, is carrying a stack of magazines with both hands and trying unsuccessfully to open a cabinet door. Without any prompting of a parent who is in the room quietly watching, these toddlers will open the door to the cabinet. These videotapes illustrate, in ways that a verbal description fails to convey, the spontaneous nature of these pro-social helping behaviors[3]. Controls consist of similar situations where it is clear to these toddlers that the adult experimenter does not need help. In this case, they will not provide help.

Another line of evidence showing an intrinsic motivation to adapt to the group or culture in which children develop can be seen in a series of experiments of three to five-year-olds attending daycare. These young children readily adopt shared values and behaviors they see in their peers and that are supported by their teachers (Schmidt & Tomasello, 2012; Tomasello, 2016). Not only do they adapt to these shared norms and desirable behaviors, but they quickly teach them to their peers, and protest when they deviate from expected behaviors (Köymen et al., 2014; Schmidt & Tomasello, 2012).

A Cautionary Note

I do not want to leave the impression that others or I think illiterate, egalitarian nomads and their lifeways represent a Garden of Eden. Based on what we know of contemporary nomadic bands, their lives are hard. Infant mortality rates and death from childbirth are high (Kelly, 2013, pp. 200–209). Compared to people living in contemporary societies, life has improved vastly for people who have access to health care and a standard of living above the poverty line. Disputes among nomadic foragers show levels of violence that are as high as some recorded in the last 200 years in poverty-stricken inner cities and slums around the world (Pinker, 2011). The improvements are the direct result of political, judicial, and policing institutions. The cultural accumulation of knowledge has accelerated at an enormous speed after the Stone Age with a series of technological, scientific, and social revolutions over the last 10,000 years that has made life much easier for billions of people (Boyd, 2018; Henrich, 2016; Pinker, 2011). This statement has to be qualified. In the last 50 years, these dramatic improvements have been deteriorating in many parts of the world as the result of globalization and neo-liberal policies that have created huge economic disparities and the polarization of societies (Pikkety, 2020).

Organized warfare, the most deadly form of violence, is the product of complex societies that emerge after the Neolithic revolution, not the product of pre-Neolithic egalitarian nomads (Bregman, 2019; Ferguson, 2013a, 2013b; Fry, 2013b; Fry & Söderberg, 2013; Fuentes, 2013). Douglas Fry, who has been one of the main scholars looking at this issue, reaches the conclusion that prehistoric nomadic foragers are typically unwarlike. Cases in which war is present often involve conditions that existed after the Neolithic among pastoralists, farmers, ranchers, and colonial powers. He notes that a few remaining nomads have been observed resorting to intergroup violence, but it is almost always in self-defence upon the encroachment of their nomadic lands by agricultural or pastoral people (Fry, 2013a).

This issue is controversial. Steven Pinker (2011) and Samuel Bowles have examined archeological and fossil data that they think shows that deadly intergroup violence was common in our species prehistory. But other archeologists and historians have looked at the same data and find those conclusions are unwarranted because they exaggerate the degree of intergroup violence (Ferguson, 2013a, 2013b) or because the fossil evidence for violent intergroup violence is ambiguous. The causes of death could be the results of accidents, caused by predators or by intragroup violence (Bregman, 2019; Fuentes, 2013). Some scholars such as Christopher Boehm make the case that you can find evidence that supports both views: prehistoric and historic nomads were capable of resolving conflicts and being peacemakers *and* engaging in intergroup violence (Boehm, 2013).

Richard Lee has undertaken a systematic review of the literature looking at different claims about intergroup violence among historic human nomadic foragers (HNF) (Lee, 2014). He weighs in on the controversy between what he calls the "bellicose group" and what others have called dismissively the "peace and harmony mafia." Lee reaches the following conclusion:

> Taking all the evidence together, the empirical basis for the bellicose school views of HNF is unsupported. The image held by the bellicose group is almost unrecognizable in light of a century of careful ethnographic research in dozens of HNF from the Artic to the Americas to Africa.
>
> (Lee, 2014, p. 223)

Although this issue is tangential to the main argument of this chapter about the prehistoric origin of egalitarianism and antiauthoritarianism, the debate is important. Tennyson's "nature red in tooth and claw" and Hobbes's view that human nature as "nasty, brutish and short" have been prevailing beliefs (Bregman, 2019; de Waal, 2013; Lee, 2014). As mentioned earlier, contemporary authors such as Steven Pinker (2011) and Robert Wrangham and Peterson (1996) support a modern version of this dark view claiming that prehistoric nomadic foragers were violent and engaged in frequent warfare. As Lee points out the views of what he calls "the bellicose group" are seen as hard-nosed empirical realists, while the views of the "peace and harmony mafia" are seen as romantic and indulging in Rousseau's myth of the "noble savage." Regardless of what bias both camps may bring to the debate, the issue is an empirical question, and the evidence does not support the bellicose group.

From what can be inferred from modern nomadic foragers, our nomadic ancestors were no angels. They can engage in violent disputes among themselves over betrayals and jealousies and can plot deadly revenges, but they were not warlike. Organized warfare is the product of societies in which conflicts arise over economic surpluses and disputes overprized rich territories. So without romanticizing the lives of illiterate nomadic foragers, there is still much we can learn from them. They were very successful in controlling bullies, one of the scourges that have plagued humans throughout their prehistory and history. Their egalitarian ethos produced a respect for autonomy and human dignity, and a generous attitude toward others. Their nomadic lives, in which there were no economic or technological surpluses that could be coveted, led to peaceful coexistence and sometimes mutual help.

There is no controversy, however, that tribal societies that emerged *after* the domestication of plants and animals, including many of them that maintained an egalitarian social organization, engaged in intergroup feuds, raids, and territorial warfare with high levels of lethality (Boehm, 1999, pp. 90–91). There are a few exceptions of tribesmen that were peaceful, such as the Yurok fisherman on the Northwest Pacific coast in the United States. The Yurok were able to remain peaceful because they were geographically isolated in a mountainous region that was very difficult to access except by boat. They had an abundance of salmon, tubers, and fruit to live from without having to worry about competition from neighboring tribes (Erikson, 1950). This is another reminder that ecological and geographic conditions can often tip the scale in determining whether groups can coexist peacefully or engage in intergroup violence and determine the type of social organization that may exist.

Part II: From Dominant-submissive Hierarchies to an Egalitarian Suppression of Bullies

Our human ancestors diverged from a common ancestor we had with the chimpanzees six to seven million years ago. Except for humans, all our great ape relatives live in dominant-submissive hierarchies in which alpha males dominate the group. There is an important exception to male dominance in nonhuman primates. As I will discuss shortly, female bonobos resist being dominated by males by forming strong alliances.

Anthropologists and evolutionary thinkers have long pondered the question of how our human ancestors could have made a transition to antiauthoritarian, egalitarian nomadic social organization. Boehm (1999) proposes a hypothesis that he called a "reverse dominance hierarchy" to explain how this transformation came about. Boehm shows that chimpanzees have an ambivalent tendency toward domination and a desire not to be dominated. Chimpanzees occasionally form alliances to overthrow an alpha male. But unlike nomadic foragers, chimpanzees immediately reestablish a new hierarchy with a dominant alpha taking control. He believes our human ancestors inherited this ambivalent attitude toward power. Boehm's main thesis is that dominance based on power among our ancestral nomadic foragers did not disappear, but was suppressed by a reversal of this power structure. Among our human ancestors, this happened as rank-and-file members of the band united to prevent any single individual from taking control of the group. In effect, they inverted the power structure of the group through various means such as sanctioning potential upstarts who would wish to gain control.

This interpretation resembles Freud's account in Totem and Taboo in which he proposed that a band of brothers united to kill the tyrannical father in order to take possession of their mother (Freud, 1913). The difference is that Boehm's explanation is based on the need of nomadic foragers to keep any individual from gaining control of food resources and females. Freud's Oedipal interpretation is wrong on several grounds. Incest avoidance among nonhuman primates is achieved by females (rarely males) leaving their natal group when they mature sexually, not be repressing sexual impulses (Chapais, 2008). With the exception of gorillas that maintain long-term bonds with a harem under their control, pair bonding in humans is unique among great apes and had many cascading effects. According to Chapais, a very important effect was that fathers, who maintained a long-term mating pattern with a female and thus stayed around as progeny grew up, were able to recognize their progeny. This led males to become less aggressive toward their sons, who they did not see as rivals. Keep in mind that among our great ape relatives, males mate promiscuously and do not recognize their kin. They see all males as potential rivals. Furthermore, when daughters began to mate with other males, those "affines," who stayed around the natal group, became less of a threat to the father.

The end result is that pair bonding inhibited endogamy (mating inside the natal group) and supported mating outside the natal group (exogamy), thus avoiding incest. Chapais' explanation is more complex, but for reasons of space I will not go into more detail. But Chapais' proposal is consistent with the explanation of incest avoidance in humans proposed by the nineteenth-century Scandinavian anthropologist Edvard Westermarck (Westermarck, 1891/1926). Westermarck proposed that incest avoidance among individuals that grow up during childhood in close proximity, whether they are kin related or not, do not develop sexual interest toward each other. For evidence supporting the Westermarck hypothesis see the work of Mark Erickson (Erickson, 1993; Erickson, 2000).

If we accept Boehm's idea of a reverse dominance hierarchy based on power dynamics, how then can we account for nomadic foragers genuine sense of generosity? Generosity is based on altruism and trust, not power dynamics. To explain this, Boehm draws on the work of the evolutionary biologist and entomologist Richard Alexander and his concept of indirect reciprocity (Alexander, 1974, 1987), and on the concept of social selection. Alexander's concept of indirect reciprocity refers to the effects of people gossiping about other members' behaviors. In small groups of nomadic foragers, gossip has powerful effects. Bad reputations and repeated offenses to the prevailing egalitarian norms can lead to ostracism by the whole group with devastating emotional effects. Boehm vividly describes this when one of his outspoken colleagues, who had become "adopted" by a powerful Inuit group member, broke rules of conduct in a well-intentioned effort to help them from being exploited by outsiders (Boehm, 1999, pp. 51–57).

The social selection concept is used by Boehm to explain how costly altruistic and generous behaviors toward conspecifics (members of the same species) could have emerged. Unlike the role of natural selection that operates *randomly* through spontaneous genetic mutations, the social selection is *targeted* and *directional*, favoring behaviors that have positive adaptive and reproductive effects. The concept of social selection was built on Darwin's concept of sexual selection (West-Eberhard, 1983). Darwin used sexual selection to explain behaviors that appear at first blush to be highly costly, such as peacocks' tails. This extravagant display of plumage is designed to court females by signaling exceptional fitness. The large energetic cost of this exotic plumage is compensated by its power to attract females. Similarly, the concept of social selection has been developed to explain the targeted selection of costly behaviors, such as generosity toward nonkin and strangers (Jablonka & Lamb, 2005; West-Eberhard, 1983, 2003). Boehm believes that over the course of 2000 generations of reverse dominance—the time needed for natural selection to have permanent effects—selective pressures favored individuals who were generous and caring toward kin and nonkin through the combined power of social reputations and social selection. In turn, the combination of these prosocial motivations paved the way for the development of egalitarian and antiauthoritarian values.

The Self-domestication Hypothesis

While in agreement with Boehm about the role played by sanctioning of social deviants through ostracism and killing if necessary the primatologists Richard Wrangham, and Brain Hare propose that there was a selection for friendliness among ancestral humans and bonobos that made them a less aggressive species through a process of domestication that occurred in the wild (Hare et al., 2012; Wrangham, 2019). They base their proposal on the remarkable experiments done by the soviet geneticist and zoologist Dimitry Belyaev and his close research assistant and colleague Lyudmila Trut (Wrangham, 2019). Belyaev decided to try to domesticate silver foxes that had been in captivity in Siberia for many generations. It was a huge gamble, but Lyudmila Trut went to Siberia and began systematically selecting silver fox puppies for one of the longest scientific experiments ever conducted with the goal of understanding the genetic basis and behavioral changes of domesticated species. Puppies were selected for breeding because juveniles in most species tend to be less aggressive and more playful than adults. The results came in quickly. By the third generation, some of these experimental populations of foxes bred for friendliness were showing significantly less aggressive and fearful responses. By the sixth generation, some of the friendly foxes were wagging their tails like dogs and whimpered to call attention.

By the fiftieth generation, friendly foxes showed the whole syndrome of domesticated animals: the retention of juvenile characteristics results in smaller, flatter faces with reduced jaws, and smaller teeth, smaller canines used as aggressive weapons. Juvenile-looking more feminized faces that make infants of many domesticated species look "cute" and endearing, and floppy ears. Another unintended side effect of domestication is the retention of playful behaviors that have important adaptive effects enhancing social learning, imitation, and developmental plasticity (Wrangham, 2019).

Wrangham and Hare argue that bonobos are much less aggressive than their almost identical cousins the chimpanzees. They think that together with humans, bonobos may be another case of domestication in the wild reached through different but convergent evolutionary paths. Bonobos develop strong female alliances through several means such as grooming each other and homosexual rubbing against each other's genitals (Wrangham, 2019). These female alliances allow bonobos to form coalitions to fend off males that might threaten or bully them and in general are less aggressive and more cooperative than chimpanzees. The significance of this observation for understanding human evolution was first made by Amy Parish and Franz de Waal (Parish et al., 2000) We should credit bonobos as being the first feminist primate species!

The self-domestication hypothesis is interesting but seems more like a metaphor for a particular Darwinian process of social selection than an actual explanation. According to Hrdy (personal communication), more docile and prosocial outcomes were more likely the result of social selection of infants and young children striving to appeal to, be accepted by, or chosen as a recipient of food by another individual (West-Eberhard, 1983; Hrdy, 2016; Hrdy & Burkardt, 2020). This process is a case of Darwinian social selection as defined by West-Eberhard (1983) and resembles Alexander's social selection concept mentioned earlier.

It Takes a Village to Raise a Child

Sarah Hrdy has proposed that this form of social selection took place through a process of cooperative infant care in which mothers allow others (allomothers) to assist in feeding and take care of their infants, technically described as cooperative breeding. (Hrdy, 2009). According to Hrdy, there are some minor degrees of provisioning by others in about 50% of primates. But only among New World small monkeys belonging to the subfamily Callitrichidae, the marmosets, and the tamarins, and in humans do we find full-blown cooperative breeders where *allomothers or alloparents,* assist in the care and provisioning of infants. Interestingly, marmosets and tamarins have high levels of cooperation and sharing despite having very small brains, but they don't have the capacity to understand the intentions of members of their same species as some nonhuman great apes have in competitive situations—see below (Burkart et al., 2009; Burkart & Van Schaik, 2010). According to Hrdy and others, cooperative care had cascading effects on already larger brained, cognitively more sophisticated apes that were in the line leading to the genus *Homo*. These cascading effects:

1. Allowed mothers to wean their infants earlier and become pregnant sooner than mothers who are exclusive providers of care.
2. Allowed hominin nomadic forager ancestors to increase their intake of calories, as mothers were free to do more gathering of foods such as nuts and tubers to feed their infants with the help of allomothers.
3. Over time, a new phenotype in infants developed in which a combination of being attractive, extra fat (that signals good fitness), and a tendency to respond with smiles to multiple caretakers from very early in development, made them a subject of directed social selection. This cemented this new phenotype in the gene pool of our human ancestors.
4. According to Sarah Hrdy, this produced a "quest for intersubjective engagement" among infants who in order to be cared for and fed needed to monitor the intentions and preference of others so as to appeal to and ingratiate themselves with potential caretakers, conditioning infants to become more "other directed" (Hrdy, 2016). This desire to be engaged not only with their attachment figures, but with others as well is what Hrdy means when she says that our nomadic ancestors became "emotionally modern" before they became behaviorally and cognitively modern equipped with language and symbolic communication (Hrdy, 2016).
5. Multiple lines of evidence show that infants with the motivation to be engaged with multiple caretakers accelerates their ability to understand the intentions, and eventually the minds of others—referred to as *mentalization* in psychoanalytic literature and "Theory of Mind" in the academic literature Hrdy, 2009, 2016). In turn, this capacity makes infants and young children dramatically better at cooperating to share experiences with others—such as when they start pointing to objects of interest with their caregivers by

12 months of age, something chimpanzees and bonobos in the wild never do (Tomasello et al., 2007; Warneken et al., 2006). It also makes them able to use this expanded joint attentional capacity to collaborate with others in joint activities and change roles with them in these joint projects—again something our great ape relatives cannot do (Tomasello & Carpenter, 2007; Tomasello et al., 2007).

According to Hrdy, the best guess of when this form of cooperative care might have emerged is 2 million years ago with the appearance of Homo erectus (Hrdy, 2016). Homo erectus had a brain size of 900 cc, double the size of the previous hominin species, the Australopithecines. Brains are very expensive organs and consume 25% of our total caloric intake. Moreover, infant brains are growing at fetal rates way into their first year, and their brains consume a whopping 50% of their total caloric intake. Mothers who were the exclusive caregivers would not have been able to provision these babies without the help of allomothers. Since the first big jump in brain size during human prehistory takes place with Homo erectus, it seems likely that the energetic demands involved would have required new ways of caring for and provisioning these very costly and slow-maturing youngsters. Cooperative childcare fitted these needs.

In summary, infants and young children who had developed "a quest for intersubjective engagement" and had become emotionally modern and other-directed, were already emotionally different apes before the evolution of big-brained anatomically modern humans with the symbolic and linguistic capacities of behaviorally modern ones. This greatly enhanced their ability to cooperate with others and set the stage for future accomplishments during human evolution. It helped to develop the type of solidarity that Boehm describes that allowed our human ancestors to reverse the power structure of our great ape societies and become egalitarian and antiauthoritarian nomadic foragers. The other-directed nature of children and adults also supported the degree of sharing and generosity seen in extant nomadic foragers around the world.

Tomasello's Joint and Collective Intentionality Hypotheses

Tomasello and his colleagues have developed an impressive body of research in the last few decades that have influenced, and in many ways complements, the work of Sarah Hrdy. According to Tomasello, selective pressures that led to the need to cooperate at high levels were the result of severe climate changes that affected Africa during the ice ages. These changes produced drastic oscillations in weather patterns, from prolonged dry periods creating savannah like environments, to very wet periods creating monsoon type of weather with lakes and overflowing rivers (Potts, 2013).

Tomasello's main proposals are that the need for higher levels co-operation favored the development of new sociocognitive capacities. These capacities consisted in the ability to coordinate intentions and goals with others, what Tomasello calls a shared or joint form of intentionality (Tomasello & Carpenter, 2007; Tomasello et al., 2005). Tomasello and his colleagues believe that during the first phase of human evolution this form of joint or shared intentionality went hand in hand with the ability to exchange roles during joint tasks. The ability to exchange roles is an early form perspective-taking capacity that helped our ancestors develop mentalizing abilities ("Theory of Mind"). These capacities show up early in the ontogeny of young children, an indirect indication that they are evolutionary predispositions of our species (Tomasello, 2014; Tomasello & Carpenter, 2007; Tomasello & Gonzalez-Cabrera, 2017).

During the second phase of human evolution, humans scale-up a two-person joint form of intentionality to a collective form of intentionality that allowed humans to coordinate complicated activities, such as the planning required for big game hunting expeditions (Tomasello, 2019). The emergence of a collective form of intentionality was accompanied by the emergence of shared social norms that further supported cooperation and paved the way for being able to live in cultures that we create (Tomasello, 1999, 2009, 2014). This second phase was also the beginning of a new form of evolution in which cultural norms begin to play a major role, and where cultural and technological innovations are transmitted from one generation to the next—what Tomasello calls the "ratchet effect" of cultural transmission (Tomasello, 2014, 2016; Tomasello et al., 2012). Over thousands of generations, these cumulative effects had led to astounding accomplishments, allowing humans to create large-scale democratic forms of governance, send men to the men, and create digital computers that have revolutionized the way we communicate and obtain information.

The second line of research that supports these general conclusions compares our great ape relatives and young children in tests that look at a general intelligence to manipulate their physical environment, and a sociocognitive intelligence that requires an understanding of the goals, intentions, and perspectives of others (Tomasello, 2014, 2016, 2019; Tomasello & Carpenter, 2005). I cannot go into details of all these comparative studies (for summaries see Tomasello's 2014 and 2016 books), but one of the major findings is that our great ape relatives are as smart as young children in intelligence tasks that help manipulate the physical world, but young children markedly outperform our primate relatives in tasks that require an understanding of the goals, intentions, and perspectives of others in *cooperative* tasks (Herrmann et al., 2007). Yet when the researchers looked at the same sociocognitive tasks that require an understanding of the intentions of others in *competitive* tasks, chimpanzees and bonobos were quite capable of understanding the goals and intentions of others (Hare & Tomasello, 2004; Melis et al., 2006a, 2006b). Taken with the work of Sarah Hrdy's work, these results support the thesis that our human ancestors developed specialized sociocognitive and emotional capacities that made us an ultracooperative species.

Part III: Re-inventing Hierarchy and Social Inequalities

Four millennia after the invention of agriculture, human societies had evolved socially, economically, and culturally to become complex hierarchical societies ruled by authoritarian leaders. As mentioned earlier, this transition is seen in the first civilizations that appear in Mesopotamia and in Egypt four and five millennia ago. But even in small agricultural communities throughout Europe during the Bronze Age one thousand years earlier, very large social inequalities had become entrenched in small villages across Europe as the result of agricultural surpluses. The patriarchal rule came with these changes as rich, high-ranking families made alliances with each other to decide whom their daughters would marry. Evidence for this comes from two multidisciplinary research projects.

This first study was done in a site near the Lech River in Germany by the archeologist Phillip Stockhammer and geneticist Johannes Krause. The study is reported by Ann Gibbons in the journal *Science* (Gibbons, 2019)

This interdisciplinary team examined 104 DNA samples, chemical clues from teeth, and artifacts left in burial sites of people living in these agricultural farmsteads. The team was trying to establish relationship patterns associated with wealth inequality in farmers that lived 3300–4500 years ago.

One-third of the women's graves of high-ranking families were lavish, with elaborate copper headdresses, thick bronze leg rings, and decorated copper pins. The DNA samples of these women and the strontium isotopes in their teeth—that reflect the minerals of the water they drank until adolescence—showed that they were all outsiders. Some of the metal artifacts found in these graves reflect valued objects these women kept from their families of origin. These prised keepsakes are typical of regions that are 350 km away in what is now the Czech Republic.

One unexpected finding is that there were no signs of these wealthy women's daughters in the burials. This indicates that the families of rich people gave away all their daughters to marry the sons of rich farmers that lived far away. In contrast, the sons of these rich families stayed in their family's farmlands. Men's graves had bronze and copper daggers, axes, and chisels, all denoting the power and wealth they held. The gravesites also show that all the sons from these rich families were also buried lavishly, showing that not only the oldest sons inherited wealth. The research team was able to establish that men kept wealth within their families for four to five generations. The gravesites of poor farmers also contained unrelated villagers, but without any signs of wealth accumulation as in the rich families.

The second study comes from Ireland at a site 25 km north of Dublin that was thought to be a Stone Age masterpiece built by egalitarian societies—the study is reported by Andrew Curry in the journal Science (Curry, 2020). The archeological site is called Neograng and has a circular structure the size of a football field with columns 12 m high. It was built 1000 years before Stonehenge and the Egypt pyramids. DNA of a middle-aged man dated 3700 BCE was found in a chamber where royalty was buried in the center of this massive structure. His DNA showed that he belonged to ancient farmers that came from Anatolia across Europe and displaced nomadic hunter-gatherers over a period of 5000 years. The DNA of this man and the other DNA samples showed that he might have been married to his sister. Marriage among close family members only occurs among royal families and is linked to royalty across the world. In these same societies, incest is taboo among the people who do not belong to these royal elites. Royal families violate the incest taboo is to keep wealth concentrated within their families. Additional DNA of more than 40 people buried in other Neolithic sites a hundred kilometers away reveal they were all very closely related. Marriage among rich family members was the norm, and social status was inherited rather than obtained in a single lifetime. Chemical isotopes of bones in these royal burial sites show that they ate more meat and animal products than their contemporaries. Thomas Kador, one of the co-authors of this study, believes that this is evidence that "a small elite called the shots like in Egypt" (Curry, 2020, p. 1299). Supporting this conclusion is the fact that most of the Neolithic sites of human remains found during this same period show people were buried together in communal tombs with no signs of wealth or hierarchy—as was the case of the previous study.

An important caveat to these studies is that the accumulation of wealth produced by farming, leading to social inequalities and social class differences during the Neolithic, are not be always associated with farming, as reported by Heather Pringle in *Science* (2015). New archeological discoveries show that resource-rich nomadic hunter-gatherers produced social inequalities as evidenced by burial sites in two places. In Eastern Mediterranean 10,800–8200 years ago, and in the Canadian Northwest Plateau 2500–1000 years ago. These findings show that a surplus of resources, however, they may come about, open the door to social inequalities.

The emergence of hierarchical societies in the form of small farming communities during the early Bronze Age and the emergence of chiefdoms, kingdoms, and modern states is not just a case of the return of the repressed as Freud would put it. It was not the return to the dominance hierarchies of great ape relatives. As societies became larger, they required different forms of segmentation and differentiation. It has been well established that any group larger than 150 cannot function informally as nomadic stateless bands do, the so called Dunbar number (Dunbar, 2010). Larger groups require a certain degree of segmentation with different roles, functions, and institutions in which rulers gain enormous power over societies. Benoit Dubreuil has studied the evolution of hierarchies from an evolutionary perspective. He concludes that once a state apparatus is in place it "gives rulers the freedom both to provide public goods and pursue exploitative strategies on an unprecedented scale. It thus transforms the state simultaneously into the most efficient and most dangerous tool under human control" (Dubrueil, 2010, p. 230).

Part IV: Attempts to Limit the Tyrannical Power of Leaders Through Democratic Institutions

This last section is very brief because it covers the well-known historical record. Democratic institutions limited to male citizens emerge in Athens and Rome during the fifth century BCE. The Roman Empire lasted five centuries and created a *Pax Romana* based on the cultural and religious tolerance of groups they conquered, in return for adopting Roman laws and paying a levy to the empire. After the fall of the Charlemagne Empire eight centuries later (end of eighth-century CE), chartered independent cities began to develop self-governance based on voluntary organizations formed by merchants and guild associations (Henrich, 2020). Commerce was no longer based on kinship networks and clans, as had been the case for millennia. Trading with strangers began to be regulated through voluntary merchant associations. Rules and institutions emerge designed to establish trust and avoid being assaulted by bandits or cheated by free riders. Self-governing cities began forming partnerships, like the powerful Hanseatic League in Northern Europe. Premodern medieval Europe was setting the stage for new forms of social organization and leadership based on a new class of merchants and guild associations.

The next transition in the West to democratic states was difficult and bloody. Despotic and tyrannical kings and the landed aristocracy were threatened by the emergence of this new merchant class, and self-governing cities. In some cases, the transition toward republican and democratic societies violently forced kings and the aristocratic class out of power, or more peacefully by giving kings and their royal families' figurehead positions in the nascent democratic societies. The landed aristocracy began to fall as people serving the aristocratic landlords and monarchies found new jobs in factories created by the industrial revolution or started their own small businesses. The first democratically elected parliament was formed in England at the beginning of the eighteenth century. By the end of the century, the United States ratified a constitution declaring that all men are created equal—except for women and enslaved Black people. The French revolution makes a "Declaration of the Rights of Man and of the Citizen." The abolition of slavery and the suffragette movements are the products of the nineteenth and twentieth centuries.

Conclusion

So, what can knowledge of illiterate egalitarian and nomadic anti-authoritarian foragers teach us today? They teach us that the desire to be treated with respect for human dignity and autonomy and live in more equal conditions with our fellow human beings has deep roots going back at least 100,000 years or more. Studying these illiterate nomads also teaches us that as long as we maintained a nomadic form of existence, we could suppress tendencies toward domination by bullies, a tendency that we inherited from a common ancestor we had with chimpanzees six to seven million years ago. As Sarah Hrdy, Michael Tomasello, and others point out, our nomadic ancestors would not have been able to shift to an egalitarian social organization if prosocial motivations and capacities that kept bullies and free riders in check. But as soon as we invented agriculture and became sedentary, tendencies for domination, hierarchy, and privilege came roaring back in the form of complex hierarchical societies divided into strict social castes. And with economic surpluses, social castes, and growing inequalities, war became an all too common and deadly outcome, becoming all the more deadly as horses were used to wage war and new technologies emerged.

Controlling bullies and tyrants have always been an uphill battle and creating democratic institutions in the past two and a half-century has been a major human accomplishment. But there is no guarantee that they will survive. The re-emergence of right wing, illiberal, and authoritarian leaders in various parts of the world are to a large extent the product of globalization and neoliberal policies that have marginalized millions of people. These leaders have been able to gain the support of millions of followers and are subverting hard won democratic gains. It is a clear warning that we should never take democratic gains for granted. Democratic institutions are based on intangibles involving social trust and social norms that support democratic institutions. When authoritarian and narcissistic leaders subvert these intangibles by sowing divisions and undermining social norms, democratic institutions can collapse.

In the immensely long arc of the timespan of our species, the desire for autonomy, social solidarity generosity, and compassion toward fellow humans have remained an intrinsic part of our nature. These better angels are not just the products of history as Steven Pinker claims, but have deep prehistoric origins. Yet as Erich Fromm (1964) put it, humans have a "genius for good and evil." We have the capacity to be selfish, power hungry, and tribalistic, and we can demonize and dehumanize human groups creating an "us versus them mentality." We also have a capacity for caring, generosity, and compassion, a thirst for autonomy and freedom and respect for human dignity. We have always needed to nurture and support these better angels in order to combat the corrosive effects of authoritarian and megalomaniac leaders and social elites that will do everything they can to maintain their privilege and power. As Jon Stokes and Robert Duckles mention in this number, we need inspirational leaders that can and bring out the best in us, and as Charles Heckscher also points out in this number, we need leaders that can stimulate new conversations and create new institutions. The quality and character of leadership play an important role in influencing which side of our conflicted human nature will prevail.

Notes

1 The domestication of dogs had begun earlier, 16,000 years ago (Hare et al., 2002).
2 The great ape family includes chimpanzees, bonobos, gorillas, orangutans, and humans.
3 You can see some of these videos by going to Michael Tomasello's web site at: http://www.eva.mpg.de/psycho/videos/children_clothes.mpg.

References

Alexander, R. D. (1974). The evolution of social behavior. *Annual Review of Ecology and Systematics, 5*, 325–384.

Alexander, R. D. (1987). *The biology of moral systems.* Aldine and Gruyter.

Balter, M. (2012). Ice age tools hint to 40,000 years of bushman culture. *Science 337*, 512.

Bloom, P. (2013). *Just Babies: The origins of good and evil.* Random House PPC.

Boehm, C. (1999). *Hierarchy in the forest. The evolution of egalitarian behavior.* Harvard University Press.

Boehm, C. (2012). *Moral origins. The evolution of virtue, altruism, and shame.* Basic Books.

Boehm, C. (2013). The biocultural evolution of conflict resolution between groups In D. P. Fry (Ed.), *War, peace and human nature* (pp. 315–340). Oxford University Press.

Bonta, B. D. (1997). Cooperation and competition in peaceful societies. *Psychobiological Bulletin, 121,* 299–320.

Bowles, S. (2009). Did warfare among ancestral hunter-gatherers affect the evolution of human social behaviors? *Science,* 324: 1293–1298. DOI: 10.112 6/science.1168112.

Bowles, S. (2012). Warriors, levelers, and the role of conflict in human social evolution. *Science, 336,* 876–879.

Boyd, R. (2018). *A different kind of animal. How culture transforms our species.* Princeton University Press.

Bregman, R. (2019). *Humankind. A hopeful history.* Little, Brown and Company.

Burkart, M. J., Hrdy, S. B., & Van Schaik, C. P. (2009). Cooperative breeding and human cognitive development. *Evolutionary Anthropology 18,* 175–186.

Burkart, M. J., & Van Schaik, C. P. (2010). Cognitive consequences of co-operative breeding in primates? *Animal Cognition, 13,* 1–19. doi:10.1007/s1 0071-009-0263-7.

Chapais, B. (2008). *Primeval kinship. How pair bonding gave birth to human society.* Harvard University Press.

Curry, A. (2020). Incest in ancient Ireland suggests an elite ruled early farmers *Science 368,* 1299.

d'Errico, F., Backwell, L., Villa P. D. I. , Lucejko, J. J., Bamford, M. K., Higham, T. F. G., ... Beaumont, P. B. (2012). Early evidence of San material culture represented by organic artifacts from Border Cave, South Africa. *PNAS, 109,* 13214–13219.

de Waal, F. (2013). *The bonobo and the atheist. In search of humanism among the primates.* W.W. Norton.

Dubrueil, B. (2010). *Human evolution and the origins of hierarchies.* Cambridge University Press.

Dunbar, R. (2010). *How many friends does a person need? Dunbar's number and other evolutionary quirks.* Harvard University Press.

Erikson, E. (1950). Childhood and society, W.W. Norton.

Erickson, M. T. (1993). Rethinking Oedipus. An evolutionary perspective on incest avoidance. *The American Journal of Psychiatry*, 150(3), 411–416. 10.11 76/ajp.150.3.411.

Erickson, M. T. (2000). The evolution of incest avoidance. Oedipus and the paychopathologies of kinship. In P. Gilbert & K. G. Bradley (Eds.), *Genes on the couch. Exploration in evolutionary psychotherapy* (pp. 211–232). Brunner Routledge.

Ferguson, R. B. (2013a). Pinker's list. Exagerating prehistoric war mortality. In D. P. Fry (Ed.), *War, peace and human nature. The convergence of evolutionary and clinical views* (pp. 112–131). Oxford University Press.

Ferguson, R. B. (2013b). The prehistory of war and peace in Europe and the Near East. In D. P. Fry (Ed.), *War, peace and human nature. The convergence of evolutionary and cultural views* (pp. 191–240). Oxford University Press.

Freud, S. (1913). 'Totem and taboo', in *The standard edition of the complete psychological works of Sigmund Freud. Vol. XIII*. The Hogarth Press, 1953, pp. 1–162.

Fried, M. (1967). *The evolution of political society. An essay in political anthropology*. Random House.

Fromm, E. (1941). *Escape from freedom*. Farrar and Rinehart, Inc.

Fromm, E. (1962). *Beyond the chains of illusion. My encounter with Mark and Freud*. Simon and Shuster.

Fromm, E., & Maccoby, M. (1970). *Social character in a Mexican village*. Prentice Hall.

Fromm. (1964). *The heart of man, Its genius for good and evil*. Harper & Row.

Fry, D. P. (2013a). War, peace and human nature. The challenge of achieving scientific objectivity. In D. P. Fry (Ed.), *War, peace, and human nature; The convergence of evolutionary and cultural views*. (pp. 1–22). Oxford University Press.

Fry, D. P. (Ed.) (2013b). *War, peace, and human nature; The convergence of evolutionary and cultural views*. Oxford University Press.

Fry, D. P., & Söderberg, P. (2013). Lethal agression in mobile forager bands and implications for the origin of war. *Science, 341*, 270–274.

Fuentes, A. (2013). Cooperation, conflict, and niche construction. In D. P. Fry (Ed.), *War, peace and human nature* (pp. 78–92). Oxford University Press.

Gibbons, A. (2019). Bronze Age inequality and family life revealed in powerful study. *Science, 366*, 168.

Hamlin, J. K., & Wynn, K. (2011). Five and 9-month-old infants prefer prosocial to antisocial others. *Cognitive development, 26,* 30–39.

Hamlin, J. K., Wynn, K., & Blomm, P. (2010). 3-Month-Olds Show a Negative Bias in Social Evaluations. *Developmental Science, 13,* 923–939.

Hare, B., Brown, M., Williamson, C., & Tomasello, M. (2002). The domestication of social cognition in dogs. *Science, 298,* 1634–1636.

Hare, B., Wobber, R., & Wrangham, R. (2012). The self-domestication hypothesis: evolution of bonobo psychology is due to selection against aggression. *Animal Behaviour, 83,* 573–585.

Hare, & Tomasello. (2004). Chimpanzees are much more skillful in competitive than in cooperative cognitive tests. *Animal Behavior, 68,* 571–581.

Herrmann, E., Hernández-Lloreda, J., Call, M. V., Hare, B., & Tomasello, M. (2007). Humans have evolved specialized skills of social cognition: The cultural intelligence hypothesis. *Science, 317*(5843), 1360–1366. 10.1126/science.1146282.

Herrmann, Hernández-Lloreda, Call, Hare, & Tomasello. (2010). The structure of individual differences in the cognitive abilities of children and chimpanzees. *Psychological Science, 21*(1): 102–110.

Henrich, J. (2016). *The secret of our success. How culture is driving human evolution, domesticating our species and making us smarter.* Princeton University Press.

Henrich, J. (2020). *The WEIRDest people in the world. How the West became psychologically peculiar and particularly prosperous.* Ferrar, Straus and Giroux.

Hill, K. R., Barton, M., & Hurtado, M. (2009). The emergence of human uniqueness: Characters underlying behavioral modernity. *Evolutionary Anthropology, 18,* 187–200.

Hill, K., Walker, R. S., Boziecocich, M., Elder, J., Headland, T., Hewlett, B., ... Wood, B. (2011). Co-residence patterns in hunter-gatherer societies show unique human social structure. *Science, 331,* 1286–1289.

Hrdy, S. (2009). *Mothers and others. The evolutionary origins of mutual understanding.* The Belknap Press.

Hrdy, S. (2016). Development and social selection in the emergence of "emotionally modern" humans. In X. L. Meehan & A. N. Crittenden (Eds.), *Origins and implications of the evolution of childhood.* (pp. 57–91). SAR Press.

Hrdy, S. & Burkardt, J.M. (2020). The emergence of emotionally modern humans: implications for language. *Philosophical Transactions of the Royal Society, B, 375*(1803). 10.1098/rstb.2019.0499.

Jablonka, E., & Lamb, M. L. (2005). *Evolution in four dimensions. Genetic, epigenetic, behavioral, and symbolic*. A Gradford Book. MIT Press.

Kelly, R. (2013). *The lifeways of hunter-gatherers: The foraging spectrum*. Cambridge University Press.

Köymen, B., Engemann, D.A., Warneken, F., Lievan, E., Rakoczy, H., & Tomasello, M. (2014). Children's norm enforcement in their interactions with peers. *Child Development, 85,* 1108–1122.

Lee, R. B. (1979). *The ! Kung San: Men, women and work in a foraging society.* Cambridge University Press.

Lee, R. B. (2014). Hunter-gaherers on the best-seller list: Steven Pinker and the "Bellicose Ssbool's treatment of forager violence, *Journal of Aggression, Conflict and Peace Research 4,* 216–228.

Melis, A.P., Hare, B., & Tomasello, M. (2006a). Chimpanzees recruit the best collaborators. *Science, 311,* 1297–1300.

Melis, A.P., Hare, B. , & Tomasello, M. (2006b). Engineering cooperation in chimpanzees: tolerance constraints on cooperation. *Animal behavior, 72,* 275–286.

Parish, A. R., De Wall, F. B. M., & Haig, D. (2000). The Other "Closest living relative": How bonobos (pan paniscus) challenge traditional assumptions about females, dominance, intra and intersexual interactions, and hominid evolution. *Annals of the New York Academy of Sciences, 907*(1), 97–113.

Pikkety, T. (2020). *Capital and ideology.* Harvard University Press.

Pinker, S. (2011). *The better angels of our nature.* Viking Press.

Potts. (2013). Hominin evolution on settings of strong environmental variability. *Quaternary Science Reviews, 73,* 1–13.

Pringle, H. (2014). The ancient roots of the 1%. *Science, 334,* 822–825.

Schmidt, M. F. H., & Tomasello, M. (2012). Young children enforce social norms. *Current Directions in Psychological Science 21,* 223–226.

Service, E. R. (1962). *Primitive social organiztion: An evolutionary perspective.* Random House.

Tomasello, M. (1999). *The cultural origins of human cognition.* Harvard University Press.

Tomasello, M. (2009). *Why we cooperate*. Boston Review Book.

Tomasello, M. (2014). *A natural history of human thinking*. Harvard University Press.

Tomasello, M. (2016). *The natural history of human morality*. Harvard University Press.

Tomasello, M. (2019). *Becoming human. A theory of ontogeny*. Harvard University Press.

Tomasello, M., & Carpenter, M. (2005). The emergence of social cognition in three young chimpanzees. *Monographs of the Society for Research in Child Development, 2019049920*(1), 279.

Tomasello, M., & Carpenter, M. (2007). Shared intentionality. *Developmental Science, 10,* 121–125.

Tomasello, M., Carpenter, M., Call, J., Behne, T., & Henrike, M. (2005). Understanding and sharing intentions: the origins of cultural cognition. *Behavioral and Brain Sciences, 28,* 675–735.

Tomasello, M., Carpenter, M., & Liszkowski, U. (2007). A new look at pointing. *Child Development, 78,* 705–722.

Tomasello, M., & Gonzalez-Cabrera, I. (2017). The role of ontogeny in the evolution of human cooperation. *Human Nature 28,* 274–288.

Tomasello, M., Melis, A. P., Tennie, C., Wyman, E., & Herrmann, E. (2012). Two Key Steps in the Evolution of Human Cooperation. *Current Anthropology, 53,* 673–692.

Warneken, F., Chen, F., & Tomasello, M. (2006). Cooperative activities in young children and chimpanzees. *Child Development, 77,* 640–679.

Warneken, F., & Tomasello, M. (2006). Co-operation and helping in 14-month-olds. *Infancy, 11*(3), 271–294.

Warneken, F., & Tomasello, M. (2007). Spontaneous altruism by young children and chimpanzees. *PLoS Biology, 5,* 1414–1420.

West-Eberhard. (1983). Sexual selection, social competition, and speciation. *Quarterly Review of Biology, 58,* 155–183.

West-Eberhard, M. J. (2003). *Developmental plasticity and evolution*. Oxford University Press.

Westermarck, E. (1891/1926). *The history of human marriage* (Vol. 1–3). Macmillan.

Wiessner, P. (2002). Hunting, healing, and *hxaro* exchange. A long trem perspective on !KIng Ju/"hoansi large-game hunting. *Evolution and Human Behavior, 23,* 407–436.

Woodburn, J. (1982). Egalitarian Societies. *Man, 17,* 431–451.

Wrangham, R. (2019). *The goodness paradox. The strange relation between virtue and violence in human evolution.* Vintage Books.

Wrangham, R., & Peterson, D. (1996). *Demonic males. Apes and the origins of human violence.* Houghton Mullin.

3

LEADERSHIP—CHARISMATIC OR INSPIRING? AN INQUIRY INTO REGRESSIVE AND DEVELOPMENTAL FORMS OF LEADERSHIP

Jon Stokes

Charismatic and inspiring leadership have fundamentally different effects on their followers. While charismatic leadership is primarily focused on the person of the leader, and their success, inspiring leadership focuses on the followers and their development. The term charismatic has been applied to very diverse leaders, in political arenas, in religious and social movements, and in business organisations. Weber (1947) defines charisma as "a certain quality of an individual personality by virtue of which he is set apart from ordinary men and treated as endowed with supernatural, superhuman, or at least specifically exceptional powers or qualities, these are such as are not accessible to the ordinary person, but are regarded as divine in origin or as exemplary, and on the basis of them, the individual concerned is treated as a leader."

As in any form of leadership, the leader must be seen as an exemplar of the followers' ideals to evoke engaged followership, but Weber's emphasis

DOI: 10.4324/9781003265122-3

in his definition is on the relationship between the leader and the followers rather than on any particular qualities of the leader. Clearly, only certain individuals could provide this exemplar, since they must be seen by the followers as an example of their ideals, but in what follows I will be focusing primarily on the relationship between leaders and their followers rather than on the necessary personality and other characteristics that the individual leader must possess.

Styles of leadership can be differentiated in terms of their outcome (constructive or destructive), the mechanism (collaborative or coercive), and their effects on the followers (developmental or regressive). Debates about the pros and cons of charismatic leadership generally hinge around whether or not the effect of that leadership was constructive (e.g., Martin Luther King) or destructive (e.g., Adolf Hitler) (O'Connor et al., 1995) (Howell & Shamir, 2005). Padilla et al. (2007) describe a toxic triangle of destructive leadership (charismatic, personalised power, ideology of hate) with susceptible followers (fearful, passive conformism, or antisocial collusion) and conducive environments (instability, perceived threat, absence of institutional checks and balances).

I want to distinguish charismatic leadership from inspiring leadership. I will be using the terms charismatic and inspiring as they apply to leadership in a pure sense for purposes of clarity and analysis. Any particular leader will use an amalgam of both styles to influence their followers, indeed the flexibility to move between these styles is a characteristic of the most effective leaders. Charismatic leadership causes emotional and cognitive psychological regression in the followers, whereas inspiring leadership enables psychological development. I shall be contrasting charismatic leadership, which is fundamentally a narcissistic process (Rosenthal & Pittinsky, 2006), whether constructive or destructive in its consequences, with inspiring leadership which is fundamentally an altruistic process. Bion (1992) contrasts narcissism and social-ism, terms which he is using in a psychological, not a political sense, as I shall explain later.

I want to argue that while charismatic leadership can be socially or materially progressive in the outcome it is necessarily regressive in its effect on the followers through the projection of aspects of the self onto the idealised leader resulting in a diminution of the capacity for independent thought, feeling, and action on the part of the followers.

The distinction between the two forms of leadership can be seen in the contrast between Napoleon (more charismatic than inspiring) who understood the dreams of his people and endeavoured to make them real, and Churchill (more inspiring than charismatic) who enabled his people to dream and have the courage and resilience to bring them to reality. Or consider the different styles of football managers Jose Mourinho (more charismatic than inspiring) and Arsene Wenger (more inspiring than charismatic). When Jose Mourinho's team loses he find something to blame, the referee, the fans, the team, rarely himself, but when Arsene Wenger's team loses he explains his own part in the failure. "Please don't call me arrogant, but I'm European champion and I think I'm a special one" says Mourinho. In contrast, Arsene Wenger describes the role of the manager as a guide. He takes a group of people and says, "with you I can make us a success; I can show you the way." Note that neither form of leadership is necessarily more effective in its results than the other, some will argue that Mourinho is the better leader, others will say that Wenger is the superior. This highlights the fact that judgements about leadership are always valued judgements depending on which outcome, scoring goals, or team morale, for example, is being sought.

Psychoanalytic Approaches to Charismatic Leadership

The psychoanalytic understanding of the intrapsychic and interpsychic dynamics of leadership have their origins in Freud's (1921) "Group Psychology and the Analysis of the Ego" where he outlines the way in which followers project their ego-ideal, the self they would like to be, onto the leader. In the type of primitive group formation that Freud was interested in the ego-ideal is replaced by the object. The individual gives up his ego-ideal and substitutes for it the group ideal as embodied in the leader. As Freud puts it "a primary group of this kind is a number of individuals who have put one and the same object in the place of their ego-ideal and have consequently identified themselves with one another in their ego".

When the leader is put in the place of the ego-ideal and idealised the members of the group become diminished through a projection of their powers onto the leader. Freud describes a series of consequences, "weakness of intellectual ability, lack of emotional restraint, an incapacity for moderation and delay, the inclination to exceed every limit in the expression of emotion and work it off completely in the form of action" or in other words massive regression into a state of collective narcissism.

Freud uses the notions of ego-ideal and ideal-ego synonymously. Subsequently, a number of psychoanalysts have argued for the distinction between these two. Hanly (1984) differentiates the ego-ideal (or self one aspires to be) as aspirational from the ideal-ego (or idealised picture of the self). It is an idealised, illusory, perfect self, with which the individual has become identified believing it to have become a reality. Whereas the ego-ideal is something that one constantly strives and works towards, but never fully achieves, the ideal-ego state happens instantly by simply believing that it is the case. Rather than experiencing a tension between the ego and the superego the individual is of the opinion that they have become their ideal-ego. It is a form of omnipotent thinking as opposed to the realistic thinking required to work towards the ego-ideal. This results in individuals who do not appear to have a superego or conscience, who "have identified their idealised self (ideal-ego) with their ego-ideal and feel at one with an internal idealised and idealising parent" (Hanly 1984). He goes on to say that the fusing of the ego and the ego-ideal results in the abolition of inhibitions and feelings of consideration for others; converting the melancholy of the previously lost and confused followers into a manic triumphant state.

Kohut and Wolf (1978) describe the mirror-hungry personality (e.g., a leader) who seeks admiration and respect from others (for example followers) who should mirror their greatness, their prestige, power, beauty, intelligence, and so forth. They contrast this with the ideal-hungry person who suffers from low self-esteem and a sense of insignificance who seeks comfort in the charisma and confidence of another person.

Post (1986) expands on these ideas. When followers are in an ideal-hungry state "the charismatic leader comes to their psychological rescue" .... "The mirror-hungry leader requires a continuing flow of admiration from his audience in order to nourish his or her famished self". .... "by conveying a sense of grandiose omnipotence and strength they are particularly attractive to individuals seeking idealised sources of strength. They convey a sense of conviction and certainty to those who are consumed by doubt and anxiety." The followers provide the continuous admiration needed by the mirror-hungry leader, the leader's charisma provides the followers with the sense of security and purpose that they feel they lack (Britton, 2003).

Charismatic leadership in its most destructive form engenders what Wieland (2017) describes as the totalitarian state of mind that encourages "omnipotent identification to protect the individual from fears of fragmentation and loss of identity. Growth is arrested and a rigid container is established that restricts the free exchange of container/contained. A super-certainty develops that allows no doubt and no interaction with new knowledge. A quasi-religious state of mind is established. The world again 'makes sense' but in a simplified way which only the faithful share. Certainty is restored but it is now related to a lack of change and a lack of exchange with the environment."

All of us when faced with fears and uncertainty, such as in times of war or epidemics of infectious disease, may move into an ideal-hungry state in which we seek mirror-hungry charismatic leaders. Post (2019) argues that the relationship between Trump and his hard-line followers is an example of this. Maccoby (2003) also argues that charisma is the product of interaction, a relationship between the narcissist and the people who are charmed and motivated by him.

Four Lenses on Leadership

I will address the distinction between charismatic and inspiring leadership in their pure forms with the help of four lenses. I want to argue that a perspective on leadership that sees it as an emerging property of a social system with evolutionary roots, provides a broader lens and a deeper understanding of the nature of leadership.

Lens 1: Leadership is an Emergent Property of a Social System

From this perspective, leadership is a product of five elements – the problem, the leader, the followers, the situation (the problem that the group is trying to solve), and the context. Charismatic leadership emerges when these five factors are in a certain alignment. Followers are anxious as a result of either contextual or more specific situational factors. Contextual factors include perceived threats to the nation or social group. Situational factors are more local, when the group faces a problem it feels unable to solve that threatens the security of the members of an organisation, or group within an organisation. To put it another way, charismatic leadership emerges when there is follower readiness, the followers are looking for and ready to follow a leader who will take them out of their current predicament which is believed to be unresolvable. When that predicament is no longer felt as existentially threatening the need for charismatic leadership fades. Inspiring leadership can emerge under the same circumstances but has a totally different emotional origin and purpose, that of progression and development rather than regression and defence. The leader does not use the followers for narcissistic ends but enables what Bion (1961) describes as Work Group functioning to face reality and to encourage and develop their capacities to solve the problem or predicament that the group faces, rather than evading this through omnipotent thought, emotion, and action.

Lens 2: Leadership is an Innate Evolved Capacity of Social Groups to Create Collective Action, The Organisation of The Group In Relation to Perceived Threats

Leadership is observable in all social animals. I wish to propose that leadership is an innate mental module (Fodor, 1983) designed to solve the problem of achieving collective action which is utilised in charismatic leadership in an omnipotent manner, in inspiring leadership in a reality-based manner. I further suggest that charismatic and inspiring leadership are rooted in two further mental modules with contrasting emotional roots and constellations. Charismatic leadership is founded on the falling-in-love mental module necessary for pair bonding in social animals. It is a fundamentally narcissistic and regressive state with an overestimation of the uniqueness of both self and other, and the relationship, and consequently neither party develops psychologically. Inspiring leadership is founded on the parent-child module of mature love necessary for the care of the newly born and their learning and development. It is a mutually beneficial symbiotic, non-idealised, progressive, and altruistic relationship in which mature love is influenced by external and internal reality and consequently both parties develop.

Inspiring leadership, based on the desire to know reality as it is, is connected with the capacity for mature love and the desire for truth.

Charismatic leadership, based on the wish to believe that reality is as one wishes, is based on narcissistic self-love, a disregard for truth, and a hatred of reality. The world of charismatic leadership is solipsistic, a closed system in which the leader has "the answer" and no further knowledge or learning is required. The world of inspiring leadership involves a focus on learning, the search for knowledge together which is always provisional and imperfect.

Lens 3: Leaders Provide a Focus and Exemplar of the Followers' Ideals

Charismatic leaders provide a focus and exemplar of the followers' ideal-ego whereas inspiring leadership provides a focus and exemplar of the followers' ego-ideal. In doing so inspiring leadership is enriching and progressive and enables emotional and cognitive development in the followers whereas charismatic leadership is regressive and inhibits emotional and cognitive development in the followers. In charismatic leadership, the leader has been put in the place of the ego-ideal, further strengthened by the mutual identifications between the members of the group. Charismatic leadership is driven by a need to be idealised; inspiring leadership is based on a desire for truth, realism, and the courage to be oneself.

Lens 4: Wilfred Bion's (1961) Three Basic Assumptions

Bion's framework of basic assumption mentality provides the conditions for three varieties of charismatic leadership: the dependency basic assumption drives the search for a leader on whom to be dependent; the fight-flight basic assumption drives the search for a leader who will fight or flee a perceived threat, and the basic assumption pairing, which I prefer to call basic assumption hope (Stokes, 2019), drives the search for a solution that will occur in a fantasised future as an escape from the current predicament. All are omnipotent states of mind offering total solutions to the group and its members but not requiring any work. Individuals drawn to charismatic leadership under the three conditions have different personality constellations suited to leading each basic assumption. As Bion (1961) puts it they have a valency for each of these conditions, a preference for either dependency, fight-flight, or hope leadership styles. In inspiring leadership, the basic assumptions are used in service of the work of problem-solving, which Bion describes as a sophisticated use of the basic assumptions (Stokes, 2019).

A Kleinian Perspective

The psychoanalyst Melanie Klein's (1946) conceptual framework provides a way of highlighting and explaining the differences between charismatic and inspiring leadership. Klein describes two fundamental mental states. The depressive state of mind, or position, in which we experience ourselves and others more or less as we are, complex, with attractive and unattractive characteristics, both good and bad. This is contrasted with the paranoid-schizoid state of mind, or position, in which the pain of facing difficult realities is avoided by the extreme splitting of the world into widely separated good and bad unrelated components. While in the depressive state the individual can experience concern for others as well as self, when in the paranoid-schizoid state concern is solely for self and for self-survival. Tuckett (2011) has labelled these two states in ordinary language as integrated and divided respectively.

Bion (1965) developed Klein's framework by arguing that the paranoid-schizoid position need not necessarily be pathological. He proposes that facing new challenges and having new thoughts may require a regression into the paranoid-schizoid state of mind from which the individual needs to emerge into the depressive state of mind in order for productive sustained development and learning to occur. These two states of mind operate in oscillation between realistic thinking in the integrated depressive state of mind and magical thinking in the divided paranoid-schizoid state. Shifts between the paranoid-schizoid and depressive positions occur in both directions depending on the mental state of the individual and are a normal part of life during the course of a day.

According to Bion our instincts are inherently bipolar, both operating as elements in the fulfilment of the individual's life as an individual, and as elements in his or her life as a social animal. There is an inherent conflict within each individual between narcissism, which is not inherently "bad" since a degree of self-love is necessary before love can be extended to the love of others, and social-ism in the expression of all instincts (Bion 1992). Like Aristotle, he takes the view that the human individual is inherently a group and political animal and cannot satisfy any emotional drive without expression of its social component. All impulses are at the same time both narcissistic and socialistic. The intensity of narcissism is accompanied by a narrowing or concentration of emotion until it becomes one, such as love or hate, attraction or fear, or any other. By contrast, the intensity of socialism is accompanied by a widening of the spectrum of emotions (Bion 1965). He believed that we are by nature conflicted within ourselves between a tendency to individualism (narcissism) and the tendency to collectivism (socialism).

The Differences Between Charismatic and Inspiring Leadership

This Kleinian perspective can be used to compare and contrast charismatic and inspiring leadership. Charismatic leadership is based on a primitive identification with the leader. Mental functioning is dominated by paranoid-schizoid mentality which splits the world into extremes of good and bad. The followers of the charismatic leader project their ideal-ego (idealised self) onto the leader with whom they become psychologically fused, as a consequence they are psychologically weakened and diminished, albeit they may feel temporarily strengthened. It results, in both destructive and constructive forms, in a negative spiral of depletion of the self by projecting strength and the capacity for thought and feeling onto the leader, who consequently feels strengthened and emboldened, pushing the leader to take ever greater risks, often leading to their ultimate downfall. One fundamental purpose of charismatic leadership is to idealise the group and provide reassurance about its specialness and longevity to defend against feelings of powerlessness. In this state of collective narcissism, feelings of concern and anxiety are suppressed and replaced by picturing an idealised perfect future and a fantasy of an immortal group, often based on a picture of a nostalgic and idealised past that has been lost, to which the group is inevitably headed.

Charismatic leadership offers to relieve the members of doubt and uncertainty by replacing them with feelings of absolute conviction and certainty (Mintchev & Hinshelwood, 2017) which the leader articulates, a Faustian pact in return for a sense of magical protection. The leader is treated as godlike, accompanied by a masochistic diminishment of the followers as lesser beings. Individuals low in feelings of self-worth and self-efficacy, and with a predominantly external locus of control, find charismatic leadership attractive both in providing solutions to their problems and taking care of them, and are as a result easily manipulated in their diminished state by their charismatic leader who describes the world in terms of extremes of good and evil, and conspiracies, as seen in cults. Internal group divisions are prohibited and punished. The charismatic leader stands in place of the follower's superego.

Inspiring leadership, by contrast, is based on an object-choice founded on a more realistic perception of the leader. Mental functioning is predominantly depressive and more integrated. The followers of an inspiring leader see their leader as an exemplar of their ego-ideal but unlike the followers of the charismatic they do not become fused with their leader. They maintain a sense of a separate self that aspires to the qualities of their inspiring leader who is not idealised. The followers' egos are enriched by the realistic perception of the qualities of the inspiring leader, the self is strengthened. The inspiring leader faces the group with the inevitable tension with its ideals, but does not relieve this through offers of certainty, or unthinking and wholescale dependence. The leader enables them to work at their ideals as aspirations to be striven after but in a realistic manner, and therefore never entirely achieved. Inspiring leadership is based on the pursuit of truth. Internal group divisions are permitted in the recognition that different perspectives are possible and that learning necessitates contact with reality, effort, and sometimes pain. The inspiring leader stands in place of the internal nurturing and developmental parent. Failure is used for learning rather than for blame. The leader works to generate a state in Bion's terms of collective socialism.

The charismatic leader persuades the group to behave "as if" it had the capacities to solve its problems which will somehow as a result be magically solved. Charismatic leadership is based on lies and fantasies, the only impediments are a failure to believe, and a lack of conviction in the rightness of the leader's solutions. The group behaves "as if" it had a solution. Neither leader nor followers develop. The inspiring leader asks "what if" we could make things better if we worked at our problems and "what if" we could find a solution together. Inspiring leadership is based on a desire for truth and for learning, it faces the group with the uncertainties it faces, and enables thought, decision, and choice. The group is encouraged to improve the solutions of their leader. Both leader and followers develop.

Under charismatic leadership any deficiencies of the leader are minimised, any failings in the group achieving its ambitions are due to the followers or external forces conspiring against the group and its leader. A failure is always an option under inspiring leadership, but when it occurs it is used for review and learning rather than scapegoating the ones who fail or blaming external conspirators. The deficiencies of the inspiring leader are acknowledged, solutions are always imperfect, and need to be worked at. The inspiring leader helps the group with its limitations and acts to improve the individual and collective performance of the members of the group, helping the followers to be themselves at their best, rather than encouraging the development of a false self.

The charismatic leader is a "phantastic object" (Tuckett, 2011) with the capacity to fulfil the followers' deepest desires to have exactly what they want, exactly when they want it. The inspiring leader is a realistic object with strengths and limitations who is not always able to solve the group's problems simply by wishing it to be so.

Charismatic leadership frequently ends in failure with self-destructive infighting of ever-smaller fissiparous extreme political groups, blaming external conspiracies as a defence against the recognition of difficulties, and in the case of cults even mutual suicide. Without the charismatic leader, the group collapses. Followers have little relationship with each other, the primary relationship is with the leader through a shared identification. Inspiring leadership results in the development of the followers. Failure may of course occur, but it is used for learning. Inspiring leadership develops relationships between followers and so the group is able to continue beyond the loss of its leader. Inspiring leadership focuses on the "we" of the group, not on the "me" of the leader and the followers.

The Elements of Inspiring Leadership

Over the past decade I have run workshops on inspiring leadership for over 700 senior managers as part of which I asked them for their views on what makes a leader inspiring. The results can be summarised under six headings which I call the Elements of Inspiring Leadership:

1. **Being the Exemplar – Inspiring leaders model the behaviours they want from their followers. They demonstrate a clear set of values in what they do as well as in what they say.**

Inspiring leaders model the behaviours they want from their followers. They exemplify in their actions, not just through what they say, those behaviours they want their followers to adopt. Leaders have distinct values about work and relationships, and followers know clearly what these are. This leads to a clear set of priorities amongst followers. Leaders also represent some ideal for their followers. They offer a figure with whom others can identify, and onto whom they can project the realisation of their hopes and ideals. This motivates the desire to follow. The difference between strong and weak leadership is not the nature of the values, but rather the forcefulness and consistency with which they are lived by the leader – this is about actions, not words.

2. **Articulating a Future – Inspiring leaders build a sense of purpose by creating a vivid picture of a future state that provides followers with focus and direction.**

The capacity to conceptualise and communicate a motivating picture of the future is a consistent finding in the literature on inspiring leaders. The ability to imagine and describe such a picture is essential to the effective sharing of lessons from present and past experience, of where we have come from, where we are now and where we are going. Implicitly or explicitly, we are always communicating a story about our ambition for the future, whether we think we are or not. The most powerful way of communicating your ambition is by telling a compelling story – we remember stories, but do not remember PowerPoint slides, strategy documents or memos.

3. **Situation Awareness – Inspiring leaders use their intuition and emotional intelligence to judge when and how to act.**

The ability to use your emotions as intelligence helps you to know how to act, how far you can go without losing your followers and when to do so. When you are able to sense situations better, people will trust you more and open up. Sensing situations occurs at three levels: reading people and their reactions to situations; being able to sense the mood and motivation of groups, teams and business units; and being able to sense likely future trends and issues that you need to pay attention to in your decision-making today – having a longer time horizon. Sensing the situation by itself is not sufficient, inspiring leadership requires being prepared to take responsibility for changing situations, to step up to the occasion.

4.   **Affirmation – Inspiring leaders enable people to feel good about themselves by providing feedback on their actual and potential contribution.**

By giving people a sense of their actual and potential contribution and worth to the organisation successful leaders demonstrate their interest in, availability to, and care for those they lead. It is always a challenge to focus on the needs of others rather than ourselves, but inspiring leaders make other people feel that they are important and valued, rather than simply telling us how great we are. Most leaders can recall a few inspiring figures in their life that have helped them become the person they are today – doing this for others builds loyalty and helps others improve their performance.

5.   **Having the Difficult Conversations – Inspiring leaders are prepared to have the difficult conversations; they do not let their desire to be liked to prevent them from telling the truth.**

Successful leaders are able to see and feel the world from the perspective of people very different from themselves. But at the same time, they identify and give people what they need so they give of their best, rather than necessarily what they want; being prepared to have "difficult conversations" and then to take tough but correct decisions. Most leaders have conversations that they need to have, but feel uncomfortable having them, so find justifications for delaying them in the hope that the problem will go away. Inspiring leaders do not avoid these conversations – such avoidance usually makes the problem worse – but rather have the courage to do the messy, awkward, difficult things that are necessary for an organisation to thrive.

6.   **Integrity – Inspiring leaders demonstrate the courage to remain true to their own values and purpose in both word and action in a way that provides a sense of consistency and integrity to others.**

By being true to themselves in a skilful way – having the capacity to stay true to their own purpose and values – inspiring leaders provide clarity and a point of focus for their followers. Authentic leaders resist the significant pressure to conform in organisations, but rather behave with an integrity and consistency that is communicated through behaviour and speech. Successful leaders are not, nor do they pretend to be, perfect. We are always revealing weaknesses to others, whether we think we are doing so or not. By acknowledging that you are not perfect, you create an environment where others are able to talk about and learn from their mistakes – one of the most consistent findings about organisations that have long term success is the ability to acknowledge and learn from mistakes.

Conclusion

I propose a distinction between two pure forms of leadership—charismatic leadership based on division, encouraging a paranoid-schizoid divided state of mind based on splitting, projection, and idealisation, and inspiring leadership based on a depressive integrated state of mind based on realism and the acceptance that each of us has good and bad aspects. Charismatic leadership creates psychological regression and the nature of the tie between members of the group is simply their shared identification with and tie to the leader. Inspiring leadership supports psychological progression in the nature of the tie between the members of the group in their shared endeavour. Whereas charismatic leadership reduces the capabilities of the group for independent thought, feeling, and action, inspiring leadership enhances and develops the powers of the members for independent thought, feeling, and action. Actual leaders use both styles to varying degrees, some are more charismatic and less inspiring, others are less charismatic but more inspiring.

Charismatic leadership, whether of a destructive or constructive kind, encourages the paranoid-schizoid state in which matters are conceived in extreme and divided black and white terms in which the leader becomes a "phantastic object." In this state ambivalence, doubt, frustration, and fears of potential defeat or disappointment in relation to a planned action are repressed. Charismatic leadership utilises a basic assumption mentality to encourage the followers not to feel or think for themselves but to remain in an immature relationship with their leader. Contradictory information stimulates denial.

Inspiring leadership encourages a depressive state of mind with an awareness of contradictions and shades of grey. Uncomfortable feelings and anxiety can remain in awareness allowing for a more reality-based approach to problem-solving. Doubt, frustration, and the possibility of failure are tolerated and serve as information for the modification of action for the group to achieve its aspirations within its actual capabilities. Basic assumption mentalities are used in a sophisticated form in the service of work. Contradictory information stimulates curiosity.

Effective leadership may draw on both charismatic and inspiring styles, shifting between these according to the nature of the problem to be faced, the state of the followers, the situation, and the context. Destructive charismatic leadership involves the generation of negative conspiracy theories, constructive charismatic leadership also involves the generation of conspiracy theories but of a positive nature, a view of the future as inevitably better than the present rather than the hard work of making the future better than the present, or even maintaining present progress, characteristic of inspiring leadership. Charismatic leadership operates by using power over others, inspirational leadership operates by using power with others.

We are all prone to the effects of charisma, the alluring simplification of the world into extremes of right and wrong, good and evil, beautiful and ugly, us and them, when we feel under threat. The complexities of the world as it is at present provide plentiful opportunities for the emergence of charismatic leadership with total ready-made solutions to the perennial challenges of the human condition. While the satisfactions produced by inspiring leadership are less immediately attractive they at least provide the possibility for us all to work at our collective problems associated with living in hyper-connected large groups, rather than simply being prey to its primitive dynamics, or retreating behind defensive boundaries.

References

Bion, W. (1961). *Experiences in groups*. London: Tavistock Publications.
Bion, W. (1965). *Transformations*. London: William Heineman.

Bion, W. (1992). *Cogitations*. London: Karnac.

Britton, R. (2003). *Sex, death, and the superego*. London: Karnac.

Fodor, J. (1983). *The modularity of mind*. London: MIT Press.

Freud, S. (1921). 'Group psychology and the analysis of the ego'. in The *Standard Edition of the Complete Works Sigmund Freud. Vol XVIII*. London: The Hogarth Press, 1955, pp. 67–143.

Hanly, C. (1984). Ego ideal and ideal ego. *International Journal of psycho-analysis*, 65, 253.

House, R. J., & Howell, J. M. (1992). Personality and charismatic leadership. *The Leadership Quarterly*, 3(2), 81–108.

Howell, J. M., & Shamir, B. (2005). The role of followers in the charismatic leadership process: Relationships and their consequences. *Academy of Management Review*, 30(1), 96–112.

Kohut, H., & Wolf, E. (1978). The disorders of the self and their treatment: An outline. *International Journal of Psychoanalysis*, 15, 261–285.

Klein, M. (1946). Notes on some schizoid mechanisms. *International Journal of Psychoanalysis*, 27, 99–110.

Maccoby, M. (2003). *The productive narcissist: The promise and peril of visionary leadership*. London: Broadway Books.

N. Mintchev & R. D. Hinshelwood (eds.) (2017). *The Feeling of Certainty, Studies in the Psychosocial*. London: Palgrave Macmillan.

O'Connor, J. et al. (1995). Charismatic Leaders and Destructiveness: An historiometric study. *Leadership Quarterly*, 6, 529–555.

Padilla, A., Hogan, R., & Kaiser, R. B. (2007). The toxic triangle: Destructive leaders, susceptible followers, and conducive environments. *The Leadership Quarterly*, 18(3), 176–194.

Post, J. (1986). Narcissism and the Charismatic Leader-Follower Relationship. *Political Psychology*, 7, No.4.

Post, J. (2019). *Dangerous Charisma: The political psychology of Donald Trump and his followers*. London: Pegasus Books.

Rosenthal, S. A., & Pittinsky, T. L. (2006). Narcissistic leadership. *The Leadership Quarterly*, 17(6), 617–633.9–36.

Stokes, J. (2019). The psychodynamics of teams. In Obholzer, A. & Roberts, V. (Eds.). *The Unconscious at Work* (pp. 28–36). London: Routledge.

Tuckett, D. (2011). *Minding the markets*. London: Palgrave Macmillan.

Weber, M. (1947). *The theory of social and economic organizations*. London: Free Press.

Wieland, C. (2017). 'The primitive container of fascism: Masculine anxieties and defences in times of trauma and uncertainty'. In Mintchev N., Hinshelwood R. (Eds.). *The feeling of certainty. Studies in the psychosocial* (pp. 129–148). London: Palgrave Macmillian.

4

CHANGING DEMANDS ON LEADERSHIP

Charles Heckscher

My discipline is not psychology but sociology, and sociologists naturally tend to see leadership as secondary to social forces. Yet the transformational experiences in many corporations over the last few decades, and the disruptive events of the Trump administration at the national level, certainly show that leaders can make a significant difference. In truth, as Michael Maccoby argues elsewhere in this volume, both dimensions are important: leadership is always a matter of interaction between personality and social context—so there is value in coming at the problem from the social end.

Most of my research since the late 1980s has focused on corporate organizations. In my career, I have seen a profound evolution from the large bureaucracies like General Motors that dominated the mid-century economy to more decentralized and—as the current buzzword has it—"agile" forms. More recently, I have examined the transformations at the societal level that have led to the "culture wars" and the crisis of trust. These shifts have placed not only severe, but *changing* demands on leadership. Good leadership of the 1980s would not be good in most contexts

DOI: 10.4324/9781003265122-4

today. And for our largest problems—the deep conflict of values that now threatens our core institutions—we cannot rely on a model of demonstrated success; the type of leadership now needed to reknit the social fabric is still in the learning phase.

Bureaucratic, Collaborative, and Charismatic Leadership

In the 1970s and 1980s, just a few companies were starting to probe the limits of the bureaucratic model of the organization; today bureaucracy is generally viewed with distaste, and concepts like "teamwork," "collaboration," and "ad-hocracy" dominate the literature much of the practice of management. These place very different demands on leaders, and indeed on all employees.

The forms of management can be characterized in two main ideal types—bureaucratic and collaborative organization—with some variants in each:

1. *Bureaucratic organization* organizes jobs in hierarchies of fixed tasks, (or "offices," in Max Weber's original analysis), which fit together like puzzle parts in a whole. Individuals are expected to stay within the boundaries of their job descriptions.

    In *simple bureaucracy*, the jobs are defined quite rigidly from above. Any individual who takes initiative will wreck the whole system, as if a puzzle piece decided it preferred a different shape. Only the higher-up leaders have sufficient perspective to see when changes are needed. This form of management has existed for millennia in governments and developed in businesses during the late nineteenth and early twentieth centuries.

    In the interwar period, as bureaucratic companies that came to dominate the economy—Ford and General Motors, Standard Oil, US Steel—many developed a modified form of bureaucracy that emphasized loyalty from employees. This added a significant element of flexibility: superiors can vary their demands to adapt to changing challenges, and employees can take a certain amount of initiative within the bounds of their loyalty to the company. I have called this form *paternalist bureaucracy* because these organizations consistently present themselves as "families" and the leaders as caring superiors. But the basic hierarchy of closely-defined jobs remained intact.

2. *Collaborative organization* developed rapidly in the 1970s and 1980s. Under growing competitive pressures from international markets, many big firms came to feel that even paternalist bureaucracy was too rigid. They needed organizations that could encourage continuous innovation and initiative from employees, without losing control. They began in a simple form with local teams, encouraging problem-solving within narrow limits, in "Quality Circles" and "Total Quality Management" teams. In their problem-solving, the teams loosened the bonds of defined jobs and focused instead on the task or project.

Over the last few decades, the scope of teamwork and collaboration has expanded rapidly. The increasing economic value of knowledge-creation has made it imperative that companies bring together people with varied kinds of knowledge to work on leading-edge, ill-defined problems. This started with small and rare cross-functional task forces, but has become steadily more common. Many analysts now believe the COVID pandemic will further increase the trend by speeding up the use of digital technologies, making it easier for people to work with others beyond the boundaries of their firms. Management scholars have begun analyzing the structuring of "ecosystems" of firms. In this context, there is a shift from corporate loyalty to independent career development.

These broad categories do not follow a linear sequence. In many organizations, all these forms of work exist in different contexts and levels, and industries differ in their emphasis. Simple bureaucracy is used where jobs are highly routinized but employees are low-skilled and turn over rapidly, such as the front-line levels of MacDonald's, Amazon, or Wal-Mart. Paternalist bureaucracy is still effective where strategies are fairly stable and work is more skilled, making employee retention more of a priority. Simple teamwork is adopted by organizations that can segment their work into small chunks with little interdependence. Complex collaboration is the leading edge, still in development, characterizing organizations (and parts of organizations) focused on innovation that crosses knowledge boundaries—particularly the high-tech industries.

These forms of the organization require and expect different types of employees and leaders. Bureaucratic organization demands leaders who know what they're doing and can tell their subordinates what to do. At the front line, the clearest example is the "scientific management" pioneered by Frederick Taylor in the early twentieth century. For Taylor, the primary quality of leadership was forcefulness:

> It is only through enforced standardization of methods, enforced adoption of the best implements and working conditions, and enforced cooperation that this faster work can be assured. And the duty of enforcing the adoption of standards and enforcing this cooperation rests with the management alone.
>
> (Taylor, 1911)

From the organizational point of view, the leadership job is to make sure each subordinate does their job in the right way. In Maccoby's psychological terms these leaders are likely to be Exacting, as Taylor himself clearly was—as one of my favorite cartoons has it: "I like things to be done in my own particular way by someone other than me."

The conception of leadership in the paternalist type of bureaucracy is best expressed in the "human relations" theories of Elton Mayo, which became popular in the interwar period. For Mayo, a good leader creates a strong relational bond with his subordinates and an overall sense of family unity. Managers in this were encouraged to ask about their subordinates' private lives, and even at the highest levels it became expected that leaders would create bonding experiences like company dinners and events.

But this orientation must be balanced by a need for continued bureaucratic discipline within a smoothly operating system. As Robert Merton wrote in 1940, such discipline

> can be effective only if the ideal patterns are buttressed by strong sentiments which entail devotion to one's duties, a keen sense of the limitation of one's authority and competence, and methodical performance of routine activities.
>
> (Merton, 1940, pp. 560–568)

The leader in this context must be a father figure who is kindly but also stern, one who demands much of his "children," and who inspires confidence that he always knows what's best. (I use the masculine pronouns here because this was very much a male world, though today women in such contexts must exhibit similar qualities.) In Maccoby's psychological terms, the ideal type seems to be a combination of caring and exacting.

Collaborative organizations require a very different mindset. In the simpler forms, the manager has to back off, give the teams space. This can be a learning experience. A supervisor in one of the very early experiments in work improvement said, "I never had so much power since I started giving it away" (Maccoby, 1983, Chapter 4). A manager of a more complex cross-functional team said of himself:

> I can't be autocratic and dictatorial to my people, as I tended to be [before]. All other things being equal, I'm a pretty good dictator. ... But if I do that, and my staff does that, it goes right down the line, and we don't have teamwork. We also don't benefit from the ideas and perspectives of the whole work force.
>
> So I've tried to learn to have patience, change my style, look for consensus, have involvement of my staff as a team, share more information, be more open. I've had to learn that you take a risk with this and not everything comes out the way you want it, but the potential payoffs far outweigh the risks.
>
> ... I didn't come to this as a natural team player. I got into this because it looked like the way this business could run best.
>
> (Donnellon & Margolis, 1990)

Organizations in which innovation is crucial do not want "team players" in the traditional sense: people who will do whatever is asked and will not cause trouble. They want people who will form effective teams—that is, who can engage others in spirited dialogue, work through conflicts constructively, hold each other accountable.

When I asked a member of a high-level cross-functional team at Citibank for his definition of the qualities of a good leader, he said:

> Enthusiastic about what they do, interested in talking about what they do—some people are just content with just managing their piece of turf and don't want anyone mucking around in it. Somebody who is

open to a new idea, who is going to feel a sense of ownership, someone who would be open to criticism or suggestions as opposed to someone who would get defensive, be scared by people meddling around. ... A lot of the role is to find out how pieces of the business are run if you don't already know. So it's important that the people you're talking to are open, and you not be overbearing and say "Here's how you have to do things." Say "Here's an idea, what do you think about it," as opposed to "Here's what we decided you should be doing." It stems from security, being comfortable with your position, and I don't mean position from an organizational perspective ... I'm trying to make a distinction between hierarchy and feeling comfortable that you know what you're doing.

These are complex personality demands, requiring substantial adaptiveness. Caring is less necessary and may be absent. Effective collaborative leaders, in my experience, are very tough about task performance: they do not let personal relations mute their criticism or standards. But they do need to be able to adapt to different situations with an array of approaches. In some situations, it may be necessary to "give someone a break" for personal reasons—as long as that is ultimately justified by its likely effect on performance. The ability to listen is very important, but so is the ability to be decisive when a decision is called for.

Thus many managers have trouble with the collaborative leadership style, and they often feel caught in dilemmas. It comes down, as my interviewee above put it, "*feeling comfortable that you know what you're doing*"—as distinct from enforcing a preset task. The best collaborative leaders I know are generally calm and patient, good listeners—but quite forceful at decisive moments. I would suggest this requires primarily a level of psychological *maturity* - perhaps what Freud would call ego-development, or Maccoby would call "productive" (Maccoby, 2003). That is, the ego must be rich enough to integrate competing needs and drives in response to a range of external pressures.

There is one more situation that I think is distinct from all of these and requires still another set of characteristics: the context of *transformation*. This may be a leader who creates a new company, or one who fundamentally reorients an old one that is failing. Steve Jobs is a prototypical transformative leader: he redirected an entire industry from a focus on engineering excellence to one on customer usability. These leaders have one shared characteristic: they hold fast to a vision. Most founders of companies are of this type, but so are leaders like Lou Gerstner, who transformed IBM from a big-systems producer to a customer solutions company after it nearly went bankrupt.

The transformative leader is close to the charismatic type described by Max Weber; in psychological terms, this involves high degrees of narcissism. These are leaders who believe so strongly in their own vision of the future that they are not deterred by failures and conflicts. Associates of Steve Jobs, the archetypal transformer, spoke of the "reality distortion field" he created—promising things that were clearly impossible yet making others believe they were possible, and so often achieving them.

These leaders can create a type of collaboration among their close followers who believe in the vision—collaboration in which there may be considerable room for debate and disagreement, but only until the charismatic leader takes a stand. But to those outside this circle, they tend to be bullies, willing to use tactics of demeaning and suppression to ensure obedience. This has been thoroughly documented in the case of Steve Jobs (Isaacson, 2011), but is visible in many other transformative leaders as well.

Conversational Leadership for a Fractured Society

Finally, there is yet another type of leadership, less familiar and understood, which is now growing in importance: the leadership of conversation.

From a sociological perspective, I have argued elsewhere that today's situation requires conversation rather than charisma (Heckscher, 2015). The charismatic, transformative leadership exemplified by Steve Jobs at Apple works when the leader can assemble her own team, or can fire those who do not join in. It sometimes works in social contexts in which people are adrift, with little sense of purpose or direction. It does not work when there is a deep divide between sharply contrasting views of the world—which was the situation before the American Civil War, and we are approaching today.

In those circumstances, I believe, the only way out is through conversation oriented not to task accomplishment, like the collaborative type, but to *understanding*. Even with deep differences, people can very often come to partial understandings—more sympathy for each others' motives, and more willingness to take steps together. This comes out of conversations that focus on values rather than tasks, that explore beliefs and feelings, and commitments in a way that goes beyond goal-focused collaborative relations.

The notion of leadership through conversation has received increasing attention because of the rapidly increasing polarization of the electorate. People have largely formed into two exclusive groups with different views of the world and visions of the future. Geographical sorting has advanced, in 1974 about a quarter of the nation's counties had "landslide" majorities for one Presidential candidate; by 2020 they had risen to almost two-thirds. Social media have also made it easier for people to read-only news that reinforces their own perspectives. It is getting more difficult for people even to imagine how a view different from theirs could be valid.

The dominant way of resolving such value conflicts since ancient times has been through conquest and suppression of one side. An alternative has developed since the seventeenth century in the West: a concept of "tolerance," in which the two sides live their different lives and interact when necessary through formal contracts and rules. For many people today these remain the only alternatives: to *win*—to impose their own view on the others—or to *secede* into a territory where everyone else agrees with them. The movers behind Brexit exemplify those who prefer secession. Donald Trump exemplifies a leader who rallies his supporters for victory. So, indeed, do all charismatic leaders, including Steve Jobs or Jeff Bezos: they inspire their followers with their visions and eliminate those who do not get on board.

But leaders of nations, as Trump discovered, cannot fire those who don't obey. If we are not to fall into civil war, we have to somehow get along with people whose views of the world are very different from our own. Even more: increasingly complex problems like climate change, nuclear proliferation, and misuse of scientific advances require close collaboration based on mutual understanding. And that presents perhaps the ultimate leadership challenge.

The philosopher Jurgen Habermas has built a formidable case that the solution to this challenge is to build conversations in which all parties are able to speak freely and to arrive at free consensus (2013). This turns out, however, to be extremely difficult to do. Habermas himself doesn't say much about leadership. Some have tried to develop models of "facilitative leadership" based on his concept of "ideal speech" (Fryer, 2012). But there is a very little solid experience to build on. Some examples I have researched in the corporate world do offer useful lessons—cases in which the leaders did not take the charismatic route and did not depend on the exercise of power to get rid of dissenters.[1]

Experiences in Corporations

IBM faced a profound crisis after 1990—first financial, which it almost failed to survive, and then cultural. By 2000, Sam Palmisano, the incoming CEO, diagnosed a deep split between employees. One set—mostly longer-term employees - believed deeply in the "Basic Beliefs" codified by the company founders. The core was an exchange of security for loyalty: the company provided an almost total guarantee of employment to employees who did their jobs dutifully. Many of the newer employees adhered instead to a sharply set of beliefs emphasizing innovation, collaboration, and flexibility. IBM had begun unprecedented layoffs in the 1990s, and Palmisano faced a revolt from the first group, who felt the soul of the company was under attack. The company was, in effect, experiencing a culture war between two value systems.

Other companies wrestled unsuccessfully with very similar problems. Xerox's leaders had begun as early as the 1980s to pursue a change in the business model and had instituted a set of top-down "cascading" programs to inculcate new values. Two decades and several CEOs later they were still trying and failing, with new programs and new cascades, none of them achieving the kind of culture change that was needed. At Hewlett-Packard, IBM's direct competitor, Carly Fiorina began in 1999 a full-out attack on the old culture using all the tools of managerial power and influence: layoffs, promotions, and demotions, hortatory speechmaking, acquisitions. She was fired by her board five years later, having lost what one insider account called the "battle for the soul of Hewlett-Packard" (Burrows, 2003).

Palmisano took another tack at IBM: he started an open conversation throughout the company. Over 40,000 employees joined in a "Values Jam" over two years, discussing online what changes should be made in the Basic Beliefs. Palmisano proposed a draft, but he and other leaders did not advocate for it, nor did they dominate the discussion.

In the first days, traditionalist employees—including many high-level managers—defended the existing value formulation and fiercely criticized the changes of the previous few years, particularly the layoffs and re-organizations. Palmisano's top advisors said to him, "You need to shut this down, it's too destructive"; but he answered, "No, let it go, it'll work out."[2] Later another senior leader set off an incendiary exchange by criticizing the Basic Beliefs. The Jam leaders said, "What are you doing?" and he answered, "I'm just participating."

Fairly quickly Palmisano turned out to be right: those who advocated the newer values began to find their voice and to articulate both principles and practices for creating collaborative projects and coordinating for innovation. By the second year, the traditionalists were still complaining, but they were fewer and more isolated; most of the participants were trying to work through the implications of the challenge of innovation and customer responsiveness.

In my interviews with a range of employees after the Jam, I heard many comments of this sort from both "old-timers" and "new IBMers":

An old-timer:

> The big difference is that when you are given a chance to express yourself on something you are much more—you feel that the values come from us as a company—300,000 people as opposed to coming from a few people in Armonk, New York. The IBMer that way feels that they own the values as opposed to being or having come from the top. And it is a really different thing.

And a "new IBMer":

> A lot of old timers still remember the Basic Beliefs, and that was something that was very important for them. And there was a lot of discussion within the values jam as to how the two compared. What we were trying to achieve now, that we were trying to evolve from the

basic beliefs to the new values. If this had come from above to the old timers, they would not have felt that these values were their own, because they would not have been given an opportunity to talk about the basic beliefs and how it relates to this. It's just a matter that if you are engaged and participate in you feel it is your own.

I think that was the magic behind the values jam. The fact that it did come from 300,000 employees participating. It did not come top down, it came from the organization. … It didn't come from Sam [Palmisano]. Sam was the catalyst. Someone came up with the idea of values jam, and obviously Sam endorsed it. So I am going to give him credit for it. It came from the organization.

There were many factors at play besides culture change. Both HP and IBM have survived and performed moderately well in the long term. But there are strong arguments that the companies that build the ability to hold extensive conversations, as IBM did, will be better positioned to deal with the increasing pace of competitive and technological changes over time (Heckscher, 2015, Chapter 6).

I have also researched a set of interventions known as "Fitness Profiling," developed by Mike Beer of the Harvard Business School, which aims to involve all employees in "conversations that matter" (Beer & Eisenstat, 2004). In this process, the top managers first define their vision of the future and the organization's strategy. Then a team of middle managers, chosen for their high credibility with their peers, conduct interviews throughout the organization around one question: "What are the strengths to build on and the barriers to address in implementing this strategy?" Then they talk to each other in a circle about what they have found, with the top management team listening from outside the circle. Very frequently the criticisms of top management's plans are devastating, triggering a painful discussion that may last several years and extend company-wide. Ultimately many of these organizations make deep changes in their operating models and visions, and some build the conversation process into their regular decision-making.

These examples remain rare, however. Purely on evidence of effectiveness, they should be much more common. But they require a degree of humility and restraint that is rare among those who have made it to the top of large corporations. It may be even rarer among leaders of societies.

Can we Rebuild our Societal Community?

These corporate examples suggest that it is *possible*, though not easy, for deliberate conversations to rebuild a sense of shared purpose at times of deep disagreement. But I started this section with the problem of the value polarization of our society. If we could advise our political leaders, what would we say?

Societal conversations are considerably more difficult than corporate ones. First, at least in democracies, the legitimacy of leadership is less solid: it depends on votes, and many of the participants may have voted against the leader. Second, the range of problems is far more complex, encompassing a wider range of values and a greater diversity of orientations.

Given these obstacles, there are far more failures than successes. Abraham Lincoln would have sought national reconciliation if he could—but history turned the other way. The Progressive Movement in the USA a century ago encouraged widespread citizen discussions, and FDR set up a large initiative through his Education secretary; these left little trace on democratic institutions later in the century. President Clinton sponsored a national conversation on race, and President Obama sought to do the same for health care; both efforts petered out with little impact.

But let me very briefly sketch two more promising cases: Dallas, Texas in the mid-1960s, and Germany after WWII.

After the assassination of President Kennedy in 1963, Dallas faced an epic crisis of confidence and self-respect. The City Council chose as mayor Erik Jonsson, the former CEO of Texas Instruments. The mayor in Dallas had virtually no power—the City manager actually ran things—but Jonsson used his influence to win support for a plan to engage a cross-section of citizens from across the city in discussions of the city's future, in a structured series of large and small meetings. The effort ran through three cycles over nearly twenty years (Allison et al., 1985).

The "Goals for Dallas" effort is generally seen as a major success. It brought together sectors of the city that had long been at odds, including—for the first time—representatives of the Black community. Citizens widely felt an improvement in their capacity as citizens. Many specific goals, such as the establishment of a system-wide public kindergarten system, were achieved over the following decade. And more than three decades later the mayors of Dallas and San Antonio returned to it as a model for further rounds of planning.

The second case is very different. At the end of WWII Germany was not only deeply divided but also shattered, and its relation to its neighbors was deeply hostile. A few decades later it was a model of relative democratic purpose and had joined with its neighbors in forming a wider community of nations.

In this case, there was no single leader, like Jonsson or Palmisano, who encouraged a widespread conversation. Konrad Adenauer pursued a policy of diplomatic and political reconciliation that was undoubtedly an essential foundation to a wider coming to terms with the past. Economic exchange and interdependence also helped in forging links. But an important element was a wide-ranging, decentralized conversation about the past and the future, conducted both within and Germany and between it and former enemies. Here, churches played a key role, but not the only one: meetings and exchanges among scientists, educators, artists, performers spread widely across Europe, with much deliberate effort.

A particularly pointed example was the development of a common German-French history book sponsored by both governments. This was an extraordinary achievement: it would be hard today to imagine a common history book written by supporters of Trump and Obama. The German-French text, coming after many decades of armed conflict and vast slaughter, took six decades to reach completion—but only because it engaged a large range of civil society actors in intense debates, reaching in the end a sufficient sense of agreement that the result was more accepted than imposed (Feldman, 2012).

Leadership of Healing Conversation

So based on these examples, what can we say about the qualities of leaders who can foster constructive conversations? I would suggest a few essential qualities.

• First, an extremely high level of *patience*; the results do not come quickly. These leaders need a good deal of security in their own jobs;

they cannot succeed in high-pressure atmospheres demanding immediate results. All the leaders I have come across in this area, from Palmisano to Jonsson to Mandela, have strongly emphasized this element of patience and restraint. Conversations do not take a straight path; they wander, they reverse. They cannot be forced, but must set their own rhythms.

- *The ability to listen*: I cannot better the description of Kevin Sharer, the CEO of Amgen:

> The best advice I ever heard about listening—advice that significantly changed my own approach—came from Sam Palmisano,1 when he was talking to our leadership team. Someone asked him why his experience working in Japan was so important to his leadership development, and he said, "Because I learned to listen …. I learned to listen by having only one objective: comprehension. I was only trying to understand what the person was trying to convey to me. I wasn't listening to critique or object or convince."
>
> That was an epiphany for me because as you become a senior leader, it's a lot less about convincing people and more about benefiting from complex information and getting the best out of the people you work with. Listening for comprehension helps you get that information, of course, but it's more than that: it's also the greatest sign of respect you can give someone. So I shifted, by necessity, to try to become more relaxed in what I was doing and just to be more patient and open to new ideas. And as I started focusing on comprehension, I found that my bandwidth for listening increased in a very meaningful way. (Sharer, 2012)

- *A high tolerance for criticism.* The IBM leadership invited criticism and emerged with their legitimacy strengthened. The Fitness Profiling process described earlier requires the leadership team to listen to often fierce criticisms from their own subordinates. They often react at first with defensive anger: *How can they say that about us? Can't they see how much we've done and how hard we're working? They don't understand.* Only leaders with a strong stomach and a brief in the process can take that with equanimity.

- *Links to the communal past.* Charismatic and collaborative leaders may be new to the community, but successful conversations need leaders with a deep understanding of the communal traditions, while still being able to stand outside them to encourage reflection and change.

At IBM, the first CEO after the near-death of the company in 1993 was an outsider with no ties to the existing culture. To a considerable extent, he trampled on the opposition and fired those who objected, driving resistance underground. Palmisano, who succeeded him, was both a long-time "IBMer" with a record of deep commitment to the company *and* an ally of Gerstner in saving it from bankruptcy. Thus he was able to win over many of the old guards through his record of loyalty. His presentation of a new set of corporate values retained many links of format and wording with the familiar and beloved Basic Beliefs, while adding crucial phrases emphasizing new values. Similarly, Jonsson's deep roots in the Dallas community were essential to his credibility in establishing the Goals dialogue.

Many of those qualities are needed to varying degrees in other kinds of leadership as well, though the pressures are greatly heightened for situations like Palmisano's and Jonsson's. One further quality is more specific to this type:

- *A strong sense of process.* Creating a good conversation on a large scale is a multi-step affair, and the steps can rarely be entirely fixed in advance. There is a need to build understanding among people who have worked separately in the past; a need to build a shared vision, or purpose, that can orient their differing contributions in the same direction; and a need for new structures and mechanisms of collaboration to implement change. These cannot be driven by top-down blueprints, the way a charismatic leader tends to do; rather, leaders need to be sensitive to new developments and areas that need focus, and help to steer the process.

Jonsson, in Dallas, laid out early on a series of steps to develop, test, refine, publicize, and build support for a shared vision of the city. He wanted to begin with issue papers developed by key leaders of the city; then choose a diverse group of 60–80 citizens for a three day offsite with much small group discussion to work over the papers; then a series of neighborhood meetings throughout the city; and finally a reconvening of the original conferees to finalize the document. This was in many respects similar to the process designed by Palmisano and his staff forty years later, which also went through multiple steps over three years. Both cases, moreover, spurred further rounds of discussion into new areas over several decades; indeed, both the IBM jam process and the Dallas Goals process are still inspiring new conversations to this day.

I would note that this description of leaders of conversation is not the same as a *facilitator*, and the now-common term "facilitative leadership" misses the mark. All these processes had facilitators, to be sure—people who managed meetings, set ground rules, mediated disputes. But these leaders need to do more: they need to make substantive judgments of value and set directions, but without suppressing the commitment and innovation of participants, and while always remaining open to changing their own views. It's a very difficult balancing act: to both push and be flexible, to guide and involve.

One might modify Freud's famous image of the horse and rider for this context: leaders, as riders, cannot effectively use power—the rest of the organization is far more powerful, but if they are sensitive to the feelings of the horse, they can guide it. Jonsson in Dallas had almost no control over the fractious community, but he made it clear from his first speech the broad beliefs which animated him: that it was essential to engage everyone in building a shared vision of the future, and that cities needed to make the most of the diversity of strengths among their citizens. These remained stable guideposts throughout the decades-long process.

In the IBM case, Palmisano and the leadership did far more than facilitating a conversation. They called for the Jam discussion and opened it by proposing a draft value statement. After the first round, Palmisano read the entire transcript and asked his team to do the same; then they revised their first draft in very significant ways—clarifying and incorporating concerns they had identified in the discussion. For example, the draft value statement "Excellence through innovation" was changed in the final version to "Innovation that matters—for our company and for the world." A number of participants commented specifically on how much that shift had meant to them in terms of restoring their pride in the company. They went on to solicit proposals for specific implementations of the values, with wide discussion and a company-wide vote to select the priorities. And they held multiple jams over subsequent years on contentious issues like the approach to changing customer demands.

A final conclusion I would draw runs partially counter to this list of principles. The German case, and others I have looked at, suggest that no one type of leadership is sufficient to bring together diverse and contentious groups. In postwar Germany, and Europe as a whole, one can see many types of leaders who played crucial roles. Some directed large organizations—corporate and political. But perhaps the largest number operated in the background, following the philosophy attributed to Lao Tzu: "A leader is best when people barely know he exists, when his work is done, his aim fulfilled, they will say: we did it ourselves."[3]

But in closing, I have to return to sociology. Leadership, no matter how skilled, no matter what the style, is never sufficient. Conversations of the kind I have sketched go far beyond the capability of any leader. Nelson Mandela did much, but grew old and tired; Abraham Lincoln would have sought reconciliation, but did not live to carry it through. It's a very long process. Consequences unfold over long periods of time and in the midst of many other environmental forces. Some would dismiss the importance of the IBM jam or the Dallas process; even Germany, which has seemed a remarkable success, is now seeing a revival of old ideologies and divisions. As Chou En-Lai reportedly said to Henry Kissinger, when asked how the French Revolution had impacted history: "It's too soon to tell."

Thus even the most effective leaders of conversation can succeed only to the degree that they are, or become, embedded in institutions. There are a few cases in which this kind of conversation has become a regular part of decision-making for a time at least: the sequence of jams at IBM; some of the "Fitness Profiling" cases sketched earlier, where the process has been repeated over multiple cycles; Johnson & Johnson where the guiding Credo has been regularly "challenged" in company-wide discussions. But the political institutions of Western democracies do not support this kind of conversation. The process is instead one of conflict and opposition—competing views in a competition seeking electoral victories, rather than aiming to build broader understandings.

To heal our wounds, we need both leaders who can stimulate constructive conversations, and new institutions that provide a framework and incentives for their continuance. There are flashes of hope, such as the

Goals for Dallas process and a growing number of community dialogues. As incomplete as they are, they cast some light on the long path ahead.

Notes

1 My discussion of IBM is based on extensive interviews and complete transcripts of the Values Jam and World Jam discussions of 2003–4. I also rely on my research at Citibank and on companies that have gone through the "Strategic Fitness" process, on my consulting experience, and on studies done by other researchers.
2 Personal interviews with company leaders, 2004.
3 This quote, like many other things, I first learned from Michael Maccoby.

References

Allison, G., Kellogg, J., & Zigman, P. (1985). *Goals for Dallas*. Kennedy School of Government, Harvard University.

Beer, M., & Eisenstat, R. A. (2004). How to have an honest conversation about your business strategy. *Harvard Business Review*, 82(2), 82–89, 123. https://hbr.org/2004/02/how-to-have-an-honest-conversation-about-your-business-strategy.

Burrows, P. (2003). Backfire: *Carly Fiorina's high-stakes battle for the soul of Hewlett-Packard*. Wiley.

Donnellon, A., & Margolis, J. (1990). *Mod IV product development team* (No. 9-491-030). Harvard Business School.

Feldman, L. G. (2012). *Germany's foreign policy of reconciliation: From enmity to amity*. Rowman & Littlefield.

Fryer, M. (2012). Facilitative leadership: drawing on Jürgen Habermas' model of ideal speech to propose a less impositional way to lead. *Organization*, 19(1), 25–43.

Habermas, J. (2013, April 26). Democracy, *Solidarity and the European Crisis*. https://www.pro-europa.eu/europe/jurgen-habermas-democracy-solidarity-and-the-european-crisis/5/. (This was an "Unpublished transcript of Lecture delivered by Prof. Jürgen Habermas on 26 April 2013 in Leuve).

Heckscher, C. (2015). *Trust in a complex world: Rebuilding community*. Oxford University Press.

Isaacson, W. (2011). *Steve Jobs (First Edition ~1st Printing)*. Simon & Schuster.

Maccoby, M. (1983). *The leader: A new face for American Management*. Ballantine.

Maccoby, M. (2003). *The productive narcissist: the Promise and Peril of Visionary Leadership*. Broadway Books.

Merton, R. K. (1940). Bureaucratic structure and personality. *Social Forces; A Scientific Medium of Social Study and Interpretation, 18*(4), 560–568.

Sharer, K. (2012). Why I'm a listener: Amgen CEO Kevin Sharer. *McKinsey Quarterly*. Retrieved from https://www.mckinsey.com/featured-insights/leadership/why-im-a-listener-amgen-ceo-kevin-sharer.

Taylor, F. W. (1911). *The principles of scientific management*. Harper Brothers.

5

LEADERSHIP IN THE INDUSTRIAL WORKPLACE

Bob Duckles

As a social-clinical psychologist, much of my career involved working with colleagues at the Kaizen Institute and working with organizations to improve their effectiveness. Sometimes the organization phrases its objective as seeking to improve productivity. At other times, the goals are richer. Since my graduate studies, my interest has been to explore how organizations bring out the best in people and how people bring out the best in organizations.

Leadership plays a critical role in the sustained success of the changes needed to reach the effectiveness objectives. Effective leadership also plays a role in bringing out the best in people.

I agree with Maccoby (2007) that leaders are those whom people follow. While we often think of leaders as mobilizing many people, some lead one or a few individuals at a time. Whether they realize it or do it without realizing it, leaders get people to do things by taking into account the thinking and feeling that leads to what their followers do.

DOI: 10.4324/9781003265122-5

I met Glen,[1] a US Department of Commerce Director, at a retreat. He described how he resolved a dilemma often faced in the federal government bureaucracy. It is tough to fire a US civil servant who does unsatisfactory work. Legal and regulatory protections prevent workers from being separated from their job. The solution sometimes devolves into writing the employee a. glowing evaluation, making it easier for the employee to find employment elsewhere in the government.

Glen told me he had inherited a secretary, whom he found inadequate, from his predecessor. She left out details when taking messages. Her typing contained many errors. He wished he could exchange her for someone more reliable. One day, he invited her into his office and told her he would like to know her better. From their conversation, he discovered she dreamed of becoming an actress.

"Look," he said, "I'm on the board of an amateur theater group in Arlington, Virginia. We produce four or five plays a year. I know the director is often looking for additional actors. I can put you in touch with him. Maybe he can find a role for you in the next play."

The secretary's face lit up. "I'd like that very much!"

She landed a small part. Over the next couple of years, she became a key player among the amateurs who acted in the theater's productions, rising eventually to perform leading roles.

"Before long," Glen said, "she improved as a secretary. She relayed accurate messages. Her typing improved. The chip on her shoulder fell away, and she became more relaxed and agreeable with everyone."

Glen demonstrates an individual act of leadership. He didn't move masses but led the secretary to do what he needed. I only met Glen this one time, but I suspect he led other people in his organization by getting to know them, understanding their hopes and expectations, and acting upon them.

Veronica, a secretary to a department head in a large multinational corporation in Mexico, attended a training program I conducted. I proposed that leaders get people to perform or make a change by acting on their ways of thinking and feeling.

"I believe I'm a leader," Veronica said. "One day, my boss returned from a meeting, furious. 'Get your notebook,' he said. 'I need you to take a letter to type up, right away!' I got my steno pad and went into his office. 'Close the door,' he ordered. Then he dictated a terrible, angry letter, full of obscenities. He said things I thought could be very damaging to other people and even to himself.

"Type the letter right now so I can sign it and send it out today," he said.

"I managed to have several other tasks compete for my time. I double-spaced the letter. We *never* double-space a dictated letter."

"I waited until he seemed calmer before taking him the typescript. 'I double-spaced it because I believe you'll want to make some changes before we mail it,' I said. He scanned the letter, smiled, crumpled it into a ball, and tossed it into his wastebasket."

"'I think I'll find another way to handle this,' he said. Later, after he had left for the day, I recovered the page from his wastebasket and put it through the shredder."

"Tell us how this was leadership," I said.

"I took into account his angry feelings. I decided it wasn't the moment to question his action but waited until he had calmed down and had a chance to consider his intention. When he arrived, I understood his actions came from strong feelings. By double-spacing the letter, I gave him a chance to think about it. If I had followed his orders exactly, he might have signed the letter and posted it."

Tony, a plant manager, always allowed one person on his staff to object vociferously to suggestions when they came from another particular staff member. Tony would let the rant ride and later return to the idea, slightly rephrasing it. By doing this, he accomplished the consensus of his entire staff around many issues.

I had a chance to sit in on several meetings led by Lyle, a general manager over several operations in Mexico. Lyle had a limited understanding of some manufacturing processes, but he never shied away from showing his ignorance.

"Now, why do we do that?" His questions often included the word, *why*.

"Sometimes he'd learn *why*. Sometimes he discovered the staff disagreed about *why*. Sometimes he'd learn no one knew *why*."

Lyle might delve deeper by asking, "Is there a better way to do that?" often finding there were several ideas of better ways, but there had never been a practical way to consider them. When opinions differed on what a better way might be. He listened and asked, "why?" repeatedly.

Over several months he achieved better teamwork, solving problems that had been festering. He challenged the managers with his questions. He supported their efforts and celebrated their successes.

When he exposed other people's lack of understanding, this could cause embarrassment, but he managed to challenge without acting judgmental.

I've met some leaders, typically founders and sole proprietors of their companies who managed to get things done without bringing out the best in their workers. In one case, Jacob, the owner, entered a meeting I was having with supervisors about improving the processes used to count and package small fasteners. Orders were often not filled on time. I had been working with them to note activities that did not add value. By finding ways to eliminate those activities, order fulfillment could improve.

Jacob listened for a few minutes. As soon as he arrived, most of the supervisors shut up. I stood at a flipchart reviewing parts of the process the group had identified they could eliminate to achieve the goal.

"I agree with Bob," Jacob said. "But we don't need him to tell us that. This is just common sense. We need just to use our common sense." He turned to me. "Bob, I'm going to ask you to step out of the room for a bit."

I gathered my gear and stepped out into the hall. As soon as the door closed, I heard the owner screaming at his supervisors. I made out some profanity and something that sounded like, "I should fire the lot of you!"

Jacob didn't understand I was reviewing items the foremen had identified, but no one could interrupt him to make that clear. After several minutes, the door opened, and the supervisors slinked out, studiously averting their gaze from me. The owner must have left by another door. I did not see him again.

Mark, Jacob's right-hand, brought me in as a consultant. Jacob hired Mark as an overall assistant. Practically, his role involved taking the brunt of the owner's tantrums, translating Jacob's wishes into results, or finding the time and way to let him know his wishes could not be realized.

I met several sole proprietors who had a number-two manager like Mark, to bring their wild or impractical ideas into fruition and smooth things over after a temper tantrum. These people exercised leadership in buffering the workforce from the boss's temper.

A Mexican truck-assembly operation was such a company. Federico, the owner, achieved loyalty and performance by acting as a godfather.

All workers could get access to him to seek financial help for a funeral or a wedding or to buy uniforms for a soccer team. Federico would figuratively pat the employees on their heads and reward them for being good and loyal. Contrition for an error usually brought forgiveness after a lecture regarding the mistake. People who showed too much independence or suggested changes that did not come from the owner were likely to have their employment come to an abrupt end. Federico rewarded those who behaved like good children.

On December 12, the company held a feast honoring the Virgin of Guadalupe with live music and gifts for the employees. All workers participated in a raffle of large appliances. This leadership managed to get people to behave as the owner wanted but infantilized them in the process. It did not bring out the best in the workers. Neither did the leadership stimulate people to contribute to bringing out the best in the organization.

One of the most interesting leaders I met was Raul. He had worked for years setting up assembly lines for the company's new products. I came in to help improve on the typical assembly line by working with a team that included assemblers and several supervisors. I helped the group see the assembly process with new eyes, identifying activities that did not add value to the final product.

"Twenty years ago, I learned that an assembly line should be a straight line with lots of material nearby from which the workers could resupply as needed," Raul told me.

After raising awareness of non-value-adding work, part of my role involved bringing some new ideas with which the group could experiment. We moved the workstations closer together, putting them into a U-shape instead of a straight line. Assemblers operating inside the cell received small quantities of material continuously from the outside of the U-shaped cell, so they never had to stop and hunt for material. The act of assembling added value. Hunting for material did not.

Raul found this revolutionary and often reminded me that he had learned to make straight assembly lines. Yet he willingly participated in our experimental U-shaped layouts. He welcomed the opportunity to implement changes to make jobs better, easier, and safer for the assemblers.

Some employees worried our activity would cause a loss of jobs. They could see that the changes would mean the same amount of units could be produced with fewer people. Raul reassured them by explaining that new products would be coming in. Any people freed up on this line would be absorbed along with additional employees to be hired.

After my week working with Raul and the team, Raul became the day-to-day leader of the improvement process, working with the assemblers. When I returned a month later, additional changes had taken place. The straight assembly line stood idle. The team had reoriented the U-shaped cell to fit a layout that included new production cells. Some of the original assemblers are now assembled full-time. Each manufactured unit flowed from one worker to the next to have components added, without a buildup between one operation and the next.

Freed-up assemblers now acted as full-time material handlers keeping the cell supplied with components on a continuous small batch basis. Raul's leadership in getting people to rethink the way they worked had made a difference.

Several months passed before I again visited the plant. I was amazed at what I saw. Fourteen U-shaped cells stood next to each other with their open ends facing a wide aisle. Forklift trucks dropped the largest components to each first operation of the cells and picked up the finished product at the end of the process—just feet from the first operation.

A few dedicated material handlers pushing carts provided a continuous flow of small parts placed within reach of the assemblers, going to a "supermarket" of components to replenish their carts. Under Raul's guidance, the assemblers were still learning how to work in the new way in some cells. He told me he was proud he had helped keep any of the lines from moving to Tijuana. That would have involved laying off workers in this plant.

He had caught onto the new idea and applied his ability to bring out the best in workers to respond to the company's increase in new products. He did not just implement a new process. He did it with the participation of the people who would do the work, permitting them to help bring out the company's best.

In many companies, process improvements come from manufacturing or industrial engineers, who tell people what to do, often causing resentment the engineers don't even notice. People need the income and benefits their jobs provide, so they don't push back. They keep quiet and fume among themselves. I've witnessed cases in which the engineers treat the employees as extensions of the equipment, not considering how new procedures make the employees' jobs more difficult or even hazardous, sometimes coming up which a change the employees knew was needed weeks earlier.

Leadership that brings out the best in people does not mean turning the process entirely over to the workers. Productive leadership involves the workers, understanding the thinking and feeling caused by changes, soliciting worker input. All too often, organizations consider all workers to fit a mold, to be the same—at least if they are "good" workers.

We learned in the Bolivar Project (Maccoby, 1981)[2] that there are social character differences in what people value about their work. In the Bolivar plant, for example, *traditional craftsmen* wanted reliable equipment, the necessary material, and clear instructions to do their job. Then, they preferred to be left alone to do the work. *Sociable workers* most enjoyed being with and talking to people. The worst thing you could do was put them off in a corner where they have no human contact. *Dutiful craftsmen* respect traditional authority. They do their duty and admire those who do their work and don't complain. Often they did not have much time for a team meeting, believing management should decide what needs doing, who does it, and how to do it.[3]

Bringing out the best in different social character types involves recognizing differences causing people to think and feel differently, sensing the best response to each person to foster their productiveness in the organization. In Bolivar, we also found some employees thrived when the joint management and union committee created education programs after work in the plant.

The best leaders understand that the organization needs to change beyond bringing in new equipment and technology. They understand the need for habits to change. One plant stands out in my memory. In my first few visits, many employees were idle for extended periods. They waited for material, equipment repair, or instructions. Apathy seemed prevalent. After a year, the whole place felt active and productive. Few people ever seemed idle. I never heard anyone express a desire to be idle again. The work pace was not frantic but sustained. It felt like a happy workplace.

Leadership by the Plant Manager and a vice-president in the parent company played an important role in making the changes happen. They both expressed a role for themselves supporting the people building the product. They displayed this role by getting quick responses to the needs of the production lines. They showed interest in and applauded people's improved work, using new approaches to getting the job done.

After a year and a half, both leaders left. The vice-president received a promotion to a job in a European operation. A recruiter found the Plant Manager an attractive and better paying job in another company.

The new vice-president played a role with little presence in the plant. The new Plant Manager did not value the thinking and contributions of the factory workers.

Some of the foremen had been slow to accept the changes and welcomed the more traditional approach of the new Plant Manager. The accomplishments no longer received nourishment from productive leaders and withered away.

Leaders often move on through promotion or leaving. In my consulting career, promising first steps died because the leaders left. Even productive leaders can fail to understand that changes in how products are produced require *changes in the total system* to survive. Active leaders who are present can see that the needs of the production system be met, without fully realizing information systems, material handling, quality systems, dealing with vendors, measuring results, and continuing to make improvements, all must also change. The longer they stay, they can discover the needed changes to the total system and implement them. Since they usually don't recognize the entire system, they don't lead the changes before leaving.

Notes

1 I've changed the names of leaders in this paper.
2 In this work, Maccoby describes, in detail, Paul Reaves, a foreman and leader who brought out the best in workers at the Bolivar Plant and Irving Bluestone, a UAW leader, who played a crucial leadership role in the Bolivar Project.
3 These are only some of the social character types we identified in the Bolivar Project. (Duckles, 1976).

References

Duckles, R. (1976). *Work, workers, and democratic change* (Doctoral Thesis). The Wright Institute.

Maccoby, M. (1981). *The leader: A new face for American Management.* Ballantine Books.

Maccoby, M. (2007). *The leaders we need, and what makes us follow.* Harvard Business School Press.

6

THE DARK TRIAD MAY NOT BE SO DARK: EXPLORING WHY "TOXIC" LEADERS ARE SO COMMON—WITH SOME IMPLICATIONS FOR SCHOLARSHIP AND EDUCATION[1]

Jeffrey Pfeffer

Research on topics such as the "dark triad" of personality traits (Furnham et al., 2013), including leader narcissism (Braun, 2017), Machiavellianism (Jones & Mueller, 2021), elements of psychopathy (Neo et al., 2018), and the effects of toxic leader behavior on individual and organizational outcomes (Braun, 2017) has proliferated. And no wonder. The world seemingly faces a plethora of problematic leaders who provide a continuing source of wonder and commentary for observers who do not understand how the narcissists and psychopaths can not only achieve powerful positions but can continue to garner support. For instance, former President Donald Trump famously quipped, "I could stand in the middle of 5th

DOI: 10.4324/9781003265122-6

Avenue and shoot somebody and I wouldn't lose voters" (Diamond, 2016). Reviewing a book on Adam Neumann, the "unusual" founder of WeWork, Walter Kirn (2020) commented that "The global pool of capital on which free-market societies float ... is a virtually bottomless reservoir of folly, vanity, mania, and caprice." People being able to shoot others and get away with it and the various ego-driven leaders of companies, some of which have flamed out in spectacular fashion (i.e., Elizabeth Holmes of Theranos) challenge fundamental ideas about the social order in general and leadership in particular.

Much, if not all, of this writing about so-called dark leadership traits and behavior proceeds from the following premises, each of which seems somewhat problematic for reasons I explore in this article. First, terms such as "dark triad," psychopathology, narcissism—which in its extreme form is a diagnosed mental disorder (Pincus & Lukowitsky, 2010)—label presumably evidence-based, scientific concepts describing individuals with language that implies at least some degree of psychological maladjustment. This terminology helps to create the impression, possibly unintentionally, that harmful, psychologically problematic leader behavior is in some sense aberrant or deviant—that even if not rare, 'dark' leader behavior is, at a minimum—dark.

The first problem with this characterization of "dark" traits is that assessments of consequences as to their usefulness depend heavily on the particular measures, perspectives, and time horizon adopted. Assessments of almost anything in the social sciences are more relative and dependent on perspective than we like to admit. For instance, measures of organizational effectiveness are often not highly correlated with each other, "supporting the notion that organizations may be effective in only some areas" (Ostroff & Schmitt, 1993, p. 1350). Measures of performance at both the individual and organizational level vary greatly over time—within-person performance variability is both acknowledged and frequently quite large (Dalal et al., 2014). This time-varying performance variability means that assessments of the outcomes of behavior depend importantly on **when** the outcome measure is sampled. Performance assessments can and do differ depending on whether one is considering longer or shorter time periods—something that holds both at the organizational and individual level of analysis. One review of the literature on narcissism, for instance, noted that while initially attractive to others, narcissistic behavior grates on others over time (O'Reilly & Chatman, 2020).

Furthermore, individual outcomes differ from organizational results, as people in high-performing companies can nonetheless lose their jobs and people in low-performing organizations can nonetheless sometimes do very well. To take one example, even as Merrill, Lynch was failing during the 2007–2008 financial crisis and reporting its largest quarterly loss ever, its CEO, Stanley O'Neal, left with a payout estimated to be $161 million (NBC News, 2007). Because research shows that narcissism and Machiavellianism both positively predict leader emergence—i.e., career success—and even, occasionally, organizational performance, whether these traits are indeed "dark" and harmful very much depends on whose perspective is being invoked, the individual being chosen for or promoted into senior positions or the people that leader will supervise, and also the particular criteria and time period that are chosen.

Moreover, the idea that motives, behaviors, and personality constituting the dark triad are deviant or problematic leads naturally and logically to recommendations as to how to prevent people with these traits from occupying positions where they lead large groups of people in ways that might cause damage (Pech & Slade, p. 200). The idea that narcissism or Machiavellianism is a personality "disorder" additionally implies that these (often quite successful leaders) need some form of intervention or treatment to change their behavior. And, an additional implication is that homeostatic organizational processes will work to rectify aberrant, harmful behavior, a perspective quite consistent with Lerner's just world hypothesis (Lerner & Miller, 1978) that people get what they deserve.

But what if, as some evidence suggests, such behaviors are common and even functional, at least in terms of advancing the interests of the individuals exhibiting them? What if such behaviors and their manifestations are actually sought by followers? In short, what if psychopathology isn't so pathological—or rare—after all? In that case, screening people out may be difficult and preventing the rise of, for instance, narcissists almost impossible.

There are two additional problems with the value-freighted characterization of dark leadership traits. First, the terminology used to describe narcissists and psychopaths, virtually by definition as reflecting some degree of mental disorder, leaves the idea of teaching people how to proactively exhibit behaviors consistent with such personality diagnoses as implausible or worse, ethically indefensible. Not teaching people about the possible positive value of narcissistic behaviors, for instance, is inconsistent with the goal of helping them acquire power and advance in their careers. That is because the research evidence is reasonably consistent in demonstrating positive effects for narcissism on people's salary, getting hired, being promoted, and often even for measures of group performance (Pfeffer, 2016). Summarizing numerous studies, recently O'Reilly and Pfeffer (2021, in press) commented: "There is evidence that in organizations, narcissists are more likely to earn more, rise to positions of power have longer tenures as CEOs, and be successful in their careers." These do not seem like particularly "dark" outcomes.

Second, the idea of traits as "dark" has led, naturally enough, to values-driven research attempting to demonstrate the harm caused by narcissists or Machiavellians. In the social sciences, scholars will mostly find what they are looking for. The problems of replicability and reproducibility in the social sciences are large enough already (Baker, 2015), without having labels such as "dark" and assumptions about harmful personality traits almost invariably operate to make the problem worse by having scholars design studies to prove what they believe, rather than what might be empirically true.

There is yet another issue raised by the idea of the "dark triad." The dominant focus on individually deviant, non-sanctioned, forms of psychopathology in leaders almost automatically renders the study of those who voluntarily select, follow, and even admire such individuals either largely ignored or, again, characterized as the study of some form of psychopathology. So to take the quote with which this chapter begins, Trump recognized, as much research only partially does, that for him to get away with shooting someone in the middle of the street and not losing votes, it is the *voters* themselves who are implicated in a psychological transaction or exchange. In the political commentary, this view of people who prefer leaders who exhibit dark triad traits has led to the mostly unproductive search for the sources of anger or social isolation on the part of otherwise regular people.

In several research domains, understanding why people follow psychologically "damaged" individuals has led to an investigation of whether people who follow so-called toxic leaders suffer from greater amounts of authoritarianism or possibly fear of death (Lipman-Blumen, 2005). This investigation of authoritarianism as a cause of people following psychopaths represents a harkening back to early research in social psychology in the post-World War II era when social scientists sought to understand why so many people willingly followed Hitler and Mussolini (Adorno, et al., 1950). But the investigation of followers of people exhibiting dark triad traits, much like Hillary Clinton's unfortunate use of the word "deplorables" (Reilly, 2016), stigmatizes many people's decisions and lodges their choices very much in their personalities and character. By so doing, it consigns the study of leadership choice—at least when such choice leads to selecting people characterized by dark triad characteristics—to a values-laden scientific endeavor that hinders the discovery of empirical regularities through the very language it uses and the frames it adopts.

In this brief chapter and overview of what has become a growing empirical literature on the psychiatric disturbances of leaders and the effects of such leaders on organizations, I want to make several interrelated and what seems to me reasonably obvious points. First, the evidence suggests that various forms of psychopathology among political and business leaders are common enough that terms that connote deviance or maladjustment should be banished, to be replaced by more value-neutral descriptions.

Second, while not for a moment denying variations in the stable individual differences that constitute personality, many of the behaviors that characterize narcissists and other forms of psychopathology, such as lying or displaying unwarranted self-confidence, are just that—behaviors—that can be strategically adopted, or dropped, according to situational exigencies. Teaching people when, why, and how such behaviors are in fact adaptive might actually be useful if we want to help people accrue power. More importantly, undertaking the associated research to be able to answer when such behaviors or more or less effective remains an important undertaking.

And third, for a leader to be a leader, there have to be followers. Except in extreme circumstances such as situations of incarceration or involuntary servitude that seldom exist in either politics or business, followers have, for the most part, voluntarily decided to follow so-called toxic or dark leaders, at least as such a term, "voluntarily," is commonly understood. Therefore, it behooves scholarly inquiry to understand the psychological transaction or affinity that binds people to leaders that many social science scholars find abhorrent. We cover each of these topics in turn.

"Dark Triad" Traits are Common Among Leaders

An early article by Kets de Vries and Miller (1985) argued that some degree of the narcissistic personality is prevalent in most leaders. As House and Baetz (1979, p. 353) noted, "leadership requires a predisposition to be influential. Therefore such traits as dominance or ascendance ... and need for power ... are ... associated with leadership." Subsequent voluminous empirical research has consistently found a relationship between narcissism, Machiavellianism, and psychopathy and leadership emergence as well as other positive career outcomes such as interviewing well, being hired, and achieving promotions. If dark traits frequently predict leadership emergence and positive career outcomes, it follows logically that leaders will, compared to non-leaders, tend to have more of these traits.

One recent review of 92 independent samples found a positive correlation between "psychopathic personality characteristics and leadership emergence" (Landay et al., 2019, p. 183), with the positive relationship stronger for men than for women, where the relationship was actually negative. A study of 439 persons observed that an element of psychopathy, "fearless dominance," was associated with professional success (Eisenbarth et al., 2018).

Judge et al. (2009) argued that lessons from The Prince by Machiavelli "are relevant today as they were in the 16th Century." They noted that Machiavellians seek leadership positions, have high motivation to lead, and are willing to do things—such as investing in their own social capital—that will help bring them into leadership roles. Not surprisingly, then, Machiavellianism is positively related to attaining leadership roles. One study (Simonton, 1986) reported that Machiavellians serve longer in national elective offices. An analysis of 793 early-career employees in Germany found that Machiavellianism was positively related to a leadership position (Spurk et al., 2015).

Of the three dark triad traits, narcissism probably has the most extensive empirical research. A study of 172 Italian CEOs found that narcissism was positively related to individuals becoming CEOs more quickly (Rovelli & Curris, 2020). A comprehensive review of the narcissism research literature reported: "Meta-analytic results ... found positive relationships between leader narcissism and leader emergence explained by leader ex-traversion" (Braun, 2017). Westerman et al. (2011) found that under-graduate business students, pursuing a major designed to place them in leadership roles, were more narcissistic than psychology students and furthermore that the level of narcissism among college students had in-creased over time. Narcissism is reliably related to people both wanting—and achieving, leadership positions. Pfeffer (2016), reviewing the leadership literature's blandishments to be modest—the opposite of being self-aggrandizing and narcissistic—cited extensive evidence that narcissism predicted being hired, being promoted, being paid more, and often even predicted various dimensions of group or unit performance.

Narcissism is a reasonably common trait among leaders. As one paper noted, "It is widely acknowledged that narcissism is a peculiar character-istic of leaders" (Rovelli & Curris, 2020), while another study commented that "narcissism ... is an attribute of many powerful leaders" (Rosenthal & Pittinsky, 2006, p. 617). Studying 32 high-technology CEOs, O'Reilly et al. (2014) found that narcissistic CEOs with longer tenure earned more, had larger shareholdings, and had a larger gap between their compensation and other members of their team.

Several problems arise from confusing what may be undesirable with what is pathological, unusual, or "dark." One is that people—observers, scholars, employees, citizens—are frequently surprised by who and what they confront in political and business organizations. Surprise may be pleasant in some situations, but surprise is seldom desirable in navigating the social world. By seeing common traits of leaders as anomalous, people risk being caught off guard by the realities of organizational and political life. As one prominent but far from unusual example, observers and, more importantly, political rivals underestimated the appeal of Donald Trump in the 2016 election because of his narcissistic, social convention-defying behavior. By the time they took him seriously, it was too late.

A second, related but distinct problem is that the assumption that common, albeit possibly undesirable, traits and behaviors are deviant and pathological logically suggests that various homeostatic, self-correcting social processes will be sufficient to, at least over some period of time, cause problematic leaders to fail and lose their positions. This reasoning is particularly the case because of the common assumptions that (a) the dark triad traits negatively affect performance and (b) performance is determinative in influencing leadership tenure. But neither assumption holds up particularly well. As I have argued elsewhere (Pfeffer, 2010), the evidence suggests at best a weak relationship between performance and keeping one's job, with numerous other factors such as credentials, demographic characteristics, organizational tenure, and political skill providing explanatory power. And the literature on the effects of dark triad traits on performance is quite mixed (Braun, 2017).

The belief that people get what they deserve, and bad behavior will be punished excuses people from taking action, mustering resources, and most importantly, figuring out effective strategies to win in the inevitable organizational political struggles that determine succession and success. Quick to believe in the just world hypothesis that fairness and justice prevails (Lerner, 1980), there is too much selective inattention to the success and persistence of problematic individuals. After all, who pays attention to temporary, or aberrant, anomalies?

Underestimation can sometimes provide the underestimated target time and space to gain leverage, and it is quite plausible that attributions of psychopathy in its various forms lead to underestimating the psychopaths until they are in power—at which point dislodging them is much more difficult because of the resources and decisions they then control.

Behaviors, Personality, and the Important Distinction Between the Two

Although personality is defined by traits and is presumed to be a relatively stable attribute of individuals, and behaviors can be presumably trained and changed, there is much confusion in the literature on the dark triad between the two, as many traits are described by behaviors. For instance, one conception of Machiavellianism defines it as the belief that interpersonal manipulation (a behavior) is the key to life success and that Machiavellians "behave accordingly" (Furnham et al., 2013). Rovelli and Curnis (2020), in their study of the relationship between narcissism and accession to CEO positions, speak about "behaving like a star." Braun (2017) writes about psychopathy as including thrill-seeking, a behavior of seeking out excitement.

Displaying confidence, a characteristic of narcissists, can be accomplished through body language (Cuddy, 2015). Some research suggests that because confidence is often conflated with competence (Anderson et al., 2012), displaying confidence—something that can be primed and adopted in the moment by instructing people in how to engage in "power posing"—results in better interview performance (Cuddy, et al., 2015). Carney (2021, p. 13) maintained that "conveying power through nonverbal behavior is easy to do" and that behaviors designed to express power are easy to select and deploy. O'Reilly and Chatman (2020) defined narcissism in part as being willing to challenge others and engaging in self-promotion. These are both behaviors that can be deployed strategically in the service of impression management. Indeed, the large literature on impression management (Gardner, 1992) provides numerous examples of using behaviors to create an image—and many of the behaviors such as intimidation and ingratiation are implicated in discussions of the dark triad.

The distinction between traits and behaviors is important because to the extent that the dark triad represents behaviors, not just traits, that fact raises the question of whether it might be desirable to teach people to exhibit, at least to some moderate extent, and in some circumstances, some aspects of dark triad behavior. Looking out for oneself—self-interest seeking—may be useful in a world in which, for decades, human resources policies have told employees they are responsible for their own careers. "Manipulation" is a word charged with negative connotations. But the essence of leadership is, in some sense, being able to get people to engage in behaviors that they would not otherwise do in the absence of that leadership. A different, less-charged word for this activity is social influence, the essence of effective leadership.

As already noted, displaying confidence can be helpful in interview situations. Being able to bluff—deceive—successfully can be useful in negotiations (Gaspar et al., 2019). The ability to charm others can be used to attract allies, supporters, and mentors, all of which is useful for advancing one's career. It is far from clear that instruction in some of the behaviors associated with the dark triad would not be useful for individuals seeking to advance in the inevitably competitive, hierarchical organizations in which most people will work. In that sense, paying more attention to behaviors and how they might be induced, and focusing less on presumably immutable traits, could be useful for both research and teaching on the topics ranging from social influence to career success to impression management. Another implication: research on the advantages of behaviors associated with the dark triad, and research on the conditions under which they are particularly effective or ineffective, would be informative.

Why do "Bad" Leaders Have So Many Followers?

As I have noted elsewhere (Pfeffer, 2016), notwithstanding a truly enormous leadership industry teaching—and preaching—leaders to be modest, authentic, truthful, and to care for others, among other virtues, such behavior is not common among successful, powerful people. Instead of or in addition to just documenting the many ill-effects of various leadership behaviors and arguing for different organizational cultures and leadership styles—an activity that has gone on for decades with little to no observable effect—progress requires understanding how and why such conditions persist. Research provides a number of possible, and not mutually exclusive, answers.

One answer to such questions is not—and cannot be—that uncovering and discerning such individuals are difficult. There are validated paper and pencil tests for various manifestations of psychopathology such as the Narcissistic Personality Inventory (Raskin & Terry, 1988), Machiavellianism (Christie & Geis, 1970), and psychopathy (Tsang, et al., 2018). Furnham et al. (2013) provided an extensive overview of the measurement of the dark triad of personality. Evidence suggests that others who have observed leaders can reliably assess them (O'Reilly et al., 2014). Moreover, there may be unobtrusive indicators—such as the use of first-person pronouns or the size of pictures (Chatterjee & Hambrick, 2007)—that help ascertain leaders' predispositions. Moreover, even if people could mask their true intentions and ways of operating, once discovered, they presumably could be eliminated—if anyone wanted to.

Nor is the search for what is "wrong" with followers likely to be productive. Although the investigation of the psychology of followers—are they beset with the fear of death, authoritarian personalities, individuals who have succumbed to pernicious social media influences, people facing economic insecurities, and so forth—may be, at first glance, reasonable conjectures, stigmatizing those who vote for—and work for—harmful leaders flies in the face of how many such leaders, and therefore followers, there are. To reprise a point already made, "abnormal" behavior cannot, by definition, be "normal" in the sense of frequent and customary, and this point is true whether we are talking about leaders or the people who follow them. It is quite possible that the attraction to leaders who exhibit dark triad traits is completely reasonable and rational and does not require the presumption that there is something "wrong" with those who vote for or work for "difficult people." Here are some possible avenues of inquiry to pursue.

Lipman-Blumen (2005) explored why people would continue to follow leaders who clearly violated the leader-follower relationship and abused the leader's power to their own self-interest. She argued that people craved safety and a sense of belonging, in part emerging from death anxiety, and that toxic leaders were effective at using these fundamental psychological needs to seduce followers into maintaining loyalty to the leaders almost regardless of the leaders' behavior. Without for a moment dismissing the plausibility and psychological insight of Lipman-Blumen's arguments, I believe the answer as to why people follow toxic leaders may be more straightforward.

Effectiveness

It is possible that leaders with dark triad traits are actually more effective, in part because they relentlessly pursue their objectives, are often visionary, and most importantly exhibit self-confidence, and are manipulative which makes it possible for them to charm—and recruit—others to their endeavors. O'Reilly and Chatman (2020, p. 13) noted that narcissists' "apparent confidence, extraversion, and willingness to challenge others fit the stereotype of a prototypical leader." Moreover, narcissists overclaim credit for their work and in the ambiguous situations typical in organizations, claiming credit is often sufficient to obtain credit, whether or not such credit is objectively justified. Because of confirmation bias and a tendency to want to believe that people get what they deserve—the world is a just and fair place—once narcissists, or anyone else, achieves a position, there will be selective attention to and remembering of their behaviors that will act to reinforce and justify their roles and status.

As Maccoby (2003), among numerous others, has noted, narcissistic leaders can be "productive," in the sense of creating highly successful organizations that market industry-leading products and services, grow to enormous size, and create substantial wealth in the process. Maccoby argued that narcissism could facilitate risk-taking and also the ability to effectively charm others, including potential investors, customers, and fellow workers. Associating with such individuals, including people like Steve Jobs and GE's Jack Welch, means being part of successful entities and befriending powerful and esteemed leaders—and what could be more rational than that?

A comprehensive review of the relationship between dark triad traits and workplace outcomes found very mixed results (LeBreton et al., 2018) with no simple answers as to whether or not the dark triad helped or hurt performance. Wallace and Baumeister (2002) noted that the context might affect the relationship between narcissism and performance. In four experiments, they found that while narcissism predicted leader emergence unconditionally, narcissists performed better when the opportunity to self-enhance was high. Nevicka et al. (2011) noted that narcissism predicted performance more strongly in teams that faced a situation of high reward interdependence, because of the ability of narcissists to succeed in influencing others.

Aziz (2005) uncovered a relationship between Machiavellianism and sales volume for real-estate agents, replicating results found earlier for stockbrokers and automobile salespeople. Deluga's (2001) influential study of American presidents found that presidential Machiavellianism was positively correlated with charismatic leadership and rated performance. Braun's (2017) comprehensive review found evidence for both positive and negative effects of narcissism on aspects of performance.

Moreover, in evaluating the effectiveness of dark triad traits, not all outcomes are equivalent. For instance, O'Reilly et al. (2018) found that companies led by narcissistic CEOs were more likely to face lawsuits, and other research has found that narcissistic CEOs acquire more companies and overpay for acquisitions and run companies that produce more variable performance (Chatterjee & Hambrick, 2007). Many studies of the effects of narcissism have emphasized the toll on interpersonal relationships. However, it is not clear that performance variability or lawsuits necessarily bother organizational members that much, depending on the financial results attained. As the case of Steve Jobs at Apple, among many other examples, nicely illustrates, people are willing to put up with a moderate amount of interpersonal abuse to be part of a successful organization and the financial results that brings.

Therefore, the first answer as to why people tolerate the dark triad in leaders is that such traits often, although not invariably, can produce good results, particularly in terms of the attained rank and earnings of individuals displaying those traits. The negative consequences that do arise are then rationalized as being necessary to create disruption or achieve power and status.

Similarity to Positive Leadership Attributes

Related to the effectiveness explanation, is another. As O'Reilly and Chatman (2020) described in an exceptionally thorough review of the literature on grandiose narcissists, many of the traits and behaviors that characterize such individuals are also descriptors of transformational leaders, and as they noted, "the concept of transformational leadership has been central to the study of leadership for the past 40 years" (p. 7). Maccoby (2003) has noted the descriptive similarity between narcissists and charismatic leaders. Because transformational and charismatic leaders are often presumed to be desirable, and because of the substantial overlap in the characteristics between such people and narcissists, observers necessarily would have some difficulty distinguishing between desirable and undesirable leaders. Therefore, following and even seeking out narcissists may be an almost inevitable consequence of the difficulty of distinguishing people with narcissistic traits from leaders who exhibit more positive, but overlapping, behaviors, and traits.

Many of the characteristics and behaviors of narcissists overlap not just with transformational or charismatic leadership but are in fact prototypical traits of leadership more generally. Nevicka (2018) has argued that narcissists "have many prototypical (leader-like) characteristics" including confidence dominance and extraversion. Because narcissists frequently create positive first impressions and actively seek positions of power, they frequently emerge as leaders. Nevicka concluded that "narcissism and leadership might appear like a perfect match." The qualities of narcissists and leaders may be almost indistinguishable, which makes the idea of people selecting narcissists for leadership roles logical and unexceptional.

Relationship to Political Skill

Gerald Ferris and his colleagues have developed and validated a political skills inventory (Ferris et al., 2005). Importantly, empirical research has documented the positive effects of political skill on numerous career and performance outcomes. For instance, Todd et al. (2010) examined the relationship between political skill and five career outcomes—career satisfaction, life satisfaction, perceived external job mobility, total compensation, and promotions--and found effects on four of them. Blickle et al. (2011) observed that controlling for general mental ability and personality dimensions, political skill accounted for a significant amount of the variation in job performance. Another study (Douglas & Ammeter., 2004) noted that political skill affected subordinates' perceptions of leader effectiveness. Being adept at organizational politics matters because fundamentally most organizations have power and politics processes at play (Pfeffer, 2010).

O'Reilly and Pfeffer (2021), in a series of studies, found that individuals higher in narcissism were more likely to see organizations in political terms. They were also more willing to engage in organizational politics. And those with higher levels of narcissism were also more skilled political actors. Given the research on the importance of political skill to both individual career outcomes and to many aspects of performance, the fact that narcissists are more skilled organizational politicians provides yet another explanation for why they are able to readily attract followers and allies.

Signals of Power and Success and the Relationship to the Self-Enhancement Motive

People want to be associated with—close to—power and success. As Cialdini and his colleagues noted (Cialdini, et al., 1976), people desire to bask in reflected glory. The self-enhancement motive (Sedikides & Alicke, 2012)—the desire to appear powerful and successful to oneself—leads to motivated cognition and to choices that make people feel good about themselves. Evolutionary theory would suggest that for people's genetic material to survive intergenerationally, one useful skill would be the ability to identify—and then associate with—those individuals with the most power.

Many of the traits and behaviors associated with the dark triad would seem to signal power in ways that would potentially attract others. As research has shown, because power provides people the latitude to violate rules and social norms, norm violators are perceived as more powerful because of the very fact of violating social expectations (Van Kleef et al., 2011). O'Reilly and Chatman (2020) specifically noted that narcissists thought of themselves as not subject to normal rules and norms. Possessing—and surviving—with dark triad traits, to the extent such traits are seen as violations of social norms and expectations, would make individuals seem more powerful.

And many of the specific traits would also possibly signal power. O'Reilly and Chatman (2020) noted that narcissism was associated with extreme self-confidence. Anderson et al. (2012), in a series of six studies, found that overconfidence produces higher social status in both short- and longer-term groups and makes individuals seem more competent. Anderson and Galinsky (2006) found an association between power and risk-taking, and risk-taking is another characteristic of narcissists (O'Reilly & Chatman, 2020).

Cheng et al. (2010) argued that, based on evolutionary logic, there were two ways of achieving social status in human societies one of which, dominance, based on intimidation, was consistent with descriptions of dark triad traits. Kessler et al.'s (2010) description of Machiavellianism noted that as originally conceptualized, it described a "rational approach to keeping power ... 'based entirely on expediency and ... devoid of the traditional virtues of trust, honor, and decency'" (p. 1869). Machiavelli's emphasis on effectively ruling (think, managing) others would seem, if effectively implemented, to imply power and success almost by definition.

Many instantiations of the dark triad are traits and behaviors that either lead to status and power or signal status and power. Because people for the most part seek to be associated with power and status, for among other reasons, self-enhancement, this logic provides yet another account as to why people might voluntarily seek out leaders who many social psychologists perceive as "dark."

Conclusion

As this brief overview makes clear, research on leader psychopathology confronts some problems. Most fundamentally, traits that are putatively deviant or maladaptive turn out to be reasonably common among leaders and predictive of career success as assessed along multiple dimensions. Second, because many of the so-called dark triad traits and behaviors either signal or create power—or both—and because people are attracted to power and status and want to be close to it for many reasons, it turns out that many individuals will willingly, voluntarily sign up to work for and by lead by "bad" leaders. What seems "bad" or "dark" to some social scientists, therefore, is common, sometimes produces success, and often attracts numerous followers in the organizational and political world. That is why I recommend focusing on behaviors and teaching people what works, why, and when.

It is far from clear to me that either leadership science or practice has been well-served by dark terminology and value-laden research, both of which have tended to cloud the observation of empirical regularities and to expending enormous effort to find what the values dictate as desirable. As I have previously noted (Pfeffer, 2016), the field of leadership is too much filled with lay preaching. This fact may explain why decades of research have failed to improve leaders, leadership practice, or to remediate leadership shortages. Nor is there much if any evidence that focusing on the dark triad or its constituent elements has caused them to be less prevalent in the world or to attract fewer followers. When a particular approach fails to work for a long time, maybe it is time to change the approach, alter judgments, and reconceptualize labels, research, and teaching.

Note

1 The comments of Charles O'Reilly on an earlier draft of this chapter are gratefully acknowledged.

References

Adorno, T. W., Frenkel-Brunswik, E., Levinson, D., & Sanford, N. (1950). *The authoritarian personality*. Harper & Row.

Alvesson, M., & Einola, K. (2019). Warning for excessive positivity: Authentic leadership and other traps in leadership studies. *Leadership Quarterly*, 30(4), 383–395.

Anderson, C., Brion, S., Moore, D. A., & Kennedy, J. A. (2012). A status-enhacement account of overconfidence. *Journal of Personality and Social Psychology*, 103(4), 718–735.

Anderson, C., & Galinsky, A. D. (2006). Power, optimism, and risk-taking. *European Journal of Social Psychology, 36* (4), 511–536.

Aziz, A. (2005). Relationship between Machiavellianism scores and performance of real estate salespersons. *Psychological Reports, 96* (1), 235–238.

Baker, M. (2015). Over half of psychology studies fail reproducibility test. *Nature*, News, 27 August, 2015. Retrieved from https://www.nature.com/news/over-half-of-psychology-studies-fail-reproducbility-test-1.18248.

Blickle, G., Kramer, J., Schneider, P. B., Meurs, J. A., Ferris, G. R., Mierke, J., Witzki, A. H. & Momm, T. D. (2011). Role of political skill in job performance prediction beyond general mental ability and personality in cross-sectional and predictive studies. *Journal of Applied Social Psychology, 41* (2), 488–514.

Braun, S. (2017). Leader narcissism and outcomes in organizations: A review at multiple levels of analysis and implications for future research. *Frontiers in Psychology, 8*, 773–795. doi: 10.3389/fpsyg.2017.00773.

Carney, D. R. (2021). Ten things every manager should know about nonverbal behavior. *California Management Review, 63* (2), 5–22.

Chatterjee, A. & Hambrick, D. C. (2007). It's all about me: Narcissistic chief executive officers and their effects on company strategy and performance. *Administrative Science Quarterly, 52*, 351–386.

Cheng, J. T., Tracy, J. L., & Henrich, J. (2010). Pride, personality, and the evolutionary foundations of human social status. *Evolution and Human Behavior, 31*, 334–347.

Christie, R., & Geis, F. (1970). *Studies in Machavellianism*. Academic Press.

Cialdini, R. B., Borden, R. J., Thome, A., Walker, M. R., Freeman, S., & Sloan, L. R. (1976). Basking in reflected glory: Three (football) field studies. *Journal of Personality and Social Psychology, 34* (3), 366–375.

Cuddy, A. J. C. (2015). *Presence*. Little, Brown.

Cuddy, A. J. C., Wilmuth, C. A., Yao, A. J., & Carney, D. R. (2015). Preparatory power posing affects nonverbal presence and job interview performance. *Journal of Applied Psychology, 100* (4), 1286–1295.

Dalal, R. S., Bhave, D. P., & Fiset, J. (2014). Within-person variability in job performance: A theoretical review and research agenda. *Journal of Management, 40* (5), 1396–1436k.

Deluga, R. J. (2001). American presidential Machiavellianism: Implications for charismatic leadership and rated performance. *leadership Quarterly, 12*, 339–363.

Diamond, J. (2016). Trump: I could "shoot somebody and I wouldn't lose voters." Retrieved from https://www.cnn.com/2016/01/23/politics/donald-trump-shoot-somebody-support/index.html.

Douglas, C., & Ammeter, A. P. (2004). An examination of leader political skill and its effect on ratings of leader effectiveness. *Leadership Quarterly, 15* (4), 537–550.

Eisenbarth, H., Hart, C. M., & Sedikides, C. (2018). Do psychopathic traits predict professional success? *Journal of Economic Psychology, 64,* 130–139.

Ferris, G. R., Treadway, D. C., Kolodinsky, R. W., Kacmar, C. J., Douglas, C., & Fink, D. D. (2005). Development and validation of the political skill inventory. *Journal of Management, 31* (1), 126–152.

Furnham, A., Richards, S. C., & Paulhus, D. L. (2013). The dark triad of personality: A 10 year review. *Social and Personality Psychology Compass, 7* (3), 199–216.

Gardner, W. I. III (1992). Lessons in organizational dramaturgy: The art of impression management. *Organizational Dynamics, 21* (1), 33–46.

Gaspar, J. P., Methasani, R., & Schweitzer, M. (2019). Fifty shades of deception: Characteristics and consequences of lying in negotiations. *Academy of Management Perspectives, 33* (1), 62–81.

House, R. J., & Baetz, M. L. (1979). Leadership: Some empirical generalizations and new research directions. In Staw, B. M., *Research in Organizational Behavior,* 341–423. Greenwich, CT: JAI Press.

Judge, T. A., Piccolo, R. F., & Kosalka, T. (2009). The bright and dark sides of leader traits: A review and theoretical extension of the leader trait paradigm. *Leadership Quarterly, 20,* 855–875.

Kessler, S. R., Spector, P. E., Borman, W. C., Nelson, C. E., Bandelli, A. C., & Penney, L. M. (2010). Re-examining Machiavelli: A three-dimensional model of Machiavellianism in the workplace. *Journal of Applied Social Psychology, 40* (8), 1868–1896.

Kets de Vries, M. F. R., & Miller, D. (1985). Narcissism and leadership: An object relations perspective. *Human Relations, 38* (6), 583–601.

Kirn, W. (2020). The cautionary tale of Adam Neumann and WeWork. *New York Times,* October 23, 2020. https://www.nytimes.com/2020/10/23/books/review/billion-dollar-loser-adam-neumann-wework-reeves-wiedeman.html.

Landay, K., Harms, P. D., & Crede, M. (2019). Shall we serve the dark lords? A meta-analytic review of psychopathy and leadership. *Journal of Applied Psychology, 104* (1), 183–196.

LeBreton, J. M., Shiverdecker, L. K., & Grimaldi, E. M. (2018). The dark triad and workplace behavior. *Annual Review of Organizational Psychology and Organizational Behavior, 5,* 387–414.

Lerner, M. J. (1980). *The belief in a just world: A fundamental delusion.* Plenum.

Lerner, M. J., & Miller, D. T. (1978). Just world research and the attribution process: Looking back and ahead. *Psychological Bulletin, 85* (5), 1030–1051.

Lipman-Blumen, J. (2005). *The Allure of Toxic Leaders.* Oxford University Press.

Maccoby, M. (2003). *The Productive Narcissist.* Broadway.

NBC News (2007). Ex-Merrill Lynch CEO to walk out with $161.5 M. Retrieved from https://www.nbcnews.com/id/wbna21549196.

Nevicka, B. (2018). Narcissism and leadership: A perfect match? In Hermann, A., Brunell, A., & Foster, J. (Eds.), *Handbook of trait narcissism,* (pp. 399–407). Springer Link.

Nevicka, B., De Hoogh, A. H. B., Van Vianen, A. E. M., Beersma, B., & McIlwain, D. (2011). All I need is a stage to shine: Narcissists' leader emergence and performance. *Leadership Quarterly, 22* (5), 910–925.

O'Reilly, C. A. & Chatman, J. A. (2020). Transformational leader or narcissist? How grandiose narcissists can create and destroy organizations and institutions. *California Management Review, 62* (3), 5–27.

O'Reilly, C. A. III, Doerr, B., Caldwell, D., & Chatman J. A. (2014). Narcissistic CEOs and executive compensation. *Leadership Quarterly, 25* (2), 218–231.

O'Reilly, C. A., Doerr, B., & Chatman, J. A. (2018). See you in court: How CEO narcissism increases firms' vulnerability to lawsuits. *Leadership Quarterly, 29,* 365–378.

O'Reilly, C. A., & Pfeffer, J. (2021). Why are grandiose narcissists more effective at organizational politics? Means, motive, and opportunity. *Personality and Individual Differences, 172,* 110557. doi: 10.1016/j.paid.2020.110557.

Ostroff, C., & Schmitt, N. (1993). Configurations of organizational effectiveness and efficiency. *Academy of Management Journal, 36* (6), 1345–1361.

Pfeffer, J. (2016). *Leadership BS.* HarperBusiness.

Pfeffer, J. (2010). *Power: Why Some People Have It—and Others Don't.* HarperBusiness.

Pincus, A. L., & Lukowitsky, M. R. (2010). Pathological narcissism and narcissistic personality disorder. *Annual Review of Clinical Psychology, 6,* 421–446.

Pech, R. J., & Slade, B. W. (2007). Organisational sociopaths: Rarely chal-
    lenged, often promoted. Why? *Society and Business Review*, 2 (3), 254–269.
Raskin, R., & Terry, H. (1988). A principal-components analysis of the
    Narcissistic Personality Inventory and further evidence of its construct
    validity. *Journal of Personality and Social Psychology*, 54 (5), 890–902.
Reilly, K. (2016). Read Hillary Clinton's "basket of deplorables" remarks about
    Donald Trump supporters. Retrieved from https://time.com4486502/
    hillary-clinton-basket-of-deplorables-transcript
Rosenthal, S. A., & Pittinsky, T. L. (2006). Narcissistic leadership. *Leadership
    Quarterly*, 17 (6), 617–633.
Rovelli, P., & Curnis, C. (2020). The perks of narcissism: Behaving like a star
    speeds up career advancement to the CEO position. *Leadership Quarterly*,
    32(3), 101–489. doi: 10.1016/j.leaqua.2020.101489.
Sedikides, C., & Alicke, M. D. (2012). Self-enhancement and self-protective
    motives. In R. M. Ryan (Ed.), *Oxford library of psychology: The Oxford
    Handbook of Human Motivation* (pp. 303–322). Oxford University Press.
Simonton, D. K. (1986). Presidential personality: Biographical use of the
    Tough Adjective Check List. *Journal of Personality and Social Psychology*,
    51(1), 149–160.
Spurk, D., Keller, A. C., & Hirsch, A. (2015). Do bad guys get ahead or fall
    behind? Relationships of the dark triad of personality with objective and
    subjective career success. *Social Psychological and Personality Science*, 7(2),
    113–121. doi: 10.1177/1948550615609735.
Sutton, R. I. (2007). *The no asshole rule*. Warner.
Sutton, R. I. (2010). *Good boss, bad boss*. Warner.
Sutton, R.I. (2017). *The asshole survival guide*. Penguin.
Todd, S. Y., Harris, K. J., Harris, R. B., & Wheeler, A. R. (2010). Career success
    implications of political skill. *Journal of Social Psychology*, 149 (3), 279–304.
Tsang, S., Salekin, R. T., Coffey, C. A., & Cox, J. (2018). A comparison of self-
    report measures of psychopathy among nonforensic samples using item
    response theory analyses. *Psychological Assessment*, 30 (3), 311–327.
Van Kleef, G. A., Homan, A. C., Finkenauer, C., Gundemir, S., & Stamkou, E.
    (2011). Breaking the rules to rise to power: How norm violators gain
    power in the eyes of others. *Social Psychological and Personality Science*, 2
    (5), 500–507.

Wallace, H. M., & Baumeister, R. F. (2002). The performance of narcissists rises and falls with perceived opportunity for glory. *Journal of Personality and Social Psychology, 82* (5), 819–834.

Westerman, J. W., Bergman, J. Z., Bergman, S. M., & Daly, J. P. (2011). Are universities creating millennial narcissistic employees? An empirical examination of narcissism in business students and its implications. *Journal of Management Education, 36*(1), 5–32. doi: 10.1177/1052562911408097.

7

THE SURPRISING RESILIENCE OF FREUD'S LIBIDINAL TYPES AND THEIR INFLUENCE ON LEADERSHIP

Tim Scudder

Introduction

Every leader brings their personality to their position. Psychometric assessment of personality is a quick, reliable way to gain insight into leaders' personalities. There are many different assessments available, from Rorschach tests that require expert analysis, to psychometrics that report on five personality factors that emerged from statistical analysis without an original theory. Psychoanalytic types offer insight into a limited number of distinct ways that leaders' personalities are likely to influence their decisions, communication, and other daily interactions. These types are grounded in theory, supported by data, and provide a simple frame of reference to understand all types of people. These insights give analysts a quick, valid, and reliable way to improve leaders' self-awareness and inform conversations about personal development and effectiveness.

Freud (1932) introduced seven normal personality types late in his life, but the article did not receive much attention. Elias Porter (1976) arrived

DOI: 10.4324/9781003265122-7

at the same seven types after a lifetime of psychometric research. Porter built on Fromm's interpretation of Freud, but Porter was not aware of Freud's seven types. Porter's psychometrics also demonstrate how affective states influence the way that motives are expressed—when people are at their best, and when they are experiencing threats and conflict. These types help explain how leaders' personalities influence the way they attempt to create meaning and purpose for the organization, what they are likely to perceive as threats to themselves or the organization, and what they are likely to do as the severity of perceived threats increases.

Rediscovering Libidinal Types

Freud's seven libidinal types were hiding in plain sight. They were first published in Psychoanalytic Quarterly, Volume 1, Issue 1, the first article. Yet they were never referenced by Erich Fromm, who expanded on Freud's concepts to present four non-productive orientations and one productive orientation (Fromm, 1947).

Fromm's non-productive orientations and psychoanalytic methods then informed the descriptions of leaders' personality types found in The Gamesman (Maccoby, 1976). Maccoby referred to Freud's types in The Harvard Business Review article "Narcissistic Leaders, The Incredible Pros, the Inevitable Cons" (Maccoby, 2000). The Productive Narcissist (Maccoby, 2003) and Narcissistic Leaders (Maccoby, 2007) included a psychometric for the reader to assess their type. These types were grounded in both Fromm's and Freud's theories, but further developed to fit the context of leadership. Fromm did not create a psychometric of his own, but Elias Porter (1953) used Fromm's four non-productive types to create a psychometric, which he refined over the years until it was offered as the Life Orientation and Strength Excess Profile (LIFO) assessment (Atkins et al., 1967). After further development, he introduced the Strength Deployment Inventory (SDI) (Porter, 1973), a new assessment with six types, based on three of Fromm's pure types, and three two-type blends. Of note, in the transition from LIFO to SDI Porter omitted the scale for Fromm's marketing orientation, citing low reliability. The next iteration of the SDI assessment included a seventh personality type, with characteristics similar to Fromm's marketing orientation, but instead of being directly measured with an independent scale as it was in the LIFO assessment, the type was identified by relatively equal scores on the other three scales and further validated by correlation with a four-scale behavioral Q-sort (Porter, 1985).

Porter described seven personality types, called motivational value systems, based on the interplay of three primary motives, which was exactly the same way that Freud constructed his libidinal types. Freud and Porter came to the same conclusion near the end of their respective careers. The SDI assessment not only has high validity and reliability, but it also offers the only current psychometric validation of Freud's libidinal typology (Scudder, 2013). Table 7.1 presents the conceptual relationships

Table 7.1 Conceptual Relationship of Typologies

Fromm's Orientations[a]	Maccoby's Leadership Types[b]	Porter's Motivational Types[c]	Freud's Libidinal Types[d]
Receptive	Erotic (Caring)	Altruistic-Nurturing (Blue)	Erotic
Hoarding	Obsessive (Systematic)	Analytic-Autonomizing (Green)	Obsessive
Exploitative	Narcissistic (Visionary)	Assertive-Directing (Red)	Narcissistic
Marketing	Marketing (Self-Developing)	Flexible-Cohering (Hub)	Erotic-Narcissistic-Obsessive
General descriptions of blended types	Specific descriptions of 12 blended types	Assertive-Nurturing (Red-Blue)	Erotic-Narcissistic
		Judicious-Competing (Red-Green)	Narcissistic-Obsessive
		Cautious-Supporting (Blue-Green)	Erotic-Compulsive
Views of Productivity			
All types are non-productive. A separate productive type can blend with the non-productive types.	All types have productive and non-productive potentialities.	All types are productive. A separate but related typology describes conflict types, based on two affective states.	All types are normal and do not represent clinical or neurotic patterns.

Notes
a (Fromm, 1947).
b (Maccoby, 2007).
c (E. H. Porter, 1985).
d (Freud, 1932).

between Freud and Porter's psychometric types, along with Fromm's and Maccoby's types.

While there are significant similarities between the typologies, there are subtle differences that can best be understood by considering the under-lying theories. Freud's typology, formed after a lifetime of observation and experience, was based on his libido theory applied to normal adults. The type names come from his earlier work on pathology, and the names tend to generate resistance—who wants to be called narcissistic-obsessive? Freud identified three pure personality types, but stated that no individual was a pure type; each individual had a mix of all three types. Fromm built on Freud's foundation, adding the concept of social character, like a macro personality that is shared by most members of society. Fromm attributed the emergence of the marketing orientation to socializing forces, such as schools, that prepare people to be successful in a market-driven economy. Fromm's four non-productive types were moralistic. Although he de-scribed some positive aspects of each type, he emphasized a single, idea-lized, productive type that he believed was the goal of human development.

Maccoby, who worked with Fromm (Fromm & Maccoby, 1996), adapted a combination of Freud's and Fromm's typology to the context of leadership and described both productive and non-productive aspects of the four primary types. The four scales in Maccoby's psychometric, based on the four types, have high internal reliability and construct validity when compared with Freud's and Fromm's types. The resultant scores facilitate the descriptions of several distinct personality types that result from the blending of primary and secondary types.

Porter, who worked with Carl Rogers (Porter, 1950; Rogers, 1951), was the first to use statistical methods to measure the effectiveness of Rogers' non-directive methods (Porter, 1943). Porter's first psychometric was an attempt to validate Fromm's four types. Porter relied on statistical analysis more than theory to further develop the assessment, which led to a disagreement with Rogers because Rogers viewed the assessment as too directive (Scudder, 2019a). Porter created several versions of the assess-ment with four scales, but was not able to achieve satisfactory internal reliability for the equivalent of Fromm's marketing orientation. It was only after Porter removed the marketing scale from the assessment that the seven types emerged from the data in a valid and reliable way. People with

approximately equal scores on the three SDI well-state scales had personalities similar to the positive aspects of Fromm's marketing orientation. It is
my understanding that Porter was never aware of Freud's seven libidinal
types, though he was obviously aware that using Fromm's types provided
a Freudian frame of reference.

My own research has connected the dots by using the SDI assessment to
validate Freud's libidinal types (Scudder, 2013). Freud's and Porter's types
are constructed in exactly the same way. There are three primary types,
three blends of two primary types, and one blend of all three primary
types. What is most remarkable about this, and is the essence of the
construct validity claim, is that these typologies were arrived at through
vastly different methods (theory vs. empiricism) and that Porter's typology
exactly aligned with Freud's—that Porter "re-discovered" Freud's libidinal
typology 40 years later without realizing it.

Leader's Personality Types

Knowing leaders' personality types can offer insight into how they will
lead. For example, while consulting with Microsoft, I had the opportunity
to observe the moment of transition between the end of Steve Ballmer's
tenure as CEO and the beginning of Satya Nadella's time in the role. Bill
Gates was also there and the three of them shared the stage. The only three
people to have held the CEO role of Microsoft in its 40-year history told
the story of the past, present, and future of Microsoft.

Consider the way each of these leaders' personalities influenced—or will
continue to influence—their engagement with the role. While I do not have
the SDI results of these three men, they are public enough figures to form a
picture of their personality types. Gates, who I infer has a judicious-
competing (Red-Green) personality type, seems most strongly driven by
concerns for both performance and process; his initial vision was based on
technical innovation. Ballmer adapted the innovations to the market. He was
most strongly driven by performance, and sometimes distracted by opportunities that were not a good fit for the organization, which sounds like an
assertive-directing (red) personality, with some characteristics of the
flexible-cohering (hub) type. Nadella seems to me have elements of
the analytic-autonomizing (green) and flexible-cohering personality types;
he seems most strongly driven by a combination of process and perspective,

exacting in his speech and acutely aware of context and how to adapt to it. Each leader has held the reins in a different part of the organization's development and faced a different context. Gates' time saw the foundation and explosive growth of the organization. Ballmer's the commoditization of the company's products and services, and Nadella has focused the organization on a shared purpose of empowering people to do more through technology.

Nadella calls himself a learner. That's a key element of his philosophy and it helps him focus on the innovations needed to continue fulfilling the purpose of empowering people with technology. But personality is more than any one assessment can measure; it is also shaped by chosen beliefs and life experiences. Witness Nadella's well-intentioned response to a woman's question at a conference. She wanted to know what Nadella thought women should do if they were underpaid and afraid to ask for a raise. Nadella replied that they should not ask for a raise, but instead have faith that the system will work—and that good karma will come back. As a Hindu, this was a well-intentioned response, one that was consistent with his philosophy. However, it was not correct in that context and he shortly thereafter apologized and corrected his response for the context saying that women should ask for raises and should expect equal pay for equal work when compared with men. And what practical value did he cite in his apology? His value of learning from his own mistake. Leaders who have a clear philosophy that is consistent with their personality can rely on their philosophy to navigate change, make difficult decisions, and adjust their approach when they do not get the results they expect. Knowing Nadella's personality, with a focus on objectivity and fairness, helps to anticipate future actions—or provide explanation and understanding of past actions.

Leadership Types in Conflict

Martin Luther King once said, "The ultimate measure of a man is not where he stands in moments of comfort and convenience, but where he stands at times of challenge and controversy." Leaders (both women and men) are often tested by conflict, and how they handle conflict can be defining moments. The way they are likely to handle conflict can also be predicted by understanding psychoanalytic personality types.

Karen Horney (1950/1991) suggested three basic approaches to conflict: moving toward a person with compliance, moving against a person with aggression, and moving away from a person with aloofness. Each of these approaches can be idealized by the person using the approach. Compliance can be self-idealized as goodness or saintliness. Aggressiveness can be self-idealized as strength or heroism. Aloofness can be self-idealized as wisdom or independence. Horney did not create a psychometric or assign these approaches to personality types. But relationship awareness theory (Porter, 1976) identifies predictable patterns of changes in motives (called conflict sequences) that influence the use of these strategies. Porter defined conflict as the experience of a threat to self-worth, and the response to conflict as having a productive intent to defend the self and return to a more productive state (not to idealize the conflict response as Horney suggested).

Based on the results of the assessment, three stages of conflict are identified for each person. There are 13 possible conflict sequence patterns, each with three stages. The stages are characterized by a range of focus during the stage, combined with a specific motive (or blend of motives) in that stage. The focus in the first stage is on the self, the problem at hand, and the other people involved. The second stage focus is predominantly on the self, and the individual's view of the problem (and therefore less focus on others), while the focus on the third stage is predominantly on the self. When combined with the accommodating, assertive, or analytical motives, we can anticipate leaders' likely actions. For example, if a leader experiences the accommodating motive in the first stage, followed by the assertive motive second, we can anticipate that initial attempts to resolve conflict will focus on restoring harmony and trust. If this fails, the second stage, which is assertive, will be deployed with less regard for others. This may come off as aggressive because the person with this pattern is likely to feel that their accommodation failed due to the other person not being open to peaceful dialogue. In this example, the third stage of conflict would be the analytical motive with a focus on the self. This would typically present only as a last resort following a prolonged fight in the second stage. This third stage would be akin to an extreme form of aloofness as described by Horney; it would likely be characterized by cutting off contact with the other party and a desensitization or detachment from the experience.

The well state (motivational value system) and conflict state (conflict sequence) are two independent, but related results that describe personality under two conditions. Combined, this yields 91 (7×13) possible types based on the interplay of three motives under two affective states. This dual-state typology is unique to relationship awareness theory (Porter, 1976), which Porter wrote to help explain what he had discovered through his psychometric research. The two states enable the presentation of one aspect of personality when leaders feel best about themselves, and another aspect of personality when leaders are experiencing conflict. Both aspects have strong validity and reliability, and as such influence leadership in good times and during the conflict.

Personality and Behavior

The SDI 2.0 (Porter & Scudder, 2018), which presents four views of a person, is based on Porter's original SDI, along with my own changes to methodology (Scudder, 2019b) that are derived from my research and experience over the last 25 years. Personality types are still presented based on motives under two conditions, while a set of behavioral strengths and their related overdone (non-productive) forms are measured in the context of work. Therefore, when leaders complete the SDI 2.0 psychometric, they are provided with insight into their personality, as well as how they tend to use (or overuse) their behavioral strengths in their roles as leaders.

The list of strengths originated with Fromm (1947). In fact, they were the original inspiration for Porter's first psychometrics. Fromm presented lists of traits with positive and negative aspects, but the positive aspects were sort of like the proverbial silver lining in the dark cloud of non-productive types. For Porter, and for myself, positive intent is essential to understanding strength.

Kurt Lewin's (1935) famous equation $B = f(P,E)$—behavior is a function of the person and the environment—is relevant to this discussion. Behaviors, or strengths, arise from the interplay of personality and situational context. We can imagine personality as something stable and enduring, like a large anchor at a harbor entrance that is attached to a buoy. The buoy moves in response to environmental conditions such as tides and currents, but the anchor remains in the same place over time and through changes in conditions. The buoy is like behavior, which is variable, but remains connected to the anchoring motives of personality.

The SDI 2.0 links behaviors in context to personality by providing example reasons that a person is most likely to choose to deploy a given behavioral strength. This is important for guiding conversations with leaders because it helps them see how to connect what they do to why it matters to them personally. As an example, we may find that two leaders share a specific strength, such as being persuasive. While the persuasive strength is most highly correlated with the assertive-directing personality type, it is not exclusive to that type. The assertive-directing leadership personality (such as Steve Ballmer) is likely to be persuasive in order to recruit people to their agenda and drive results—but a flexible-cohering leadership personality (such as Satya Nadella) is likely to be persuasive in order to be more inclusive and promote consensus.

Fromm provided lists of traits to help differentiate his four non-productive personality types. I have taken a different approach because my data showed that strengths correlate with personality but do not define personality. Therefore the SDI 2.0 provides explanatory connections between all possible combinations of 7 personality types and 28 behavioral strengths set in the context of work. For analysts engaging in developmental conversations with leaders, this offers a powerful and accurate entry point to discuss the deployment of leaders' strengths in their roles and relationships.

Strengths may also be overdone, and these are similar to the negative aspects of the traits that Fromm described for the four non-productive orientations. Overdone strengths, in contrast with Fromm, begin with positive intent. When a strength, such as being persuasive, is generally effective for a leader, they come to rely on it and sometimes use it to excess. The psychodynamic explanation for this is akin to expectancy. When a leader expects persuasiveness to produce the desired result, but the result does not manifest, the leader may continue to be persuasive—believing that a bit more application of the "right" strength will, in the end, produce the desired result. But people on the receiving end may find excess persuasiveness unpleasant, perhaps coming across as manipulative, abrasive, or demanding. When an overdone strength becomes a patterned behavior, it can lead to conflict in relationships, limit a leader's effectiveness, or become a derailment factor for an executive.

The key to controlling overdone strengths, or mitigating their negative impact, lies in positive intent. Within the SDI 2.0, the overdone strengths that are the most likely risk factors are presented alongside the underlying personality. This way, positive intent can be compared to potentially negative impacts, which opens a dialogue about the intentional selection of behavioral strengths that are more likely to be effective within a given context.

Personality and Purpose

As stated at the start of this article, leaders bring their personalities to their positions. And sometimes they leave an indelible mark on the organizations they lead. Ralph Waldo Emerson said "Every great institution is the lengthened shadow of a single man. His character determines the character of the organization." While I do not subscribe to the absoluteness or gender bias of such a statement, there are certainly enough examples of it to see why the idea persists. Henry Ford. Jack Welch. Steve Jobs. Jeff Bezos. Elon Musk.

What I see instead, is that leaders (women and men) project their personalities onto their organizations. They find a way to lead that reflects their personal drives and motives—or they interpret the organization's purpose in a way that connects with who they are as a person.

I worked recently with a social welfare organization whose leadership team had people with many different personality types. I asked each of these leaders several questions, including "What is the purpose of your organization?" and "What are the greatest threats facing your organization and how do you think the organization should respond to them?"

Answers to the purpose question meshed with the well-state of personality. For example, the altruistic-nurturing leaders described the purpose of helping people who were currently unable to help themselves. Contrast this with the purpose as viewed by the analytic-autonomizing leaders who saw the purpose as defending people's rights and promoting their independence. And the assertive-directing leaders saw the purpose as transforming entire communities. And they were all right. They actually shared a common mission, but they internalized it in different ways, which led them to establish different measures of success.

Answers to the threat and response questions meshed with the first stage of conflict. Leaders with assertiveness as their first response to conflict (regardless of their well-stated personality) wanted to take immediate action in response to threats; they wanted to mobilize people and resources in a direct attack on the problem. However, leaders who analyze as their first response (again regardless of their well-state-personality) wanted to stop the action in order to assess the situation; they wanted to have all the facts before taking any action so they would have the best chance of solving the correct problem in the best possible way—and they wanted to avoid any impulsive action that could worsen the situation. Leaders who tend to accommodate first in the face of conflict talked about their desire to protect their team, restore harmony, and their overriding concern to not do anything that would damage the reputation or relationships of the organization.

For leaders, awareness of personality type goes beyond self-management or leadership team dynamics. Leaders also need to communicate in a way that engages followers—followers who have diverse personalities. Understanding the way personality types are constructed also offers a clue to effective communication. Freud described that every person is a blend of three primary types, Porter identified the same structure with the SDI. Every personality is a blend of three primary motives. Simply stated, these primary motives are concerns for people, performance, and process. Leaders who overemphasize their own primary concerns are likely to alienate people with different personalities. Overcommunication about performance can leave people feeling overlooked or neglected—or wondering exactly how the desired performance can be produced. Similarly, overcommunication about processes can leave people feeling stuck in an impersonal, slow-moving bureaucratic environment. A more effective technique for leaders to communicate purpose, values, and goals is to give about equal time and emphasis to the people, performance, and process elements of any strategy or plan. These three pillars will align with the three primary motives that blend to create every personality.

Conclusion

The importance of understanding personality can hardly be overstated. Without this understanding, a leader may inadvertently create a lengthening shadow of themselves and end up recruiting and retaining similar types—and alienating diverse personalities. As organizations become increasingly complex and leadership teams become more common, diverse personalities can lead to deep, intractable conflict—or they can lead to healthy opposition, debate, and innovation. Psychometrics can offer leaders insight into themselves and others, along with a common language to talk about personalities in the organization—in good times and during conflict. In my own experience, leadership teams who embrace the personality types measured by the SDI 2.0, and use them in daily meetings, messages, and conversations build strong bonds and strong organizations that are resilient in the face of challenges. And this speaks also to the surprising resilience of Freud's libidinal types.

References

Atkins, S., Katcher, A., & Porter, E. H. (1967). LIFO: Life orientations and strength excess profile. Los Angeles, CA: Atkins-Katcher Associates.

Freud, S. (1932). Libidinal types. *Psychoanalytic Quarterly*, *1*(1), 3–6.

Fromm, E. (1947). *Man for himself: An inquiry into the psychology of ethics.* New York: Henry Holt and Company.

Fromm, E., & Maccoby, M. (1996). *Social character in a Mexican Village.* New Brunswick, NJ: Transaction Publishers.

Horney, K. (1950/1991). *Neurosis and human growth: The struggle toward self-realization.* New York: W. W. Norton & Company.

Lewin, K. (1935). *A dynamic theory of personality.* New York: McGraw-Hill.

Maccoby, M. (1976). *The Gamesman.* New York: Simon & Schuster.

Maccoby, M. (2000). Narcissistic leaders, the incredible pros, the inevitable cons. *Harvard Business Review*, January, 68–77.

Maccoby, M. (2003). *The productive narcissist.* Broadway Books.

Maccoby, M. (2007). *Narcissistic leaders.* MA: Harvard Business School Press.

Porter, E. H. (1943). The development and evaluation of a measure of counseling interview procedures: Part II the evaluation. *Educational and Psychological Measurement*, *3*, 214–238.

Porter, E. H. (1950). *Introduction to therapeutic counseling.* Chicago: The Riverside Press.

Porter, E. H. (1953). *The person relatedness test.* Chicago: Science Research Associates.

Porter, E. H. (1973). *Strength deployment inventory: First manual of administration and interpretation.* Pacific Palisades, CA: Personal Strengths Assessment Service.

Porter, E. H. (1976). On the development of relationship awareness theory: A personal note. *Group & Organization Management, 1*(3), 302–309.

Porter, E. H. (1985). *Strength deployment inventory: Manual of administration and interpretation.* Pacific Palisades, CA: Personal Strengths Publishing.

Porter, E. H. & Scudder, T. (2018). *Strength deployment inventory 2.0.* Carlsbad, CA: Personal Strengths Publishing.

Rogers, C. R. (1951). *Client centered therapy.* Boston: Houghton Mifflin.

Scudder, T. (2013). *Personality Types in relationship awareness theory: The validation of Freud's libidinal types and explication of Porter's motivational typology* (Doctor of Philosophy Dissertation). Santa Barbara: Fielding Graduate University.

Scudder, T. (2019a). *History and Development of the SDI 2.0.* Carlsbad, CA: Personal Strengths Publishing.

Scudder, T. (2019b). *SDI 2.0 Methodology and Meaning.* Carlsbad, CA: Personal Strengths Publishing.

8

AESTHETICS AND LEADERSHIP

Rafael Ramirez

Introduction

In September 2016, President Donald Trump stated

> *We will build a great wall along the southern border, and Mexico will pay for the wall... They don't know it yet, but they're going to pay for it. And they're great people and great leaders but they're going to pay for the wall. On Day One, we will begin working on intangible, physical, tall, power, **beautiful** southern border wall.*
>
> (Morin, 2019)

This chapter examines the use of the term "beautiful" in that statement, indeed the very notion that the wall was meant to be a thing of beauty (Cillizza, 2019).

The aesthetics of the presidency was also mobilised to assess the process which determined whether it would continue on to a second term or not. Thus, in its September 5, 2020 *The Economist* described the November 2020

DOI: 10.4324/9781003265122-8

US presidential election as "ugly" with their cover story titled "America's ugly election: How bad could it get?"

After the election had taken place, the British daily *The Guardian's* "Fashion" page published a piece titled "Bye-Don: a farewell to the Trump aesthetic" where Cartner-Morley (2020) underlined how much looks mattered to Trump, and she suggested that "when populism is centre stage, then style, show and swagger are at the heart of politics." So un-surprisingly, when Reilly wrote about how Donald Trump had exaggerated his credentials while introducing him, and he asked Trump why he had done this, the president responded that "it sounded better" (Reilly, 2019).

Leaders—populist or not—have forever attended to aesthetics, whether in terms of the pageant, uniforms, and official settings for government or in *"grands travaux"* such as French President Mitterand remodelling of the Louvre (more recently) or Emperors designing and building great pyr-amids in Egypt and Mexico (earlier). Well before social media-enabled widespread application, the Nazi party's leadership developed what Dege (2019) aptly called "aesthetics for the masses"; and unsurprisingly, the Soviet leadership also resorted to aesthetics to occupy the mental and physical spaces which their political ambitions sought to master (Dobrenko and Naiman, 2003). Eidinow and Ramirez (2016) argued that deploying aesthetics can be usefully seen as a technology with which one articulates arguments that are taken in as plausible. They contrasted this technology of aesthetic storytelling (for manufacturing plausibility) to that of the spreadsheet (used to calculate probabilities). Kay (2013) showed how very important plausibility is in determining outcomes in settings such as courts of law. So, the suggestion from Eidinow and Ramirez is that leaders who articulate aesthetics may often do so to manufacture plausible narratives, which have been shown to be effective even if the narrative ends up taken to be absurd (Cappellaro et al., 2020).

Studies Relating Aesthetics with Leadership

Assessing leadership as aesthetic is not unproblematic. English and Papa (2020) underlined how contrarian to established views on leadership it can be to propose considering leadership as aesthetic. In their case, this took place in the context of educational administration and leadership, where they tell us that an aesthetic take is considered too emotional and too unscientific. Yet treating leadership through the lens of aesthetics is not novel.

In a paper studying the aesthetics of "beau geste" acts by leaders (such as one where CEO's may donate their bonus to charity), Bouilloud and Deslandes (2015) summarised the situation in the field as follows:

> To start with, let us note that aesthetics emerged at a fairly recent period in the development of leadership studies
> (Gautier, 2011; Guillet de Monthoux, Gustafsson & Sjöstrand, 2007; Hansen & Bathurst, 2011; Hansen et al. 2007; Strati, 1992, 1996, 2000; Ten Bos & Spoelstra, 2011).

> Nonetheless, this specific work tended to remain apart from mainstream lines of research on leadership: development of leaders and/or leadership (Day, 2000; Day, Fleenor, Atwater, Sturm, & McKee, 2014; Day, Harrison, & Halpin, 2009), personalities and leadership (House, Shane, & Herold, 1996), importance of feedback (Atwater & Waldman, 1998), evaluation of their skills (Mumford, Campion, & Morgeson, 2007), charismatic or non-charismatic leadership theories, ethical and gender dimensions, influence of contexts, diversity, emotions, etc. (Dansereau, Seitz, Chiu, Shaughnessy, & Yammarino, 2013; Day et al., 2014; Dinh et al., 2014). Despite this intellectual effervescence, no scholar is truly interested in the aesthetic dimensions potentially present in the actions performed by leaders in the 29 approaches to leadership that were listed by specialists (Dionne et al., 2014) or the "web of belief" of leaders
> (O'Connell, 2014).

> As a matter of fact, current developments in research on aesthetics and leadership generally adopt two distinct approaches.

> ... the first one focuses on analysing the experiences of aesthetic sensations within organizations in connection with the perceptions of leaders by their followers
> (Hansen et al., 2007); ...

> ... it otherwise views sensations as mechanisms that produce representations of organizations or generate a specific relationship to space, etc.
> (Linstead & Höpfl, 2000; Ramirez, 1991; Strati, 1992, 2000)

.... the second one refers to art, for instance describing the figures of leaders as artists (Degot, 2007 Dobson, 1999; Hatch, Kostera, & Kozminski, 2004).

Contrary to such approaches, the purpose of this paper is to analyse the behaviour of leaders in an aesthetic perspective (Brady, 1986; Kersten 2008; Ladkin, 2008; Taylor & Elmes, 2011). *Accordingly, instead of relying on the common notions of aesthetic sensory experiences and the model of leaders as artists, our intention is to engage forcefully and specifically in an exploration of "beau geste" viewed as a specific behaviour* (p. 1097)

As is stated in their summary of the field, my own work has been on the aesthetics of organisations, not on the leader's own work, nor on the specific behaviour of a given leader.

Yet the Trump presidency can be thought of as an organisation, organising the upper echelons of the US federal government, the Republican states, the Senate, and other institutions. In this vein, the Trump presidency can therefore be considered in aesthetic terms: as attractive (as it was to over 74 million American citizens who voted to re-elect him in November 2020, only to be thwarted by 81 million who did not) or as an "abomination," in the words of the above-cited article by Cartner-Morley. Back in 2016, democratic candidate Hillary Clinton already referred to Trump supporters in aesthetic terms–according to her half of them were a "basket of deplorables" (BBC, 2016). This aesthetic assessment most likely did not earn her any votes.

The choice of field I have worked on with aesthetics—that which concerns the beauty (or ugliness) of given organisations and the clarity of strategy, does not mean that I take the alternative approaches Bouilloud and Deslandes offered to be without interest—on the contrary. Thus, in the second type of study proposed by them, I like books such as the one by Daas (2015) on how the second-longest term president of MIT, Charles M. Vest, focused so much of his attention and work on architecture, as "*the architecture of an organization is a fundamental organizational artifact that provides the most tangible, spatial, and material continuity for an organizations' mission, identity, and meaning*" (p. 5). In the same way, the book *The Art Firm* by Guilllet de Monthoux (2004) examined people like Wagner, who created firms to create art. Guillet de Monthoux examined the "Shwung" (as he called them) pendulum relations swinging back and forth from substance to form and from the real to the ideal, and also among the audiences, culture, artists, and technicians with which art firms work. He suggested that two extremes of how artworks work are totality and banality—this very much affects (in my view) how one might consider the aesthetics of leadership. Let us take each in turn. Social media has helped with totality-approximating 24/7 messaging in ways that Nazi propagandists could only dream of, appearing on every screen (PC, laptop, phone) several times per hour, with the average American being exposed to media 11.8 hours per day (Illing, 2019). Stanley (2015) suggested that news as propaganda now takes up a near-totality of one's attention, and that this endangers democracy. As to banality, one might suggest that the piece by Cartner-Morley cited above, considering Melania's role in the Trump presidency's aesthetics, offers a good example of how this works today:

> But soon after, she switched to a soldierly wardrobe that intensified the combative mood music around Trump. A vague air of abrasiveness turned sandpaper-rough in June 2018, when she wore a Zara jacket with a faux-graffiti slogan reading "I Really Don't Care, Do U" to visit a shelter for unaccompanied children. Black and olive green became her signature colours. Had you not known that the woman standing next to the president was his wife, you might have assumed—when she was wearing a pith helmet or a severe Alexander McQueen suit in army green with snap-button pockets—that she was a military leader, on stage to remind the audience of the muscle behind the government machine."

Ladkin (2008) explored "the territory of leading as an embodied activity through the lens of the aesthetic category of 'the beautiful', considering the linking of leading between followers and leaders in those terms" (p. 32). That perspective can be built into the design of leadership development activity, as Carroll and Smolović Jones (2017) did when they assessed leadership development as an aesthetic project—as

> a felt experience, where any leadership concepts are known and experienced through the lens of a vivid milieu of affective, visceral, sensory, embodied and relational processes, which aesthetically shape what participants come to recognise as leadership (p. 187).

Taylor (2007) assessed the extent to which leaders attend to the aesthetics as artists might, displaying this facet of the practice alongside those implied by other roles that are more widely used in the literature. I now want to return to how aesthetics might consider Trump's leadership during his presidency.

Not Just a Question of Taste

The Trump presidency manifested deep divisions across the United States. These divisions in turn manifested as a very polarised set of views on Trump's leadership. Many pundits have proposed the difference to be one of the values (big State vs. small State, centralised vs. devolved political power, internationalist vs. nationalist, etc.). An aesthetic reading would propose that such differences, real as they might be, are dependent on a deeper difference in aesthetics. Such differences are not a difference only of "taste," differentiating those who like cowboys who gallop into town and take over the ageing sheriff from those who dislike macho sexists who break up institutions and norms.

In his book *La Distinction*, Bourdieu (1979) suggested that a given group might like the opera while another group in society might like attending dog races and that such preferences distinguishing one group for another were manifested as tastes. What is interesting for my reading of aesthetics is not that there are differences in taste which distinguish one group from another—differences which Trump's leadership style reinforced and more violently contrasted; but that *all* groups, and *each* group, and that *each* individual in those groups or even outside them, finds something—some thing—beautiful.

Yes, the flashy aesthetics which Trump favoured may have made his tastes hard to hide, but it is not the taste itself nor its manifestation which matter for an aesthetic reading of leadership. Instead, an aesthetic reading of leadership will contend that what matters is how the underlying aesthetic shapes a particular taste, as this taste articulates values, shapes preference, informs priority, and forms action.

A good example of how this more fundamental level upon which taste depends on works in practice was offered by Schalg's (2002) study on how judges interpret American law. He suggested that if a given individual judge thinks of the law as a field of forces, while a different judge is one who considers the law to be a question of what category a particular case fits into, the distinct way each judge will interpret what to me, a priori, might appear to be the "same" case in a way where each aesthetic defines the outcome. Each judge will interpret what for a third party might look like the same case in a distinctive manner that differs, fundamentally from that of the other because, Schlag contends, they have an underlying aesthetic of the law which determines these contrasting outcomes, and the ethics and tastes which each aesthetic entails. Schlag's proposal is that it is the underlying aesthetic that shapes the ethics and values and priority-making entailed in judging. In the same manner, I contend in this chapter that this also applies to one's leadership style ("style" itself being an aesthetic construct, to be noted).

I think of this aesthetic foundation as a "framing" device, where one's aesthetics frames one's understanding of the world, one's experiencing that world, that to which one gives most importance, and the forms one will bring forth to in-form oneself. If one's actions affect those of others, as is the case of judges and leaders, this forming will be not only an in-form-ation to oneself but will also give forms that which affect (and can indeed, shape) the lives of others (Ramirez, 1987, 1991).

Aesthetics as Framing

Building on Schlag's propositions, if aesthetics is the foundation of how any individual accesses and manifests and produces and shares form, leaders are those who manifest form(s) in ways that resonate for their followers. If they have many followers, they are considered effective (or "great") leaders.

One might argue that it is this very re-framing which makes leaders significant. That is certainly what my colleague Richard Normann proposed in his book "Reframing Business: when the map changes the landscape" (2001); and which my colleague Angela Wilkinson and I suggested in our book "Strategic Reframing" (2016). We must note that such reframing is not always for the good, even if it can manifest a "great" leader. In a damning editorial in The Financial Times Martin Wolff (2020) suggested at the beginning of his piece that

> Historians will view Boris Johnson as one of the UK's more significant politicians. In terms of his impact on his country, for good or ill, he may rank not far behind Clement Attlee and Margaret Thatcher among post-war politicians.

He ended the piece by stating that

> Mr Johnson is not a serious man. He is unlikely ever to govern competently ....
> Mr Johnson has already broken big things that cannot be put back together again. This
> has made him a truly important politician, but a damaging one, alas.

The aesthetic which undergirds Johnson's premiership and upon which Trump's presidency was based is one where what had become established is something that needs to be brought down; where accepted norms must be disregarded or, if possible, broken; where politeness can be (or must be) ignored or trampled upon. The image it conjures for me is that of the cowboy (not necessarily from out of town) who takes over the frontier town by force or might. In 2016, many Americans (though, let us remember, not the majority of those who voted) welcomed the cowboy and cheered him to take on the role of sheriff. In the same way, Johnson won an eighty-seat majority in the House of Commons.

The aesthetic that drove these two individuals to power is one of simplicity, where "too complicated a world" assessments can be swept aside and replaced with simple slogans such as "Make America Great Again" and "Get Brexit Done." This aesthetic is also the aesthetic upon which conspiracy theories are based, according to an opinion piece posted by Harari (2020) in The New York Times.

Conclusion

Gareth Morgan (1986) suggested, based on reading Vico, that one's images of organisation are inevitably themselves premised on an underlying figure or form. This guiding figure plays the role of metaphor and organises our cognition and experience—in his case, of organisation. This too applies to organisational phenomena such as leadership and hierarchy and office designs and uniforms, which at a very fundamental level we take in as disgusting or beautiful (Ramirez, op. cit.).

Trump was perhaps rawer in manifesting the aesthetic of his presidency, via Twitter and power suits and orange-tinted skin and golf courses, than more subdued leaders might manifest that of their own leadership. His brash style embodied and outwardly manifested what he stood for and—as the basis of other more superficial (in the sense of closer to the surface, not in the sense of "shallower") forms of cognition, as Schlag identified them—this strident style provoked a more primary reaction from opponents than policy documents or budget announcements might. To call ugly walls beautiful and fail to issue any comments when his wife wore a coat that read "I do not care, do you?" when visiting border detention facilities where children of migrants were separated off from—and caged away from—their parents, is an aesthetic of "*there is a new sheriff in town who does not care for the old order.*"

The Democrats failed to provide an aesthetic that was as appealing to their own supporters and which manifested what they stood for, as did the anti-Brexit pro-European "remainers" in the UK. Both decried the aesthetic of simplicity and both failed to manifest an alternative aesthetic that was as attractive to their own supports as that of their opponents was to their own teams.

The big challenge for those opponents is to create a compelling aesthetic that takes in complexity (instead of rejecting it in over-simplistic one-liners or slogans fitting Twitter word limits, as Trump and Johnson have done). My proposal is that clarity rather than simplicity will be a potential avenue in this regard (Ramirez, 2008). Let us hope that in times affected by rising inequality among and within countries, climate change imperatives, ageing and still growing populations, increases in armed capabilities, and massive debt issued to avert the worse effects of COVID-19, new leaders will manage to muster an aesthetic of clarity that is as convincing and riveting as that of simplicity has been in the last few years. They might get inspired by reading the beautiful books authored by Edward Tufte (readers are directed to the website he curated—https://www.edwardtufte.com/tufte/), to avoid their aesthetics being about either totalities or banalities.

References

BBC. (2016). *Half of Trump's supporters Basket of Deplorables*. https://www.bbc.co.uk/news/av/election-us-2016–37329812.

Bouilloud, J-P. & Deslandes, G. (2015). The aesthetics of leadership: *Beau Geste* as Critical Behaviour. *Organization Studies. 205, 36*(8), 1095–1114. doi:10.1177/0170840615585341.

Bourdieu, P. (1979). *La Distinction: Critique sociale du jugement*. Les Editions de Minuit.

Cappellaro, G., Compagni, A, & Vaara, E. (2020). Maintaining strategic ambiguity for protection: Struggles over opacity, equivocality, and absurdity around the Sicilian Mafia. *Academy of Management Journal*. doi:10.5465/amj.2017.1086.

Carroll, B., & Smolović Jones, O. (2017): Mapping the aesthetics of leadership development through participant perspectives. *Management Learning, 49* (2), 187–203. doi:10.1177/1350507617738405.

Cartner-Morley, J. (2020). Bye-Don: A farewell to the Trump aesthetic. *The Guardian*. Retrieved from https://www.theguardian.com/fashion/2020/nov/11/bye-don-a-farewell-to-the-trump-aesthetic.

Cillizza, C. (2019). *Trump's big beautiful border wall: A history with Chris Cillizza*. [Video]. YouTube. https://www.youtube.com/watch?v=tN4XjlF597A.

Daas, M. (2015). *Leading with aesthetics; The transformational leadership of Charles M*. Vest at MIT. Lexington Books.

Dege, S. (2019) Nazi design, from megalomaniac to kitsch. *DW Magazine*. Retrieved from https://www.dw.com/en/nazi-design-from-megalomaniac-to-kitsch/a-50329053.

Dobrenko, E., & Naiman, E. (Eds.). (2003). *The landscape of stalinism: The art and ideology of soviet space*. University of Washington Press.

Eidinow, E. & Ramirez, R. (2016). The aesthetics of story-telling as a technology of the plausible. *Futures, 84* Part A, 43–49. doi:10.1016/j.futures.2016.09.005.

English, F.W. & Papa, R. (2020). Aesthetics of leadership. *Oxford research encyclopaedia, education*. Oxford University Press. doi:10.1093/acrefore/9780190264093.013.646.

Guilllet de Monthoux, P. (2004). *The art firm: Aesthetic management and metaphysical marketing*. Stanford University Press.

Harari, Y.N. (2020). When the world seems like one big conspiracy. *New York Times*. Retrieved from: https://www.nytimes.com/2020/11/20/opinion/sunday/global-cabal-conspiracy-theories.html.

Illing, S. (2019). How propaganda works in the digital age. *Vox*. Retrieved from: https://www.vox.com/policy-and-politics/2019/10/18/20898584/fox-news-trump-propaganda-jason-stanley.

Kay, J. (2013). A story can be more useful than maths. *Financial Times*. Retrieved from: https://www.ft.com/content/b22182d4–7f49-11e2–97f6–00144feabdco

Ladkin. D. (2008). Leading beautifully: How mastery, congruence and purpose create the aesthetic of embodied leadership practice. *The Leadership Quarterly*, *19* (1), 31–41.

Morgan, G. (1986). *Images of Organization*. Sage.

Morin, R. (2019, January 8). A quick history of Trump's evolving justifications for a border wall. *Politico*. Retrieved from https://www.politico.com/story/2019/01/08/trumps-evolving-reasons-border-wall-1088046.

Normann, R. (2001). *Reframing business: When the map changes the landscape*. John Wiley and Sons.

Ramirez, R. (1987). *Towards and aesthetic theory of organisation* (Doctoral dissertation). Social Systems Science department, The Wharton School, University of Pennsylvania (Michel Crozier and West C. Churchman, co-supervisors).

Ramirez, R. (1991). *The Beauty of Social Organisation (Studies of action and organization)*. Accedo.

Ramirez, R. (2008). Scenarios providing clarity to address turbulence. In R. Ramírez, J. Selsky, & K. van der Heijden (Eds.) *Business Planning in Turbulent Times: New Methods for Applying Scenarios*. Earthscan, London. doi:10.4324/9781849770644-22.

Ramirez, R. & Wilkinson, A. (2016). *Strategic reframing: The Oxford scenario planning approach*. Oxford University Press.

Reilly, R. (2019). *Commander in Cheat: How Golf Explains Trump*. Hachette Books.

Schlag, P. (2002). The aesthetics of American Law. *Harvard Law Review*, *115*(4), 1047. February.

Stanley, J. (2015). *How propaganda works*. Princeton University Press.

Taylor, S.S. (2007). The three faces of leadership: Manager, artist, priest. *Journal of Organizational Change Management*, *20*(1), 150–153. doi:10.1108/09534810710715342.

Wolff, M. (2020). Boris Johnson has secured a questionable legacy. *Financial Times*. Retrieved from https://www.ft.com/content/d7f7e0f7-fd57-46d3–87f2–53254ff348f1.

9

WHY PEOPLE LEAD AND OTHERS FOLLOW: THE BLACK PERSPECTIVE

Robert L. Cosby and Janice B. Edwards

Introduction and Overview

Historical Development of African American Leadership

To understand our current Black leaders, we must look at how history, in context, has influenced the present. Beginning 400 years ago, slavery, as practiced in the US, provided a difficult and painful legacy that has damaged our society. There is a growing historical record told by Black people or by Black leaders of the time. The names of Black leaders we recognize from the period around the Civil War have become icons: Sojourner Truth, Harriet Tubman, Frederick Douglass, and Alexander Augusta. People are less familiar with Dr. Augusta, who moved to Canada to earn his medical degree at the University of Toronto before returning to serve as the Union Army's highest-ranking Black officer during the Civil War. After the war, he practiced medicine and became the first Black medical professor and one of the original faculty members of the new Medical College at Howard University, where he stayed until 1877. He was

DOI: 10.4324/9781003265122-9

the first Black officer to be buried in the Arlington National Cemetery in 1890 (Fennison, 2009).

Leadership Development Over the Years

Black leadership and leadership styles have evolved in the twentieth and 21st centuries. This chapter discusses the formative educational process of leaders and suggests that in defining their leadership style one must recognize that what shapes leaders are influenced by experiences throughout the life course. Effective leaders can come from different cultural foundations. We find that examples of effective leadership are usually viewed through the lens of the dominant cultural group, which is White. White "ideal leadership" assumes the attainment of an end goal most easily achieved with no hidden obstacles along the way. Jim Collins in his book *Good to Great* (2009) suggests that great leaders have two qualities that make them great—personal humility, putting the interests of others ahead of the self, and the will to succeed (Sosik, 2015). These qualities are not just important, they can be defining principles for great leadership (Cosby, 2021). Maccoby adds a third quality, courage. As Samuel Johnson wrote, "Courage is reckoned the greatest of all virtues; because, unless a man has that virtue, he has no security for preserving any other" (Johnson, n.d., p. 109; Boswell, 1873, 1998). In short, without courage, the other qualities are useless. Sosik (2015) suggests that people with courage also have other virtues such as bravery, integrity, persistence, and vitality. This can be the case for leaders, regardless of color, to work to achieve leadership goals in helping businesses, groups, movements, and organizations succeed.

The Difference Between Black Leadership and White Leadership

There are differences between Black and White leadership. Black leaders have had to overcome many obstacles simply to be given the opportunity to lead, often without the same tools and opportunities as their White counterparts.

Because of the recognition of domination from slavery, many Black leaders must tell stories that are linked to slavery again and again and must begin again and again with the recognition that Blacks have to first overcome the oppression of slavery (Crenshaw, 2019). This may sound like a simple meaning of besting oppression where wisdom is conferred upon the leader, but the reality is that this is exceedingly difficult because of the recognition that the playing field is not level. Blacks still face economic, health care, housing, and education barriers to equality and equity.

Positive leadership is defined by an understanding of humility, a burning in the belly to make a difference, to chart change, and possess the courage to act. Consequently, the ability to compete at a high level for followers to follow and supporters to support is hard. We know that there are recognized resources that are enjoyed by some and not others. This means that some people became leaders because they have an impact on followers and others become leaders because they seize the opportunities presented.

One opportunity is intergenerational wealth; it is as old as slavery in the US with little signs of abatement any time soon. With wealth come opportunities for gathering and sharing information, for accumulating additional wealth that can be used to train and mold leaders for the future. Black leaders must consider that a different path to leadership is necessary to gain trust, supporters, and followers.

The Language of Black Leaders

In the past, the language of Black leaders included self-recognition, as among White leaders, but there must be more to support the Black leader. There must be an awareness of self within the Black community and the perception of the individual and leader within other communities (Du Bois, 1897). For example, members of the Southern Christian Leadership Conference (SCLC) from Martin Luther King, Jr., Ralph Abernathy, Ralph Bunch, Andrew Young, Jesse Douglass, to Jesse Jackson, and A. Philip Randolph provided direction and also competition among White liberals who sought to provide support to Black leaders (Fairclough, 2001). This support was offered in terms of money and resources. It can be argued that this help also sought to co-opt Black initiatives so as to control the Black masses through their nonviolent leadership (Fairclough, 2001). The daring to take action can be seen as overweening confidence, but we believe that the ability to put the interests of others first as one dares to take action is a balancing act that requires a depth of personal confidence. Political strategist Donna Brazile addresses it so: "Why you? Because there is no one better. Why not? Because tomorrow is not soon enough" (Brazile et al., 2018).

When Blacks look at their successes over 10 generations compared with Whites, Blacks are, in almost every category, still disproportionately getting the short end of the stick. Malcolm X (1964) spoke in one of his speeches of the ballot or the bullet, pointing out that some Black Christian leaders were given money to distance themselves from Malcolm X, who was labeled radical. This quid pro quo was offered in exchange for the White organizers' money. Blacks were offered these resources if they would stop criticizing certain economic injustices that to this day continue to permeate US society (Bass, 2021; Malcolm X, 1964). Such economic injustices have included earning potential, employment opportunities, education, and housing.

This makes selecting effective leaders more difficult. The old Civil Rights mantra of many southern Whites during the 1960s allowing the Negro to get close, just not too high, have continued to be areas that Black leaders point to in the struggle for not just equality going forward but equity or fairness (Bonilla-Silva et al., 2004). To bring attention to the Black populist view, Malcolm X spoke of supporting Black businesses, building Black infrastructure, providing effective schools, and ways of helping communities, including standing up to injustices and fighting back. The role of the Black church has continued to be a safe haven, supporter, spiritual teacher, network convener, and incubator for Black leaders (Gates, 2021).

Since the time of slavery, communication among the oppressed has always been an area that has provoked distrust, anger, and fear (Tobin & Tobin, 2000). The palpable fear of White enslavers was that teaching an enslaved Black person to read might lead to their insurrection, to their rejection of oppression, and of oppressor as with Denmark Vesey and Nat Turner (Egerton, 2004; Wolf, 2006). Therefore, such insurrection had to be stomped out, even with a knee to the neck of the Black man. As one Black leader suggested, insurrection was not part of the game, but instead, suggesting an eye for an eye was fair. "Even Stephen" was one way to stop the brazen actions of lynching and shooting of Black people by White supremacists well into the twentieth century (Malcolm X, 1964). This type of language caused some reaction in the 1960s, perhaps not as overtly as during slavery and post-slavery times, but resulting in swift White retribution. To some extent, with the Black Lives Matter (BLM) movement in the past decade, this remains an area of concern among White leaders today (Small & Garrett, 2020). This has led to different opinions on what constitutes effective Black leadership and who should lead. There is no plurality of support for BLM across many groups (Reynolds, 2015), but today there is a change in how leaders are found and molded.

Political Leaders

Voters have coalesced around some leaders who promote Black issues. They are both Black and White. For example, in the Georgia 2020 US Senate race, Stacy Abrams (political analyst and former Georgia gubernatorial candidate) and others have stated that success is not dependent on one group but upon a multicultural, multiethnic, and multigenerational coalition. The result in Georgia demonstrated that change was possible even in the deep South. The result saw the youngest White senator elected and the first African American elected senator in the history of Georgia (Cramer, 2021).

Black Political Leaders

Justice Thurgood Marshall learned well from his professors at Howard University College of Law. Black people referred to him with the utmost respect because he had education and exemplified what was needed to uphold the Black race. Marshall was a highly successful attorney who argued 29 cases in front of the US Supreme Court, winning 26 of them in the 1940s and 1950s. The apex of his work as an attorney was arguing four cases that all came under the one title Brown v. Board of Education in 1954. The politics of race was revealed at the highest federal court in challenging the doctrine of "Separate and Equal." The law was reversed and resulted in changes in educational systems and long-standing pillars of Jim Crow, killing segregation and promoting the integration of schools across the US. In 1967 in large part based on his Brown v. Board of Education success, President Lyndon Johnson nominated him for appointment to the US Supreme Court on August 30, 1967.

Justice Marshall built on his knowledge, skills, and experience with personal experiences of Jim Crow and helped in shaping the federal law based on the US Constitution and the Bill of Rights (Rowan, 1993). He became a steadying hand in helping the Courts interpret federal laws to live up to the intent expressed in the Bill of Rights from removing Jim Crow laws to shaping opportunity in laws for the underprivileged and disenfranchised persons. In addition to being known as a "Race Man" (Carby & Carby, 2009), a term used by W.E.B. Du Bois and many Black persons to respectfully address those who stood up as leaders, Marshall became known as Mr. Civil Rights up until his death in 1993 (Rowan, 1993; U.S. Courts, n.d.).

Raphael Warnock, raised in the Black Church tradition, excelled to become pastor at Ebenezer Baptist Church in Atlanta, GA. He preaches and espouses the liberation of oppressed people (Warnock, 2020) in the tradition of Martin Luther King, who pastored the same church. In his book *The Divided Mind of the Black Church* (2013), Warnock acknowledges that the Black church is not unilateral in its positions or its mission to serve. Rev. Warnock has pushed his position of rising from oppression to serve and now serves as the first Black man to be a US Senator from the State of Georgia. Senator Warnock has built his support on being a multiculturalist and a free thinker (Galeotti, 2002). This would imply that he is taking on similar roles as MLK in preaching nonviolence and representing all constituents in Georgia, not just Black residents (Mellow, 2020).

Senator Warnock has developed an active affirming and reaffirming role of leader. His message, consistent with his Senate campaign, is built on a platform that he will represent all Georgians, even those that did not vote for him. A vocal number of Georgians did not support Senator Warnock and have been able to change the messaging, getting the attention of Georgia State legislators and those with similar views in other states. These vocal members of racially motivated groups have successfully lobbied for future laws to suppress voter registration and ballot counting in Georgia that target Blacks. The leadership in Georgia can be compared to post-Civil War Reconstruction and the ensuing backlash of Jim Crow and related laws (Waldman, 2021). If Senator Warnock is to be successful and effective, his multicultural followers and supporters will have to organize and express their positions in future elections from local to state to congressional.

US Vice President Kamala Harris has ascended to the Vice Presidency of the United States, the second-highest federal position in the USA. Kamala Harris grew up in a very supportive and demanding household where both of her parents were highly educated university academics. As the eldest child, Vice President Harris was shaped by both parents. Her mother of Indian heritage and her father of Jamaican heritage instilled the importance of education as a conduit for promoting change and for succeeding in society. As the eldest of two children, both could be said to be overachievers.

Taught in the State of California schools and augmented with two academics' beliefs in hard work, Harris built upon this culture of success. In *The Truths We Hold*, Harris (2019) writes of what it was like to grow up in northern California influenced by the confidence of self-expression in Berkeley and Oakland, and in the University of California at Berkeley shadows where her parents taught. Harris attended Howard University as an undergraduate. At every step, she built upon her resilience and successes going from undergraduate to law school to District Attorney's Office in San Francisco to California Attorney General, to junior US Senator, and to her current role as Vice President of the United States (Harris, 2019; Weatherspoon-Robinson, 2013). It is clear that both parents valued her as she came to believe in herself, to learn about perseverance from both parents, Donald Jasper Harris and Shyamala Gopalan Harris. Both parents were leaders in their fields as college professors in Economics and in Biology, intellectuals who met while studying at the University of California (Berkeley). It was her parents as scholars, researchers, and political activists who shaped their children to become overachievers (Sanghvi, 2019).

In her book, Kamala Harris provides a glimpse of her approach to leadership. She writes "We cannot solve our most intractable problems unless we are honest about what they are; unless we are willing to have difficult conversations and accept what facts make plain. We need to speak the truth: that racism, sexism, homophobia, transphobia, and anti-Semitism are real in this country and we need to confront those forces" (Harris, 2019, p. xv). Both of her parents overcame cultural norms to push for change, and in the process, found each other. It is clear that her mother was a force that embodied her need to strive for more and to accept power as a construct to be seized and used. Most often, boys are taught these skills, but Kamala was taught that they can be wielded by a woman. Each of these leaders, Thurgood Marshall, Kamala Harris, and Raphael Warnock, had a drive to succeed tempered by the ability to follow but willing to expand upon the rules.

There have been changes in voting blocks and differences both in voting styles and voter make-up. Younger voters and more educated voters are registered to vote now in Georgia than in recent times. How we see Black leadership may be influenced by the complexity of different constituents who may or may not be followers.

Is there an important distinction between leaders who believe in integration (MLK) and those like Du Bois and Elijah Muhammad who believe that only by being separate can Blacks maintain their dignity? Dignity may be an old saw in this new age of twenty-first-century leadership. Younger Blacks do not gather around leaders in the march for dignity in the same way as with past leaders (Garza, 2020; Weddington, 2018). Rather, discussions around dignity are seen by many younger leaders, followers, and supporters as not part of the equation. The current question is, do we have equality and equity? Yes, or no?

The new leaders are expected to answer how their leadership will propel Blacks to collective empowerment and address the issues of getting women in boardrooms and maintaining positions of power. It doesn't matter whether a leader is a womanist (Howard University, 2018) or self-described empower-er of people; rather, the changes in lived life experiences must challenge oppression more vigorously than before. The challenges and oppression are not new. A White woman still makes 78 cents to every one dollar made by a White man (White House Briefing Room, n.d.) and the differences in earnings for Black men and Black women are even greater.

Black leaders, before they can discuss issues, must first overcome the subtext of the subjection of slavery and oppression as the backdrop to successful leadership, even in the twenty-first century. MLK recognized this and used it as a vehicle to create solidarity of message. The BLM movement and the "I Can't Breathe" reference to George Floyd's final words may be the new solidarity of message (Szetela, 2020). MLK spoke of the imagery and songs of enslaved ancestors and common language that Black people embraced and was made into the language of the Civil Rights movement, such as "We shall overcome." The language is telling as is the discussion of leadership in the context of the past injustices and the new leadership struggles that still must embrace change with similar backdrops of Black persons dying indiscriminatingly with strong prejudice. If Black leaders must always overcome, how do they focus on the same issues as White leaders without the accompanying baggage of oppression?

The BLM leadership has offered a new paradigm for the twenty-first century that is not weighed down by the testosterone-rich indignation and righteous anger of men (Garza, 2020). The three founders of the BLM are women who have led not with the traditional trappings of a central leader and lieutenants with various counsels that all report up in the hierarchy, such as the SCLC of MLK and Ralph Abernathy (Garza, 2020; Szetela, 2020). This new paradigm offers leaderless groups that have no central or national leaders. Rather, they have identified local community leaders who are empowered by their local affiliates (Buchanan et al., 2020). MLK had local leaders who briefed national leaders. SCLC board member Rev. Dr. Jesse Douglass, one of the Selma-to-Montgomery March organizers, stated that MLK developed personal covenants of all marchers with local pastors who kept signed copies of each participating person in their church. Each covenant document showed that they agreed to a vow of nonviolence and a next-of-kin affidavit. This covenant was powerful and was turned over to MLK at each major march or gathering. MLK received the original and the pastor kept the carbon copy covenant with signature page. This proved to be an effective leadership tool but also a way that leaders could identify next of kin for those who were incarcerated or killed (Douglas, 2015).

Black Religious Leaders

The new paradigm offers a reflection in the water of the past as current leaders pivot and stand to look at what may be yet to come. Religious thought is built on tradition and interpretation of sacred texts, and the ability to understand the sacred and the profane requires religious grounding. Each of the following leaders presents slightly different positions as Christian leaders. Among African Americans, religious leaders are primarily from the Christian tradition.

The Very Reverend Dr. Kelly Brown Douglas is a leader who has been seasoned by scriptural interpretation and recognition that the Word requires new discipleship. As the Dean of the Episcopal Divinity School at Union Theological Seminary, Douglas has traditional authority as both Dean and Professor. In addition, Rev. Dr. Douglas wears many hats. She has served as the Canon Theologian at the Washington National Cathedral and Theologian in Residence at Trinity Church Wall Street. What makes Dean

Douglas interesting as a leader is her ability to address secular and religious issues like shame, stigma, and bias against LBGTQ+ persons. Her book *Sexuality and the Black Church: A Womanist Perspective* (2018) was one of the first to speak of the way congregations and clergy treated LGBTQ+ persons. Her views remain fresh even today. She is one of the leading womanist scholars who is also a religious leader. She has written on racism, sexism, and radical discipleship. Her book, *Stand Your Ground: Black Bodies and the Justice of God* (2015) continues to bring attention to Black women. Her recent article, "Theological Methodology and the Jesus Movement" (2020) critiques Presiding Episcopal Bishop Michael Curry and his work with the Jesus movement. Having built on the foundation of her mentor, Rev. Dr. James Cone, she has embraced what it means to be oppressed in today's society and still push for change in educational and church settings so that graduates of Union Theological Seminary are prepared to go forth into the world as disciples and future leaders.

Bishop William Barber II serves as the President and Senior Lecturer at Repairers of the Breach and co-chair of the Poor People's Campaign: A National Call for Moral Revival.

Bishop Barber has shaped his ministry and his mission as a Civil Rights activist in the Baptist tradition (Wilson-Hartgrove, 2016). He has spoken forcefully on the oppressed who are forgotten and patterns himself in the mold of Martin Luther King as a moral conscience for the masses. In his books written with Barbara Zelter, they write about their Moral Monday Rallies ministry for the everyday person, preaching scripture and civil rights, suggesting a moral imperative as with the Trayvon Martin court case verdict and Uniting Women in the fight for social justice.

Episcopal Presiding Bishop Michael Curry is the leader of the Episcopal Church in the United States, composed of approximately 2 million members, part of the 85 million Anglican/Episcopalians worldwide. He leads at a time in which the Episcopal Church has wrestled with many issues, including LGBTQ+ issues in the Church and declining numbers of active Episcopal church parishes. As a leader of his flock, he has taken on issues of political and spiritual strife at a time when other Black spiritual leaders are seeking larger followings, preaching from a Black context. Presiding Bishop Curry has embraced a different model during this time of unrest during the COVID-19 pandemic, which has exposed health disparities, racial unrest, and economic inequities. He has taken the position that we must first build on Jesus Christ's teaching "to love one another" (Curry, 2013). As fundamental as this framework is, it has been seen as radical both for its simple message, and radical for the Episcopal Church to have a Black man as priest and leader of the largest body of Anglican/ Episcopalians who are predominantly White. Presiding Bishop Curry has offered ways of building linkages with the Church of England and the Worldwide Anglican Communion, addressing social justice issues and by seeking common ground in the Anglican tradition. He has attracted many new followers through traditional and nontraditional models of evangelism with prayer vigils and revivals, outreach, and homiletics (preaching).

Black Thought Leaders

Patrisse Cullors, Alicia Garza, and Opal Tometi are recognized as the founders of the BLM movement. As Black women, they have led in a nontraditional manner by saying they are simply people in the community who are saying that change must occur (Black Lives Matter, 2018). They say they are just like daughters, mothers, wives, and significant others in communities across the nation where too many Black people die. The data shows that more young Black boys and men are killed, but also young girls and women have been killed due to violence disproportionately affecting Black, Brown, and Indigenous people. Dismissed for many years as radical and racially charged, these three Black women have demanded change. More recently other groups nationally and internationally in places like England, Australia, Thailand, Korea, and Japan (GatwirI et al., 2021; Reddie, 2019; Mallard et al., 2020) are making the case for seeking common ground among not just people of color but groups in power, such as Whites, by stating that violence against Blacks has to stop and the police role in the violence has to change. Their position has presented oppressors and Blacks being killed as the oppressed. The three women have collectively built their platform around advocacy for Black lives and providing information to educate persons on why these lives matter. Groups opposing the BLM movement have tried to mischaracterize the BLM message by stating that ALL Lives Matter or Blue Lives Matter, etc., suggesting that the BLM movement is misguided in its scrutiny of other groups such as the police and fail to see that police officers are working under harsh circumstances and are misunderstood.

Patrisse Cullors, Alicia Garza, and Opal Tometi have continued to make the case that the common denominator in most of these shootings is police officers. Their approach is to embrace social justice for all. They have as the founders and among current local autonomous groups used an organizing strategy that empowers local persons with strong and organized local messaging to lead and protest. The local BLM groups have picked up the mantra as nonelected officials, to say maintaining the status quo is no longer acceptable because left alone the outcomes remain the same, Black lives are ended or incarcerated. The three women suggest that power can be seized if advocated for by strong, willing, and able people interested in changing the power dynamics of the oppressors and the oppressed. They have been very successful in building followers using social media.

Dr. Linda A. Hill is a thought leader recognized for her work identifying leadership qualities and identifying common threads that help marry leadership with innovation to achieve future innovation and success. This work has evolved into other works that study how businesses recognize and groom future leaders. Dr. Hill serves on the faculty at Harvard Business School. In her role as the Wallace Brett Dorham Professor of Business Administration, she is recognized internationally as an expert on leadership. Beginning in 2013 with her forward thinking on the role of leaders in business, she has worked to build synergy between leaders using technology innovation and strategies to lead highly successful companies. In Dr. Hill's book *Collective Genius* (Hill et al., 2014), she discusses how innovation and effective leaders sustain innovation in businesses. These leaders use innovative strategies and practices to lead and motivate teams and inspire workers to build businesses that consistently succeed. Her premise that she continues to build upon is that effective leaders stay on the cutting edge of innovation, lead by giving staff people the ability to get out in front and directing them from behind as might a shepherd (Hill et al., 2014, p. ix; Mandela & First, 1990). Dr. Hill attributes the example relayed by her to Ahmed Kathrada, a friend of Nelson Mandela and fellow prisoner on Robben Island (Hill et al., 2014). Her teams are both intergenerational and multidisciplinary. As a result, winning teams are not just about technology, or smart people, or research money, although all of those may indeed help. She posits that effective and innovative leaders lead to the future. They create environments that in turn create synergy and champion improved and sometimes radical ways of seeing a challenge and finding effective solutions that affect both business longevity and the ability to stay ahead of the market.

Dr. Desmond Upton Patton serves as the Associate Dean for Innovation and Academic Affairs at Columba University School of Social Work. He is the founding director of the SAFE lab and co-director of the Justice, Equity and Technology lab, also at Columbia School of Social Work. Dr. Patton has charted a bold course in making artificial intelligence (AI) that is culturally sensitive and less biased. As a leader, he has followers who are listening to what he is saying. Some AI programmers and IT experts are developing code that may have latent or overt biases related to race and sex built into the code. As a result, AI code is being developed with these biases that may perpetuate racism and perhaps other isms (Patton, 2020). The future of technology from driverless cars to banking systems to online education, health care, food production, and business practices are all directly or indirectly related to advances in AI. Therefore understanding how AI can be developed to take out these biases can go far in being more helpful AI without the isms. Leaders who can help chart the course of future AI will be extremely helpful for inclusion in innovation effective technology and services that are developed to help and care as opposed to limit, exclude, and neglect. The new landscape for our society can be better shaped by leaders who understand and lead followers and supporters who can promote diversity, at the same time work to address and limit biases, hate, and divisive behaviors.

Dr. Dorie Ladner, recognized as an activist, social movement, and Civil Rights leader, is often overlooked when looking at contributions of Black leaders, particularly women (Payne, 1995; SNCC Digital Gateway, n.d). However, Dr. Ladner is a former leader in the Student Non-violent Coordinating Committee (SNCC). She learned from the cauldron of activism in Mississippi early in the Civil Rights movement, and she and her family were involved with the local and statewide National Association of Colored Persons (NAACP; Crosby, 2014; Mosnier, 2011). Her work with SNCC leadership was developed in a different way than within other civil rights organizations. SNCC allowed youth and college students to hold positions of authority and built an education component into their training outreach and advocacy (Lowe, 2009; SNCC, n.d.). Dr. Ladner was mentored by Medgar Evers (Evers, 2005), a leading political and social activist in Mississippi, assassinated by the Mississippi KKK (Evers, 2005). Social justice issues were part of Dr. Ladner's upbringing. Ladner said that she was "born a rebel against oppression" (Mosnier, 2011; SNCC, n.d.). Women, although an integral part of the Civil Rights movement, were often asked or told to defer to their male counterparts (Scanlon, 2016).

Ladner has continued to advocate for social justice issues. She went on to obtain her MSW degree at Howard University School of Social Work and worked in the largest public hospital in the Washington, DC, area (DC General Hospital). Ladner advocated for better health care, stable housing, and employment opportunities for patients and local community residents.

Mellody Hobson is a business leader, investor, and the co-CEO of Ariel Investments. She leads as part of a new group of business leaders who are demonstrating the importance of diversity (Hobson, 2016). Ms. Hobson directs a multibillion-dollar portfolio and leads one small but growing segment of CEO leaders looking at diversity (Hobson, 2019; Manyika, 2020).

Ms. Hobson's record shows what can be achieved through diversity and how it can actually increase the bottom line. For example, her company, Ariel Investments, supports "After School Matters," the largest after-school program in the world, and it is the largest employer of teens in Chicago in the summer (Manyika, 2020). Her work speaks to the importance of diversity and the intersectionality of belonging for Black women but also surviving and thriving in a White male business world (McCluney & Rabelo, 2019). This message has merit in that many Black leaders, particularly Black women, are always trying to address levels of visibility because of how they are perceived. McCluney and Rebelo speak of this in terms of precarious visibility, invisibility, hyper-visibility, and partial visibility. Hobson speaks to the importance of always improving and listening to feedback. She says "Tell me how I could be better. Tell me what I could do to improve" (Manyika, 2020, p. 13). Hobson further offers that leaders, Black, in particular, must know the numbers related to business direction, growth, and comparisons to other leaders in that field and know what that means. She says the math does not lie (Manyika, 2020).

What makes her relevant to the discussion of Black leadership is her innovative approach to challenging leaders in diversity to bring in different people in education and finance. She describes what successful leaders do, describes their work ethic, their curiosity, and willingness to continue learning.

With the BLM movement, this identification was not employed and thus linkages to leaders are more diffuse. As a result, Black leaders have a less-defined leadership hierarchy (Szetela, 2020). Rather, local BLM leaders have "street cred" or credibility in the community to call what they see as wrong and identify what is necessary to make it right, for example, with the death of Breonna Taylor, the Black Emergency Medical Technician (EMT) in Louisville, Kentucky, who was killed while sleeping in her own bed by police officers who broke down the door of the wrong home (Better, 2020). A recent historic settlement by the City of Louisville acknowledged that there was a severe travesty of justice but made a financial settlement to make up for the wrongs of that day. Black local leaders made the case for going to court that resulted in the settlement.

Among many African Americans, there is considerable angst around the viewing of the death of George Floyd due to forced asphyxiation (Kim, 2020; Lim et al., 2021). The cry for his mother by Mr. Floyd became a rallying cry for all mothers of color who could see and feel the pain of a son being taken away. Leaders have had to embrace this in the context of recognition that Black lives and other minority lives are still being taken. This is another fatality in a long line of deaths. BLM has brought a different type of leadership that continues to focus on the goal of no Black deaths and thereby no deaths due to brutality (Szetela, 2020) because people recognize that Black lives are being taken at disproportionate rates that have little to do with "protect and serve" but much more to do with law and order. In bringing national attention to this issue of being killed for being Black, the BLM and other Black leaders have attempted to bring attention to what was believed by many to be minimal and a Black problem (Rojas, 2020; Szetela, 2020).

For Black leaders, it is not just a discussion about leadership, it is the recognition that they must embrace the call for leaders to shape discussions around these issues. As was shared for the first time on national television in 1965, police batons, tear gas, and whips were used against Black demonstrators during March 7, 1965, Selma to Montgomery March for voting rights (Combs, 2013; Maddox, 1965). There were three days of attempted marching, but that day became known as "Bloody Sunday." A host of Black leaders linked arms as they walked in solidarity during the Selma march. The Selma march helped to galvanize the fight against racial injustice, leading to the passage of the Voting Rights Act of 1965

(Davidson & Grofman, 2021; Garrow, 1978). What made those Black leaders successful? And were they any more successful than BLM affiliates?

The supremacists of old and many of the silent majority of today might judge how the justification is added only after BLM and others ask for it, the justification that was clearly designed to cloud the facts and suggests that there was just cause to kill a young sleeping Black woman. Many Black leaders of today would say that this was no different from the police killing a sleeping Fred Hampton, an Illinois Black Panther local leader who was killed by the FBI (Williams, 2013). There were similarities in that they both were killed while they were sleeping, and both Taylor and Hampton were Black. But one was a blatant attack and one was a wrongful death and cover-up. Both Black leaders and Whites always need to shape the message. Yet regardless of whether one says that sleeping Blacks were doing wrong, there is for Black leaders a level of righteous indignation that can be used very effectively when asking why these victims were shot while sleeping (Lutze, 2021; Szetela, 2020).

Why is this important in a discussion about Black leaders? Because BLM in the minds of the three women founders believed that people at the local level knew the issues and could provide leadership and a unified position in addressing a social justice issue now that before had been overlooked (Lutze, 2021). Over the decades there has been a tacit recognition for Blacks that it is more important to survive, but if you were White leaders, racist or not, the goal would be to promote stability and ensure law and order (Beckett, 1999; Currie, 2015). The unwritten message received by Black people in the community is it matters less who was aggrieved and more that "law and order" was achieved. Yet, when speaking of justification for similar police actions for White communities there was the need to "protect and serve." Whether subtle or nuanced, in short, White leaders could request that the White community circle in support of their call for calm. Yet when Black leaders are called, they are asked to find answers for the pain of their oppressed brothers and sisters. While MLK, the elected leader of the SCLC, did not condone rioting, he spoke eloquently of rioting in the following way. He said for Blacks:

> I think America must see that riots do not develop out of thin air. Certain conditions continue to exist in our society which must be condemned as vigorously as we condemn riots. But in the final analysis, a riot is the language of the unheard. And what is it that

America has failed to hear? It has failed to hear that the plight of the Negro poor has worsened over the last few years. It has failed to hear that the promises of freedom and justice have not been met. And it has failed to hear that large segments of white society are more concerned about tranquility and the status quo than about justice, equality, and humanity.

(King & Willis, 1967; Rothman, 2015)

Dr. King went on to say, "Our lives begin to end the day we become silent about things that matter" (King & Willis, 1967).

BLM leaders recognized that the language of the oppressed is spoken in ways that make the message more easily understood, unifying around common goals and themes of organizing, directing attention to wrongs, and empowering individuals to collectively stand up through peaceful rallies, as one tool in the toolbox of change to go along with pressure on the government. They also shared decentralized messages with social media, allowing Black leaders locally and in other communities to assess the reaction and to move swiftly to share more loudly, to educate the masses. Many Whites do not know that it is possible to be killed while walking or driving Black.

The Ability to Lead

Leaders can't be timid or so biased that they lose their objectivity at the expense of the cause. Some leaders prefer to be in the background until needed, pushing an agenda consistent with the cause. "Racism is what we see in the workplace, where only a certain number of Black people make it to the top and there are systems at work to prevent them from doing that," said an associate professor who teaches organizational behavior at Babson College (Opie & Roberts, 2017). Among Black leaders, these challenges of pushing a cause may be in fact made worse because of issues and obstacles of race and racism that are layered onto the leadership role (Gaines, 2012). To say race and racism are not significant challenges is neither realistic nor practical. Mayor Chokwe Antar Lumumba of Jackson, Mississippi, speaking about a forced water shortage in his 80% Black city, has stated that "I don't deny how racism has factored into the city's underfunded infrastructure ... I think that if we're honest with ourselves, we have to recognize the role that that plays. Often, we're a bit skittish of having those conversations. But we have to realize that issues of race are as American as apple pie" (Schimmel, 2021).

To suggest that Black leaders do not have to address these issues and that they are not relevant to the leadership discussion is to suggest that we live in a post-race and post-racism society (Bonilla-Silva, 2015). The election of Barack Obama, a Black man, as the president of the United States suggested for some that the argument could be made for post-race leadership (Bonilla-Silva, 2015; Gaines, 2012). His mixed success and inability to lead without the tools of Executive Orders gave lie to the notion that we live in a post-race era that accepts Black leadership. To add an exclamation point, our society is perceived as somehow better than the ugliness of racism and White supremacy, yet our country followed Barack Obama with a sharp swing the other way to a reactionary election of Donald Trump. It is fair to note that the USA would come to see that President Trump was an avowed racist and White supremacist masquerading as a populist. There was a failure of Black leaders not just to call out this fact, but for some Black American followers to be duped by billionaire candidate Trump who rhetorically asked Black voters in 2016, "What have you got to lose?" suggesting that Blacks had been taken for granted by prior presidential administrations and had not been treated well (Homolar & Scholz, 2019).

That question revealed that there was heterogeneity among Black voters, thereby weakening a united voting bloc, and suggested that Black leaders did not have an ability to speak with a united position on what was necessary for change. The prevailing view in 2016 was this was the hand that had been dealt by voters, so Blacks must meet with Donald Trump to ask for his support to simply get along. It is not unusual for Black leaders to work to get the best deal possible for Black communities and constituents. It is clear that Black leaders were not able to convince the masses of Blacks and Whites that to win the White House in a new bipartisan or multinational way required broader coalition building, often recognized as at the heart of community organization and statewide delivery of voting blocks. Black leaders needed more coalition building to show poor Whites that they had more in common with poor Blacks than not, and that to not join forces was voting against their own self-interest, that was not beneficial to either group. Instead, poor Whites supported the wealthiest top 10% of the country because it was a way to deliver a blow against Blacks.

Black leaders have not been unified in their solution to White supremacy. A result was the Unite the Right Rally in Charlottesville, Virginia, in August 2017 to show solidarity of White supremacy groups, which did not surprise most Black leaders. Instead, it showed what Black leaders had stated, "Now you see what has been really happening" (Jackson, 2019, 2020). Despite these revelations, it further split the vocal and the silent majority who refused to acknowledge many warring factions of the left, from progressives to moderates who have suggested that "America is better than that" and that groups have the right to assemble in support of the First Amendment rights. For Black leaders, this has made it clear that you cannot lead without the middle; because of the strife, there is no plurality. This has allowed conservative groups to paint moderates and centrists as left-wing liberals, White and Black, thereby allowing the fringe and far right to be accepted as legitimate, recognized parties, and groups.

For example, conspiracy theorists, the Proud Boys, Qanon, and the Three Percenters (an American and Canadian far-right, anti-government militia movement (Jackson, 2019, 2020)), and others have become more accepted in the eyes of the general electorate. This gave purchase to believers and supported more polarized viewpoints, helped along in large part by social media that kept people glued to their screens using biased algorithms that find similar content that supports a particular belief or conspiracy group. This practice has allowed Black leaders to be silenced. Groups once seen as extreme or fringe receive more visibility because such groups have been considered more mainstream by many media outlets, allowing for more one-to-one equivalent comparison of Blacks to far-right groups, suggesting that they are equal in their legitimacy as mainstream groups. Black leaders are among the many who have not yet stepped forward to condemn the media for such equivalency comparisons and related actions.

Black leaders have made their support for the US government known, yet many examples of peaceful protests and the right for peaceful assembly as with BLM has not fared well among White leaders and media. This changed with the May 25, 2020, death of George Floyd, a Black man restrained and asphyxiated by a Minneapolis police officer, captured on video and shared over social media worldwide. Prior to that event Black leaders were not uniformly supported. But after George Floyd's murder, millions of Blacks and Whites demonstrated with peaceful protests across the US during May and June 2020. These overwhelmingly peaceful protests were recorded in every single state and the District of Columbia. "When there was violence, very often police or counter protesters were reportedly directing it at the protesters" (Chenoweth & Pressman, 2020). Some of the assemblies became unruly with the tear gassing of peaceful protesters.

In DC on June 1, 2020, then-President Donald Trump ordered federal authorities to bring in the National Guard from several states to return law and order to Washington, in opposition to Black DC Mayor Muriel Bowser who indicated that there were for the most part peaceful demonstrations in and around the city (Hsu et al., 2021; Smith & Santiago, 2021). Hundreds of people were arrested and jailed within hours and over the next 3 days. It was later revealed that DC prosecutors dropped most of the charges. Black leaders have pointed out that a number of the people jailed were Black. This is contrasted with the insurrection of 10,000 people who stormed the US Capitol on January 6, 2021, pushing through the Capitol Rotunda and into Senate chambers, attempting to stop the ratification of the Electoral College votes. This resulted in five dead but no arrests on the day of the revolt (Hsu et al., 2021).

Despite the federal property being destroyed or stolen, Congressional House and Senate members running for their lives and hiding under desks and cowering on the floor, the result is alleged to be the disparate treatment of White violent protesters and Black peaceful protesters.

The point for many Blacks and Black leaders in these contrasting scenarios is recognition that Whites and Blacks are treated differently in practice, if not in law.

It is with this complex example that Black leaders are asked to follow a new path that strives for excellence not tied to ego, or financial stake, or advancement of self. It is this recognition that the goal and the cause are bigger than themselves, and the burden of carrying the leadership mantle is not about them but about the cause, the organization, the movement.

Aesthetics and Unique Characteristics of Leadership in the African American Community

Many leaders find their stride while leading. By this we mean they are thrust into positions of power and must lead. They may make mistakes that help educate or define them as they learn to lead. To lead, some of our great Black leaders such as Martin Luther King, Jr., present the message as salient, but maybe not attainable, but if you are with me, like I am with God, then there are possibilities. Throughout the 1950s, during the Civil Rights era beginning with the death of Emmett Till on August 28, 1955, we can see that MLK refined the "I have a dream" speech. This example shows how leaders refine their craft and use different ways of connecting with listeners, who may grow to become followers or supporters. Over time the speech was refined with examples, with imagery, for different audiences and vocal variety and with a casual yet emphatic urgency that led you to believe MLK was speaking to you alone. The culminating moment was when he was introduced on the anniversary of the death of Emmett Till on August 28, 1963, as the keynote speaker at the Lincoln Memorial for the Washington March for Jobs and Freedom.

The prepared speech was not well received in the sweltering heat of the day. It was a follower, allegedly Mahalia Jackson, one of the most influential vocalists of the twentieth century, who told him in the middle of his speech to give them the "I Have a Dream" speech. His leadership style would suggest that he listened and could adjust his presentation on the spot to change his address to the estimated crowd of 250,000 people. This leadership style surprised some people and made others feel that there is nowhere they would rather be than following this leader. Another example was Malcolm X in his "ballot or the bullet" speech, given on April 12, 1964, in Cleveland, Ohio, which also builds on those same skills and abilities. Many non-Blacks saw Malcolm X as being revolutionary, even if he did not suggest that people riot.

Upon closer examination, he purported to challenge those that harm Blacks so that Blacks need to support Black businesses, build upon Black economic security, and if necessary, consider the King Hammurabi code, of an eye for an eye, the principle that a person who has injured another person is to be penalized to a similar degree by the injured party. In softer interpretations, it means the victim receives the estimated value of the injury in compensation. The intent behind the principle was to restrict compensation to the value of the loss. The concept of reciprocal justice in the Old Testament was considered the law of the land in the period 1755 BC. However, for Malcolm X to use it in the 1960s as believed by many Whites, including the FBI's J. Edgar Hoover, was the basis for insurrection.

In context, the death of George Floyd in 2020 and the re-awakening of the BLM movement have called into question these many years later what can be done for aggrieved parties whose loved ones are killed as if no Black person's life mattered. For leaders of the 1960s, the time considered the halcyon days of the Civil Rights movement, Malcolm X was embracing logic based on similar principles from the Talmud, and this was profoundly radical for reporters, law enforcement, and others not because Malcolm X was a Muslim, but because of prior messages stating that the White man could not be trusted based in history. This message could be interpreted as saying that Black slaves could rebel against White masters. Going back to the days of John Brown and the insurrection at Harper's Ferry, this style of leadership was seen as presenting messages that were heretical and not common to the American way of life. Once again, a simple message was introduced by the leader, based on logic and a historical precedent that was a thousand years old. These types of leaders make it difficult not to be moved one way or another by the oratory skills and presentation.

Some of the characteristics in Black leadership have been found to show clear oratory and written language skills, the ability to integrate thoughts and put them into context with an oratory style. This has been done with leaders sharing dreams, telling stories, with examples of what is needed to improve, to be better, and to fit into categories of leaders, followers, admirers, or supporters. There has been a range of leadership oratory styles. These include calm, measured, deliberate presentations, as well as following the Black church pulpit preacher style, or the folksy storytelling style. These styles of presentation are familiar to followers and may be offered with humor, or the laser-focused demand for change that implores the follower to leave what they are doing and to follow now. Persuasive in approach, whether it is to open your purse or wallet, send your check, donate your rent money, pay what you want, tithe what you need, each leadership style promotes a common thread as being an influencer of opinion and promoter of action.

In identifying prominent leaders we emphasize the relational connection with the community and how this connection serves as tremendous healing and hope for the African American community. Looking at the numbers of elected officials, we see significant growth in African American leadership.

Understanding Leadership in the United States

There are many examples in history of leaders who have led, influenced, or guided an organization, group, or nation. We would add that the best leaders lead to overcome adversity and build upon a greater good even at the expense of negative discourse or criticism. Abraham Lincoln's efforts succeeded in preserving the Union of the United States. He is credited with abolishing slavery. Although his efforts led to the passage of the 13th Amendment outlawing slavery (National Archives, 2019), Lincoln's efforts preserved the Union of the United States. He worked diligently to secure the 13th Amendment to the US Constitution, abolishing slavery, followed soon by 14th and 15th Amendments, known collectively as the Civil War Amendments.

This is profound because together the three amendments did what had not been done before. However, Lincoln never got to realize the success or the impact due to his assassination at Ford's Theatre on April 14, 1865 by a confederate sympathizer. The emancipation proclamation did not truly end slavery in 1863, but did allow Blacks to serve in the US Army and Navy, seen as necessary to raise the number of troops to fight on the Union side of the Civil War. Lincoln also reinforced the federal government, modernized the US economy, and sought to heal the nation with reconciliation at the end of the war.

Frederick Douglass is another example of a historical leader who demonstrated his leadership while overcoming his status as an escaped slave and became a great abolitionist orator, elected official, and editor and owner of the North Star newspaper. He supported women's right to vote. Douglass was supported by Elizabeth Cady Stanton, abolitionist and women's rights advocate. However, when Congress secured enough votes to pass the 13th and 14th amendments they did not include women, seeing the passage of the amendments as very close. Douglass argued that Black men should go first over women suggesting women's turn would be next. Stanton felt betrayed by Douglass. The 19th Amendment giving women the right to vote passed in August of 1920 some 50 years after the Civil War Amendments. Douglass saw himself as an ideal pragmatist who helped with the passage of at least the three Civil War Amendments at the height of the Reconstruction period. Yet, the women's right to vote was greatly impeded by men, including Douglass. Douglass was the first African American to receive a vote for president of the United States at the Republican National Convention. One of his greatest speeches was on ending slavery in his Moorsfield (England) reception speech:

> What is to be thought of a nation boasting of its liberty, boasting of its humanity, boasting of its Christianity, boasting of its love of justice and purity, and yet having within its own borders three millions of persons denied by law the right of marriage?... I need not lift up the veil by giving you any experience of my own. Every one that can put two ideas together, must see the most fearful results from such a state of things.
>
> (Foner & Taylor, 2000)

Why Do People Follow Black Leaders?

Black leaders speak out eloquently and speak truth to the moral outrage of racial barriers, oppression, systemic inequality, and consistent violations of human dignity. They give personal voice to the silence of despair that Black Americans experience in response to the relentless inequalities encountered in all areas of Black American life, including the political, social, and economic. In these areas, charismatic and inspirational Black leaders provide a caring leadership, the much-needed "warmth of belonging" (personal communication, Cosby, 2021) that offers restoration of hope. Their voice and individual personalities give permission to stand up and never acquiesce or to succumb to the morally objectionable experience of relentless physical, psychological, and cultural exclusion in a deeply repressive society. In doing so, they soothe the emotions associated with the deep pain of the unremitting mental tax of racism. When one consistently suffers from the psychological thirst of despair and helplessness, the need to drink from the fountain of security and develop a positive vision is essential. For Blacks, the identification and idealization of Black leaders are emotionally soothing as they restore pride, hope, and promise for a better future. This restoration speaks to the psychoanalytic perspective of the self-other.

The "Being like me [self-other identity] concept speaks to the identification of the self with other individuals as like me" (Gallese, 2005, p. 103). The warmth and positive response to "Being like me" stimulates a biological neuronal response. This neuronal activation helps to "understand the meaning of the actions performed by others and of the emotions and sensations they experience" (p. 24). The activation of these neural networks is helpful in understanding social identification and the associated sensations, affect, and emotions relating to why African Americans follow Black leaders. Gallese (2009) explains that these mirror neurons and other mirroring mechanisms in the human brain activate when in connection with a meaningful other. These mechanisms "mediate our capacity to share the meaning of actions, intentions, feelings, and emotions with others" (p. 519). This is the foundation of "our identification with and connectedness to others," the empathic sense of "we-ness" which is the underpinning of our being. And, it is this 'we-ness' that underpins the why of why Blacks follow Black leaders. As suggested by Freud (1926), it is only by the empathy that we know the existence of psychic life other than our own (p. 104).

The psychological thirst for healing and relief from the cumulative effects of persistently experiencing racism and the retriggering of psychological trauma associated with slavery and oppression can be severe and disabling. This relentless battle has both physiological pain and psychological strain, and the energy associated with it is assuaged by the rise of Black leaders who offer from the "we-ness" intrapsychic relief and a vision of hope from the battle fatigue experienced in the African American community. There is an emotional relief with the "we-ness" connection that enables Blacks to freely express emotions, knowing there is safety in how these poignant emotions are held by the Black leaders with whom they identify. Winnicott's extant notion of the "holding environment" (Winnicott, 1960) refers to Chace's (2019) "[protective] container that fosters growth" (p. 50). This environment, although referring to infants, also applies throughout the lifespan and refers to the anxiety that Winnicott claims ascends from the fear of annihilation. Annihilation is a very real fear of all African Americans as they daily witness attacks on members of their community and feel the constant pressure of the "knee on the neck." This container/holding environment created from the "we-ness" of Black leadership encourages Blacks to access their innate power. Their leadership, guided by the magnetism of their personalities, induces followers to choose, adhere to, and emulate selected Black leaders (Cox, 1966; Huggins,1990).

Conclusion

This chapter opened with an idea of what the future may hold for Black leaders. Leaders develop to pursue a goal and in the process, followers and supporters find the leaders. The thirst for current leaders who retain authenticity, street credentials, education, and understanding is growing. Black leaders are not all cut from the same cloth, are not homogeneous nor accepted by other Blacks simply because they are in leadership roles. We hope we will advance to see a new paradigm that builds from the "content of a person's character" (King, 1963) as MLK would say, and advances to a new way of seeing people embrace change. In this new paradigm leaders will share their messages using technology across many platforms, streaming content, smart technology, and social media that build and shape opinions largely because of improvements in automation, AI, improved computers, and robotics. Together, depending on what else may come, these advances along with the leaders of tomorrow, Black and White, will require fewer traditional workers and more workers who can adapt to exponential changes in the industry, education, culture, and health care. The future for Black leaders must utilize ways of sharing common messages and building coalitions not only in the immediate future but for future generations.

References

Bass, S. J. (2021). *Blessed are the peacemakers: Martin Luther King Jr., eight White religious leaders, and the "Letter from Birmingham jail."* LSU Press.

Beckett, K. (1999). *Making crime pay: Law and order in contemporary American politics.* Oxford University Press.

Better, S.L.E. (2020). *Civil lawsuits lead to better, safer law enforcement.* Center for Justice & Democracy, New York Law School.

Black Lives Matter. (2018). *Black lives matter. Peace insight.* Retrieved from https://www.peaceinsight.org/en/organisations/black-lives-matter/?location=usa&theme.

Bogel-Burroughs, N., & Garcia, S. (September 28, 2020). What is Antifa, the movement Trump wants to declare a terror group? *New York Times.* https://www.nytimes.com/article/what-antifa-trump.html.

Bonilla-Silva, E., Lewis, A., & Embrick, D. G. (2004). "I Did Not Get that Job Because of a Black Man…": The story lines and testimonies of color-blind racism. *Sociological Forum*, 19(4), 555–581. doi:10.1007/s11206-004-0696-3.

Bonilla-Silva, E. (2015). The structure of racism in color-blind, "post-racial" America. *The American Behaviorist, 59*(11), 1358–1376.

Boswell, J. (1873, 1998, November 19). *The life of Samuel Johnson.* William P. Nimmo.

Brazile, D., Caraway, Y., Daughtry, L., Moore, M., & Chambers, V. (2018). *For colored girls who have considered politics.* St. Martin's Press.

Buchanan, L., Bui, Q., & Patel, J. K. (2020). Black Lives Matter may be the largest movement in US history. *The New York Times, 3.*

Carby, H. V., & Carby, H. V. (2009). *Race men.* Harvard University Press.

Chace, S. (2019). Uses of a holding environment as container for stepping up and stepping back in the context of truth and reconciliation. In H. E. Schockman, V. A. Hernandez Soto, & A. B. de Moras (Eds.), *Peace, reconciliation and social justice leadership in the 21st century* (pp. 49–66). Emerald Publishing Limited.

Chenoweth, E & Pressman, J. (2020, October 16). Washington This summer's Black Lives Matter protesters were overwhelmingly peaceful, our research finds. *Washington Post.* Retrieved from https://www.washingtonpost.com/politics/2020/10/16/this-summers-black-lives-matter-protesters-were-overwhelming-peaceful-our-research-finds/.

Collins, J. (2009). *Good to great: Why some companies make the leap and others don't.* HarperCollins.

Combs, B. H. (2013). *From Selma to Montgomery: The long march to freedom.* Routledge.

Cosby, R. (2021). *Leadership styles. Notes from "The Flash Performance of Swissness"* [Lecture].

Cox, A. (1966). The Supreme Court, 1965 term. *Harvard Law Review, 80*(1), 91–272.

Cramer, P. (2021). Jon Ossoff: Everything you need to know about the new Jewish Democratic senator. *The Times of Israel.* Retrieved from https://www.timesofisrael.com/jon-ossoff-everything-you-need-to-know-about-the-new-jewish-democratic-senator/.

Crenshaw, K. (2019). *On intersectionality: Selected writings.* New Press.

Crosby, E. (2014). " I just had a fire!": An interview with Dorie Ann Ladner. *The Southern Quarterly, 52*(1), 79–110.

Currie, E. (2015). Shouldn't Black lives matter all the time? *Contexts, 14*(3), 17–18.

Curry, M. B. (2013). *Crazy Christians: A call to follow Jesus*. Church Publishing.

Davidson, C., & Grofman, B. (Eds.). (2021). *Quiet revolution in the South: The impact of the Voting Rights Act, 1965–1990*. Princeton University Press.

Douglas, K. D. (2015). *Stand your ground: Black bodies and the justice of God*. Orbis Books.

Douglas, K. B. (2018). *Sexuality and the Black church: A womanist perspective*. Orbis Books.

Douglas, K. D. (2020). Theological methodology and the Jesus Movement. *Anglican Theological Review, 102*(1), 7–30.

Du Bois, W.E.B. (1897, August). Strivings of the negro people. *The Atlantic*. doi:10.5422/fordham/9780823254545.003.0004. https://www.theatlantic.com/magazine/archive/1897/08/strivings-of-the-negro-people/305446/.

Egerton, D. R. (2004). *He shall go out free: The lives of Denmark Vesey*. Rowman & Littlefield.

Evers, M. W. (2005). *The autobiography of Medgar Evers: A hero's life and legacy revealed through his writings, letters, and speeches*. Civitas Books.

Fairclough, A. (2001). *To redeem the soul of America: The Southern Christian Leadership Conference and Martin Luther King, Jr*. University of Georgia Press.

Fennison, J. (2009, March 29). *Alexander T. Augusta (1825–1890). Black past*. Retrieved from https://www.blackpast.org/african-american-history/augusta-alexander-t-1825–1890.

Foner, P., & Taylor, Y. (Eds.). (2000). *Frederick Douglass: Selected speeches and writings* (p. 390). Chicago Review Press.

Freud, S. (1926). Inhibitions, symptoms and anxiety. *Standard Edition of Complete Works, XX*, 77–174. Retrieved from https://www.pep-web.org/document.php?id=se.020.0075a.

Gaines, K. K. (2012). *Uplifting the race: Black leadership, politics, and culture in the twentieth century*. UNC Press Books.

Gallese, V. (2005). "Being like me": Self-other identity, mirror neurons and empathy. *Perspectives on Imitation: From Cognitive Neuroscience to Social Science, 1*, 101–118.

Gallese, V. (2009). Mirror neurons, embodied simulation, and the neural basis of social identification. *Psychoanalytic Dialogues, 19*(5), 519–536.

Galeotti, A. E. (2002). *Toleration as recognition*. Cambridge University Press.

Garrow, D. J. (1978). *Protest at Selma: Martin Luther King, Jr., and the Voting Rights Act of 1965*. Yale University Press.

Garza, A. (2020, October 20). Black Lives Matter's Alicia Garza: Leadership today doesn't look like Martin Luther King. *The Guardian*. Retrieved from https://www.theguardian.com/world/2020/oct/17/black-lives-matter-alicia-garza-leadership-today-doesnt-look-like-martin-luther-king.

Gates, H. L. Jr. (2021). *The Black church: This is our story, this is our song*. Penguin Press.

Gatwiri, K., Rotumah, D., & Rix, E. (2021). BlackLivesMatter in healthcare: Racism and implications for health inequity among Aboriginal and Torres Strait Islander peoples in Australia. *International Journal of Environmental Research and Public Health, 18*(9), 4399.

Harris, K. (2019). *The truths we hold: An American journey*. Penguin Press.

Hill, L. A., Brandeau, G., Truelove, E., & Lineback, K. (2014). *Collective genius: The art and practice of leading innovation*. Harvard Business Review Press.

Hobson, M. (2016). The importance of diversity in good governance. *Investment Magazine, 125*, 30–31.

Hobson, M. (2019). Mellody Hobson: Diversifying personnel as well as portfolios. *Journal of Investment Consulting, 19*(1), 6–14.

Holomar, A., & Scholz, R. (2019). The power of Trump-speak: Populist crisis narratives and ontological security. *Cambridge Review of International Affairs, 32*(3), 344–364.

Howard University. (2018). *The womanist movement*. The Howard University School of Law–Law Library. Retrieved from https://library.law.howard.edu/civilrightshistory/womanist.

Huggins, N. I. (1990). *Black odyssey: The African-American ordeal in slavery*. Vintage.

Hsu, S., Hermann, T., & Davies, E. (2021, March 15). Two arrested in assault on police officer. *Washington Post*. Retrieved from https://www.washingtonpost.com/local/legal-issues/two-arrested-in-assault-on-police-officer-brian-d-sicknick-who-died-after-jan-6-capitol-riot/2021/03/15/80261550-84ff-11eb-bfdf-4d36dab83a6d_story.html.

Jackson, S. (2019). "Nullification through armed civil disobedience": A case study of strategic framing in the patriot/militia movement. *Dynamics of Asymmetric Conflict, 12*(1), 90–109.

Jackson, S. (2020). *Oath Keepers: Patriotism and the edge of violence in a right-wing antigovernment group*. Columbia University Press.

Johnson, S. (n.d.) The Samuel Johnson sound bite page #109. Retrieved from http://www.samueljohnson.com/courage.html.

King, Jr., M. L. (1963). 'I Have a Dream,' Address delivered at the March on Washington for Jobs and Freedom. *King Papers. The Martin Luther King, Jr., Research and Education Institute, 28.*

King, Jr., M. L., & Willis, A. (1967). The other America. Retrieved from https://rolandsheppard.com/?page_id=879.

Lim, G. H. T., Sibanda, Z., Erhabor, J. & Bandyopadhyay, S. (2021). Students' perceptions on race in medical education and healthcare. *Perspectives on Medical Education, 10*(2), 130–134.

Lowe, M. (2009). "Sowing the Seeds of Discontent": Tougaloo College's Social Science Forums as a prefigurative movement free space, 1952–1964. *Journal of Black Studies, 39*(6), 865–887.

Lutze, T. (2021). *"Up against the system!": Investigating systemic problems; inventing systemic solutions.* Illinois Wesleyan University.

Maddox, E. A. (1965). The National Medical Association's contribution to the Selma-Montgomery march. *Journal of the National Medical Association, 57*(3), 243–244.

Malcolm X. (1964, April 3). *The ballot or the bullet. Speech given at Cory Methodist Church, Cleveland, OH.* Retrieved from https://www.rev.com/blog/transcripts/the-ballot-or-the-bullet-speech-transcript-malcolm-x.

Mallard, W., Lawson, H., Kerry, F., & Liffey, K. (2020, June 6). *Protests worldwide embrace Black Lives Matter movement.* Reuters Staff Worldwide.

Mandela, N., & First, R. (1990). *No easy walk to freedom.* Heinemann.

Manyika, J (2020, June 18) *A happy warrior: Mellody Hobson on mentorship, diversity, and feedback.* McKinsey Global Institute.

McCluney, C. L., & Rabelo, V. C. (2019). Conditions of visibility: An intersectional examination of Black women's belongingness and distinctiveness at work. *Journal of Vocational Behavior, 113,* 143–152.

Mellow, N. (2020). An identity crisis for the Democrats? *Polity, 52*(3), 324–338.

Mosnier, J. (2011, September 20). *Interview with Dorie and Joyce Ladner.* Retrieved from https://www.loc.gov/item/2015669153/Rights.History.

National Archives. (2019, April 17). *The Emancipation Proclamation.* Retrieved from https://www.archives.gov/exhibits/featured-documents/emancipation-proclamation#:~:text=Although%20the%20Emancipation%20Proclamation%20did,expanded%20the%20domain%20of%20freedom.

Opie, T., & Roberts, L. M. (2017). Do Black lives really matter in the work-place? Restorative justice as a means to reclaim humanity. *Equality, Diversity and Inclusion: An International Journal, 36*(8), 707–719.

Patton, D. U. (2020). Social work thinking for UX and AI design. *Interactions, 27*(2), 86–89.

Payne, C. M. (1995). *I've got the light of freedom: The organizing tradition and the Mississippi freedom struggle.* University of California, Berkeley Press.

Reddie, A. G. (2019). Do Black lives matter in post-brexit Britain? *Studies in Christian Ethics, 32*(3), 387–401.

Reynolds, B. (2015, August 24). I was a civil rights activist in the 1960s. But it's hard for me to get behind Black Lives Matter. *Washington Post.* Retrieved from https://www.washingtonpost.com/posteverything/wp/2015/08/24/i-was-a-civil-rights-activist-in-the-1960s-but-its-hard-for-me-to-get-behind-black-lives-matter/.

Rojas, F. (2020). Moving beyond the rhetoric: A comment on Szetela's critique of the Black Lives Matter movement. *Ethnic and Racial Studies, 43*(8), 1407–1413.

Rothman, L. (2015). What Martin Luther King, Jr., really thought about riots. *Time Magazine.* Retrieved from https://time.com/3838515/baltimore-riots-language-unheard-quote/.

Rowan, C. T. (1993). *Dream makers, dream breakers: The world of Justice Thurgood Marshall.* Little, Brown & Company.

Sanghvi, M. (2019). Gender and intersectionality in political marketing. In M. Sangvi, *Gender and political marketing in the United States and the 2016 presidential election* (pp. 61–100). Palgrave Macmillan.

Sosik, J. J. (2015). *Leading with character 2nd edition: Stories of valor and virtue and the principles they teach.* Information Age Publishing.

Scanlon, J. (2016). *Until there is justice: The life of Anna Arnold Hedgeman.* Oxford University Press.

Schimmel, R. (2021, March 12). *Jackson, Mississippi, residents enter 4th week of water crisis.* NPR Morning Edition Interview. Mississippi Public Broadcasting.

Small, M., Garrett, L. (2020, December 13). *Thousands of Trump supporters rally in DC, clashes ensue with counter-protesters.* WTOPnews. Retrieved from https://wtop.com/dc/2020/12/pro-trump-supporters-to-rally-again-in-dc/.

Smith, R. J., & Santiago, A. M. (2021) The storming of Washington, DC: The city of love against the city of White supremacy. *Journal of Community Practice*, 29(1), 1–10. doi: 10.1080/10705422.2021.1894866

Student Non-Violent Coordinating Committee (SNCC). (n.d.). *Digital gateway*. Retrieved from https://snccdigital.org/people/dorie-ladner/.

Szetela, A. (2020). Black Lives Matter at five: Limits and possibilities. *Ethnic and Racial Studies*, 43(8), 1358–1383.

The White House Briefing Room. (n.d.). *Did you know that women are still paid less than men?* Retrieved from https://obamawhitehouse.archives.gov/equal-pay/myth.

Tobin, J. L., & Tobin, J. (2000). *Hidden in plain view: The secret story of quilts and the Underground Railroad*. Anchor.

U.S. Courts. (n.d.). Justice Thurgood Marshall Profile - Brown v. Board of Education Re-enactment. Retrieved from https://www.uscourts.gov/educational-resources/educational-activities/justice-thurgood-marshall-profile-brown-v-board.

U.S. Senate (n.d.) Civil War Amendments, the Thirteenth, Fourteenth and Fifteenth Amendments. Retrieved from https://www.senate.gov/artandhistory/history/common/generic/CivilWarAmendments.htm.

Waldman, M. (2021, March 31). Georgia's voter suppression law. *The Brennan Center for Justice*. Retrieved from https://www.brennancenter.org/our-work/analysis-opinion/georgias-voter-suppression-law.

Warnock, R. G. (2013). The Gospel's meaning and the Black church's mission. In *The Divided Mind of the Black Church* (pp. 53–74). New York University Press.

Warnock, R. G. (2020). *The divided mind of the Black church: Theology, piety, and public witness*. NYU Press.

Weatherspoon-Robinson, S. (2013). African American female leaders: Resilience and success. Theses and Dissertations. 377. Retrieved from https://digitalcommons.pepperdine.edu/etd/377.

Weddington, G. (2018). The fall of 2014: Recovering the roots of the Black Lives Movement. *Race, Politics, Justice*. [blog]. Retrieved from https://www.ssc.wisc.edu/soc/racepoliticsjustice/2018/09/01/the-fall-of-2014-recovering-the-roots-of-the-black-lives-movement/.

Williams, J. (2013). *From the bullet to the ballot: The Illinois chapter of the Black Panther Party and racial coalition politics in Chicago*. UNC Press Books.

Wilson-Hartgrove, J. (2016). *The third reconstruction: How a moral movement is overcoming the politics of division and fear.* Beacon Press.

Winnicott, D. W. (1960). The theory of the parent-infant relationship. *International Journal of Psycho-Analysis, 41,* 585–595.

Wolf, E. S. (2006). *Race and liberty in the new Nation: Emancipation in Virginia from the Revolution to Nat Turner's Rebellion.* LSU Press.

10

HOW PAUL ELOVITZ USED WHAT HE LEARNED ABOUT CHILDHOOD, LEADERSHIP, LISTENING, AND PERSONALITY TO BECOME A PRESIDENTIAL PSYCHOBIOGRAPHER OF TRUMP AND BIDEN

Paul Elovitz

The Making of a Presidential Psychobiographer

While growing up I was fascinated by the American dream of unlimited opportunities for ordinary people, including immigrants and their children. "Honest Abe" Lincoln, Franklin Delano Roosevelt, Andrew Carnegie, Booker T. Washington, Lou Gehrig, and Thomas Alva Edison were among those who inspired me. However, I was a shy and lonely boy who fantasized about growing up to be a great baseball player, Superman-like hero, or president, but I did poorly on the playing field and dismissed my presidential daydream as a silly fantasy. When I was terrorized by events, nightmares, and waking dreams as a four and five-year-old living in a dangerous neighborhood, my idealistic mother would calm me down by

DOI: 10.4324/9781003265122-10

describing a perfect world "with a fence around it," which inclined me to search for utopian solutions. This contrasted with the hardheaded realism from my father who I idealized and aspired to be like, despite my mother raising me to become an intellectual (Elovitz, 1997).

In the classroom, I would become a good student, although I never saw myself as being very smart, partly because of undiagnosed learning disabilities. On the playground, I was anything but a leader. Leadership remained a fantasy for me in dealing with the rough and tumble of boys' sports as I felt lucky to not be beaten up as one of the few Jewish kids living in a tough neighborhood. In retrospect, an exception was that sometimes I would hang out with another kid and lead him in activities that didn't involve a group. A barrier to my being a leader on the playground was my self-image, reinforced by my mother sometimes declaring that I "had two left arms and feet, and if my head wasn't sewn on" I'd forget it someplace or another. I also followed her advice that it was wrong to fight, which meant I was easily bullied.

When my father told me to fight back and not take any abuse from bullies, he said: "you might lose, but they will find someone else to pick on." This advice was lost on me as I would emotionally sink into the ground as he modeled shadowboxing to show me how to do it. I felt lonely and apart from the kids, I grew up with. Standing alone for what I believe in, especially psychoanalysis and psychohistory, is perhaps part of the legacy of my childhood experience of wanting but not needing the approval of the group. Ultimately, I would eventually create, or help to create, my own groups to lead. During analysis in my 30s, one step I took to change my self-image as only being good for academics was to personally build an apartment, doing all of the carpentry, plumbing, and the safer aspects of the electrical work myself.

The exception to my not fighting back was when I refused to be bullied if I happened to be sick when I came to school or if a friend of mine was facing abuse. During one big fight, when all the kids gathered around on the vacant lot and the fight was a draw as we wrestled around, I finally said to myself, "this is stupid," so I just let the other kid get on top of me and win. Humiliated by not having been able to have an easy victory over a supposed pushover, he proceeded to pummel me after I said "I give up" until the gathered kids started yelling, "enough, we gotta get back to school." Clearly, I was not going to be a leader in the rough and tumble of the playground and the unorganized sports of my childhood. But I could study leaders and dream of myself as a type of comic book superhero.

While I made friends in and out of the classroom, I was too self-doubting and excited when I spoke in certain situations to see myself or be seen as an actual leader. Thus, in my Junior Achievement Club, during freezing winter weather, I outperformed everyone else when it came to selling the product we created door-to-door. But a more readily articulate girl from another one of our city's Junior Achievement Clubs was chosen to be the representative at the state championship. In graduate school, among the safety of academia, I established and led a history graduate student organization. At the New Jersey Institute for Training in Psychoanalysis, I would also help establish and then lead the candidates' organization. An academic model for my leadership was established. As a young professor, I led a committee that played a key role in getting a colleague, who had introduced me to psychoanalysis and psychohistory, to be the Director of the Ambler Campus of Temple University and go on to play a decisive role in the university's administration. A pattern of my helping a person one-on-one was established.

When I became enthusiastic about something, I would forget that my self-image was such that leadership for me was only an issue of fantasy as I studied historical and contemporary leaders. Consequently, after reading Rachel Carson's *Silent Spring* (1962) and becoming increasingly distressed by environmental degradation, I said something ought to be done about it. I found a receptive audience as America awakened to this problem. Shortly before the first Earth Day in 1970, along with a biology professor, I organized a very successful Environmental Studies Week at the Ambler Campus of Temple University.

Applied psychoanalysis, that is, psychohistory, became and remains my passion. The first three-day summer workshop of the Institute of Psychohistory was such an intellectual feast that I suggested we not wait until the following summer for the next workshop but instead have monthly or bi-monthly meetings for those who were in or could travel to the New York metropolitan area. I asked the female colleague who had enthusiastically seconded my motion to be the co-convener, feeling insecure about leading the group on my own. In these early, hesitant steps toward leadership, I needed a partner in this uncomfortable role. Also, with my focus on the causes of history, graduate school, environmentalism, psychoanalysis, and psychohistory, I overcame my hesitancy about being a leader, which violated my self-image. Looking back, I realize that my being devoted to causes is related to my family history since both my parents were young organizers who helped workers in the Great Depression (Elovitz, 2018).

The barriers to acknowledging my self-leadership actions and capabilities were based on more than self-image and the sense that leadership was just something to be dreamed about or studied. One of my greatest fears in life has been not being understood. As a young child, only my mother and sister could understand my speech. In speaking I sometimes would become very excited, which often resulted in garbled speech. Because of a lisp, I was briefly sent to speech therapy. Little did I know that my future wife would find my lisp to be very attractive.

So, with the dread of not being understood, why did I become a college professor who makes a living by communicating with others? Teaching was not my first choice. Rather, I wanted an adventuresome life like that of my father who came alone to this country as a 14-year-old political refugee after supporting his family, in part during the aftermath of World War I and the Russian Revolution. Dad traded goods in the name of the family business, took boots off dead soldiers to sell, and brought home food to his mother and younger siblings. Then, after the Polish nationalists won the struggle, he escaped after he was arrested for showing the Bolsheviks a strategic river crossing. Dad taught himself simply by observation as he swept floors to be a talented furrier, became a union organizer, and when blacklisted by employers for his union activities, started his own business at the height of the Great Depression. However, I had been raised by my immigrant mother to be a secular Yeshiva bucher (a Jewish religious student) and was not well-equipped to fulfill my unrealistic dreams.

The closest I got to the adventurous life of my father was allowing myself to be drafted into the US army and laboring in a long stream of mostly part-time jobs while in grad school and my early years as a professor. These jobs included driving trucks, cleaning offices as well as working in warehouses, workshops, and factories where I got to test my abilities among ordinary people as opposed to academics. Falling in love, marrying, and quickly having children made it essential that I find a way to make a living. Fortunately, there was some initial support from both families on the condition that we continue our undergraduate educations.

Aside from being the leader of my new family, I would have to become a leader in the classroom.

Having a captive audience was a starting point, but as an idealist, I was determined to share my curiosity and love of knowledge with my students, which was no easy matter with undergraduates who were taking a required history course. Teaching Western Civilization was quite a challenge. Frustrated that I was not listened to by the students with the same rapt attention that I usually paid to my professors, I went to the speech department for help. A kind professor there quickly realized that my problem was a lack of confidence and experience, rather than my lisp. My struggle to find my niche in life led me to leave Temple University for an underpaid fellowship at my graduate institution while struggling to get my dissertation completed. After a year, I returned to Temple but went to the smaller campus where I could make my mark and hone my pedagogical craft. It was there that my life was transformed by the discovery of psychoanalysis and psychohistory.

In learning to become a confident teacher, I had to dispense with the unrealistic notion I started with of stuffing students' heads full of knowledge. I was learning to listen carefully to students (including their resistances), bringing humor and contemporary life into the classroom, and always keeping in mind that learning is something they do and my job is to create the best possible educational environment for it to happen. Leadership in the classroom meant getting my followers, that is the students, to turn to me for what I had to offer. Students were called upon to play a much more active role in the learning process. This was especially the case after I "perished rather than published" at Temple University and needed to find a student-centered teaching institution.

Writer's block was a major obstacle to my success since college professors are expected to publish. My first memory of writing was an inability to do so as my mother told me to write a letter to her father, who my father disliked, and I did not even know. In school, I would often procrastinate writing and eventually do it right before the final deadline to avoid disgrace. I overcame this block by working on it in my own analysis, coming to the realization that I had much to share with others, co-authoring studies, and acknowledging my competitive feelings with colleagues. As a result, I now have hundreds of publications. In writing this chapter, it has come to me that this block was related to my identification with my very smart immigrant father's inability to write more than a few words in English since he had barely attended any school in America where he arrived as a teenager who quickly had to go to work.

I became a founding faculty member at a new interdisciplinary, student-centered, liberal arts school, Ramapo College, where publication was not then emphasized. In the early days of Ramapo, I could teach any subject that I wanted, provided it could be made interesting to the students. This meant teaching courses such as Children in History; Darwin, Marx, and Freud; Leadership; Presidential Elections; the Psychology of Creativity; and the Psychology of Greatness. The emphasis was on discussion and students were often divided into small groups to work on projects as I walked around answering questions, encouraging them with ideas, and keeping them on track. In studying resistance analysis in psychoanalytic training, I was able to confront educational resistances much better than in my early days. Student fears and hopes became clearer to me.

The resistances of anti-psychoanalytic colleagues, especially among my fellow historians, had to be confronted. Some disdained the very concept of psychoanalysis and psychohistory. Several saw me as an easy target due to my being closely associated with the first woman academic leader at my college who they feared attacking. While she was extraordinarily good at defending herself and playing academic politics, I was less adept. Consequently, I would have to fight to receive tenure and had to invite a dozen students to the all-college tenure committee meeting to speak to the quality of my pedagogy in my successful bid for academic security. Presently, I am the only "Founding Faculty Member" still actively teaching at Ramapo and presented the 50th anniversary lead-off lecture with the talk, "My Half Century Love Affair with Ramapo College." Regrettably, my type of interdisciplinarity has diminished. I now mostly teach freshman and sophomore required courses, which I enjoy, but I still miss the more challenging courses in my field of expertise.

In the classroom, listening involved many different modalities. Over time, I increasingly structured my courses to be student-centered. This involved implementing major interactive activities for the students, in-cluding debates and student-led discussions with students receiving extra points in the course for successfully involving each class member in a discussion of historical documents. In teaching, I continually listened for the emotions and motivations of the students. As with my patients, students were quick to pick up on my emotions: my boredom or passion readily influenced what happened in the classroom. Becoming keenly aware of my teaching countertransference feelings helped keep me engaged with my students. Utilizing my transference feelings in doing presidential psychobiography would subsequently prove to be quite helpful.

While doing psychohistory, my focus increasingly has been on the emotions of the country, especially revolving around the selection of presidents. As a political psychobiographer, I found most students did not have a great deal of political interest. In presidential election years, the ideal course to teach was the senior seminar, the Psychology of Election. It became clear to me that these young people were drawn to the emotions of the candidates far more than their actual policies, although after making an emotional connection, the interest in policies greatly increased. Regrettably, in a general assault on the interdisciplinarity of the type we established at Ramapo in our early years, the college basically turned the senior seminars to the disciplines, which made them far more traditional and effectively ended this very helpful interdisciplinary modality.

At a critical juncture in its history, Ramapo was threatened with being shuttered as the Chancellor of Higher Education was seeking to oust the founding president during a severe budgetary crisis. Ramapo was vulnerable because the students and their parents were turning, in very large numbers, away from the liberal arts and in favor of business, psychology, and nursing, which were deemed to be much more "practical." In listening to the wishes of our audience, I started teaching related courses. The longest-running and most successful of these was the senior seminar in Business Leadership and Career Development. Indeed, it was students from this course who played a key role in my being chosen for the first (and only to the best of my knowledge) Ramapo Alumni Association Faculty Award for Leadership, Teaching, and Dedication in 1990. What I liked most about this class was that students shared their career goals and realistic barriers to success. Then we could work through these obstacles as well as some of their intrapsychic conflicts thwarting the achievement of their goals.

It was no accident that in my analysis at the time, I was identifying and working through some of my own internalized conflicts about doing for myself as opposed to helping others, at which I have almost always been good (Elovitz, 2020a). In analysis, it was becoming increasingly clear to me that my own life choices were related to my childhood and personal conflicts. Also, having to speak as a college teacher meant confronting my lifelong fear of not being heard and continually searching for ways to reach the students more effectively. Related to my inclination to have a single-follower friend was my preference for mentoring people on a one-on-one basis.

There was a crisis of confidence among the historians at Ramapo in the mid-1980s reflected in the depressed head of the program telling me that since "there are no jobs for history majors that we should not encourage students to major in our discipline." This troubled me since I love history. Consequently, I founded the History Club to encourage students to see the value of the field as well as give faculty a venue to present their research and knowledge. The students were enthusiastic, the administration eventually provided funds, and during the 20 years of my being adviser, we mostly brought in scholars who gave well-received psychoanalytic and psychohistorical presentations without being labeled as such. As a result, we increased enrollments and helped revitalize the history program.

My Role as a Psychohistorical Leader

Psychoanalytic therapy in which the patient comes to treatment and often does not consciously know what they are really searching for, but are listened to quite carefully by the analyst, became an important part of my model for nurturing scholarship. Starting at our Saturday workshops of the Institute for Psychohistory, colleagues were invited to present their research, which would be read ahead of time by the participants. We then sat around a seminar table to help the scholar or therapist deepen their knowledge. As in analysis, the tone was nonjudgmental as we listened to the presenter. Before long, it became quite apparent that the presenter's transference to his/her historical subject was an important ingredient.

Without necessarily knowing much about a particular period or subject, clinicians especially could pick up on essential elements. Thus, when Professor Donald Hughes was roleplaying a dream of Xenophon (430–354 BCE) in which he and his fellow Greek mercenaries are depressed and demoralized in a foreign land after the murder of their leaders, Montague Ullman suggested to the historical biographer that the essence of the dream was "awaken" (Ullman & Zimmerman, 2019). These Greek soldiers of fortune did save themselves by awakening and fighting their way back home. Often historians and political scientists would need the insights of clinicians, while clinicians would also benefit from the input of historians and other academics. The essential principles governing these seminars are that the scholar/clinician chooses the subject, the participants read the presenter's research paper, and then they meet to assist the process of understanding in a non-judgmental manner.

As an organizer, I see myself as a midwife of knowledge. At our meetings, as in my classroom, my goal is to see to it that everyone has an opportunity to share their thoughts and develop their ideas. The Institute for Psychohistory originally sponsored the workshops and provided an elegant Broadway conference room for meetings, but after seven years lost interest in sponsoring them. So I, rather anxiously and with a younger colleague, started the Psychohistory Forum in 1982 and these meetings continue to this day. I variously call myself the director/convener, pay membership dues, and take no pay for my considerable efforts, which also led to the creation of the refereed journal Clio's Psyche in 1994 (cliospsyche.org).

Presidential Psychobiography

American presidents have enormous power and influence in the world resulting in their being the subject of innumerable studies. Regrettably, there are not nearly enough in-depth psychodynamic explorations starting with detailed studies of childhood, mechanisms of psychic defense, and personality. The political misuse of a 1964 survey of American psychiatrists to pathologize Republican presidential candidate Barry Goldwater led to the American Psychiatric Association (APA) prohibiting their members from this important endeavor (Renshon, 1996). The Watergate affair led to a focus on Richard M. Nixon's misdeeds and self-defeating tendencies, resulting in publications on presidential personality (by non-APA members) who generally were not well-trained in scholarly methodology.

In the wake of Watergate, upon reading Jimmy Carter's Why Not the Best? (1975), I suggested at the 1976 summer Institute for Psychohistory Workshop that someone should go to Plains, Georgia, to research an unusually open presidential candidate. Despite much hesitation, I became that "someone." In Plains, Georgia, before the election, I established a relationship with one of Jimmy Carter's sisters and his mother, who gave me access to unusually revealing diaries and school materials (Elovitz, 1977). Almost immediately, a crucial decision I made as a researcher was to avoid psychopathologizing terminology in my extensive work on candidates and presidents. While diagnostic labels can be so valuable in clinical settings, they are inclined to close the door on the further inquiry of politicians and are misused. Upon finding myself titling a chapter, "Jimmy Carter as a Self-Defeatist," I dropped my plan to write a book on the 37th president, but still wrote a number of articles and teach extensively about him (Elovitz, 2007, Elovitz & Shalaan, 1991). Subsequently, I researched and wrote about more than 15 candidates and presidents.

As a psychoanalyst, I am well-trained in using my countertransference in treatment. One night I dreamt that I was the President's psychoanalyst, which told me a lot about my countertransference, as well as my belief that Carter needed help. Another example of my being informed by my countertransference is when I typed "Bore" instead of "Gore" several times. In a 2016 dream, I was determined to keep Donald Trump, as one of my students, from cheating on my Holocaust examination. Consequently, for the first time, I publicly revealed my political preferences (Elovitz, 2016). During the Reagan presidency, I focused more on the relationship of the leader to the group than previously and during George H. W. Bush's presidency, I found his birth order's influence on his personality to be a crucial element in his success (Elovitz & Jeansonne, 1991).

The American Public's Changing Standards for Presidential Leadership

After making some observations on the preferences of the electorate, below I will probe the impact of childhood and personality on Trump and Biden. A striking aspect of the choice of presidents is how many men in my adulthood have achieved the White House despite the political pundits' belief that they would not be eligible for it. According to the wisdom of the day, JFK was barred as a Catholic; Carter as a Southerner with a thick Georgia accent; Reagan as an actor, divorcee, and 70-year-old; George H. W. Bush as a sitting vice president, which hadn't happened since 1837;

Clinton as a draft-avoiding Vietnam war protester in a time when the military experience was still considered essential in the post-WWII era; Obama as an African American; Trump as a president without any prior governing, military, or political experience; and Biden as a man who will be 82 years old at the end of one term.

The electorate sometimes makes radical switches, such as electing the multi-racial Obama and then Trump, who based his political following on questioning if his Hawaiian-born predecessor was a legitimate American or of Kenyan birth like his father. Today the presidency has become more of a popularity contest than it was earlier in our history. In 2008, the electorate overwhelmingly chose a junior senator whose road to the nomination began with his 2004 keynote speech to the Democratic national convention, which decried pundits dividing the country into "Red and Blue States" and declared "that there is not a liberal America and a conservative America—there is the United States of America" (Obama, 2004). In his losing 2020 bid for reelection, President Trump achieved a record number of over 74 million votes by focusing on the divisions in America.

The Impact of Childrearing on the Politics and Life of President Trump

Donald Trump is an unusual politician and president in that he mostly only listens to what he wants to hear. For over four years I have been probing the nature and origins of his personality, resulting in numerous scholarly articles and a chapter of the book *Psychoanalytic and Historical Perspectives on the Leadership of Donald Trump: Narcissism and Marketing in an Age of Anxiety and Distrust* (Elovitz, 2020, pp. 43–57). A lack of care at an early stage of his development, as well as the style of childrearing and discipline in the Trump household, had an enormous impact on his politics and life.

Donald Trump's birth on Flag Day (June 14, 1946) made him the second son and fourth of five children to a workaholic builder father and a Scottish immigrant mother who was the tenth child of a poor family. The turning point in his childhood came when his brother was born when Donald was 26 months old. His mother was simply overwhelmed, and then nine months later she hemorrhaged and almost died, undergoing a hysterectomy, peritonitis, and additional surgeries. She suffered from severe osteoarthritic, and her health would never be fully restored, leaving her with little time and energy for her needy son. Emotionally she was "often unstable and needy, prone to self-pity and flights of martyrdom." She was unable to perform the essential mirroring Donny needed (M. Trump, pp. 21–25). The boy turned inward, in psychoanalytic terms becoming his own self-object. He demanded attention all the time, often in an angry manner, bullying his baby brother, and as a five- or six-year-old throwing stones at a neighborhood toddler in a playpen. His second-grade music teacher said that he was a disruptive student requiring constant attention. His oldest sister said he was "a Brat" (O'Brien, 2005, p. 49).

In contrast, his siblings were well behaved and there seems to be no indication that his incessant need for attention was dealt with beyond being hit with a wooden spoon or by simply being ignored. Donny probably had undiagnosed attention deficit disorder with hyperactivity (ADHD)—an employee would clock his attention span as 26 seconds (Hurt, 1993, p. 18). His niece suspects something similar calling it "a learning disability ... making it difficult to process information" (M. Trump, 2020, p. 13). The coldness and rigidity of Donald Trump's upbringing left a profound impact on the future president. The focus was on "proper behavior" and traditional gender roles, strictly enforced for his three sons and two daughters. His father, Fred Trump, dressed formally in a jacket and tie for dinner and insisted that there be no arms on the table, no nicknaming each other, reports every night on schoolwork, no lipstick, and typically no snacks. He lectured on the power of positive thinking and ambition. Freddy was mocked for wanting a pet. Maryanne, nine years older than her future president brother, was expected to marry and have children, not go to law school, and become a federal judge, which she did only after the failure of her first marriage and as a mature woman.

After his father's death in 1999, Donald reported that he "wasn't the kind of dad who took us to the movies or played catch with us in Central Park. He was better than those fathers. Instead, he'd take me to his building sites in Brooklyn and Queens, he'd say 'let's make the rounds,' and we'd be on our way" (D. Trump, 2004, p. xv; Donald had to learn by watching, not being told by his father, who didn't believe in praising his sons but was quick to point out mistakes. Donald's education in real estate came partly through a process of osmosis). As a young child, Donny strongly identified with his builder father, as reflected in his playing with blocks.

"Borrowing" his younger brother's blocks, he would make a taller structure that he liked so much, to the point that he glued it together without regard for his brother's possessions or feelings.

Fred Trump cared about his sons and wanted them to grow up to be winners, killers, and kings (D'Antonio, 2015, p. 39). Being "a winner," "a killer," and "a king" were the mantras Donny was raised with, but he grew up in the shadow of his big brother Freddy, who had a very different personality. His father's namesake was an easygoing, handsome, likable, fun-loving boy, eight years older than the Donald. When Freddy went into the family business, as was expected of him, he withered under his father's lack of praise and intense criticism. He would eventually establish himself as an airplane pilot but ultimately die at age 42 of heart failure brought on by alcoholism that bordered on being "suicidal" (Blair, 2001, p. 320). According to the family biographer, "Donald appeared shaken by his older brother's death and would speak over the years of a deep sense of loss as well as a certain guilt for having benefited from seeing his brother's mistakes" (Blair, 2001, p. 320). Grievance, rather than loss and guilt, is the emotion most associated with Donald Trump.

Donny was quite different from his older brother, with his insatiable drive for attention marking his interpersonal relationships. He talked back to his teachers and parents, disrupting classes at the private schools he attended to the point where fellow students referred to detention by his initials: "DT." Being bad got him the attention he craved from other kids. They would laugh when he said something wrong, such as a mispronunciation of a name, but he would continue to repeat it since this brought more attention. Donald became a bully, disrupter, loudmouth, and show-off. At parties, he threw water balloons and cake. He writes that he wanted to be the toughest kid in the neighborhood (D. Trump, 1987) and was finally sent off to the New York Military Academy to learn some discipline.

Some valuable thoughts on the family dynamics come from Trump's niece, the psychologist Mary Lea Trump, who wrote *Too Much and A Never Enough: How My Family Created the World's Most Dangerous Man* (2020). In the most unflattering terms, she describes her grandfather as "a sociopath" and the great enabler of her Uncle Donald who "meets the criteria for antisocial personality disorder" (M. Trump, 2020, p. 13). Dr. Trump writes of her uncle seeing no values in empathy and quotes her aunt Maryanne calling her brother in 2015 "a clown" with "no principles" after he began his presidential run. She was "traumatized" by her uncle's election since "it felt as though 62,979,636 voters had chosen to turn the country into a macro version of my malignantly dysfunctional family" and felt that his reelection would spell "the end of American democracy" (M. Trump, 2020, pp. 15, 17).

As a 12-year-old, Fred Trump had suddenly suffered the loss of his own father to the Spanish Flu in 1918 and therefore had less of a model of successful parenting than most men. The question arises as to why Fred Trump, who drove his eldest son to alcoholism and an early death, was so supportive of Donald to the point that he bailed him out when Donald's real estate ventures failed (M. Trump, 2020, p. 26)? Perhaps he feared the same might happen with his next son. Clearly part of the answer is that Donald loved real estate and that he shared his father's Hobbesian views of human nature. Whereas his eldest son cringed in the face of criticism, his middle son talked back, which he associated with strength. Donald was a fighter, and with the counsel of his mentor Roy Cohn, he led the defense of the Trump organization when rightfully accused of discrimination in rentals. In typical Donald Trump fashion, they claimed the loss as a victory (Elovitz, 2020b). Fred was uncomfortable in the public eye and with public speaking, while Donald thrived as he worked early on to become a celebrity businessman.

Unlike his father, Donald was determined to stand out so long as he was not called a loser. In one of his most revealing books, Think Like a Billionaire (Trump, 2004), he proudly asserted his "large ego," "alpha personality," "narcissism," and "vision" bordering on "lunacy" (Trump, p. xvii). In describing himself as "a counter-puncher," he was unconcerned about contradicting himself. He invents conspiracies and denigrates his competitors and critics with derogatory nicknames. Trump uses denial, projection, and splitting to an unusual degree even for the most irresponsible of politicians. In all my psychobiographical studies, I have never found a politician who projects to the extent that he does. More than anything else, he thrives on the adoration of his followers at his rallies, as he says "I love you," making his supporters feel like the "good people" supporting their leader against the "fake news," "bad people," Democrats, and whoever irked him at that moment. When criticized and not denying what he is accused of, he inclines to double down on the point as a way of showing he is strong. His life and personality contrast greatly with President Joe Biden.

Joe Biden: An Ambitious Man Raised to Listen and Serve Others

Joseph Robinette Biden Jr. had a very different childhood than Trump and has a radically different personality and style of leadership. Joe and Jean Biden raised their four children to be fair, stand up for one another and the needs of others, and practice empathy. In *Promises to Keep: On Life and Politics* (2007), Joe wrote that "When any of us had a problem, we'd go to Mom and she'd set us straight" (Biden, p. 12). The family was devoutly Catholic and Joe attended only parochial schools before college. But when a nun made fun of his stutter, Joey walked out of the classroom and reported the disrespect to his mom. With a toddler in her arms, she went to the principal's office demanding that the teacher be brought to the office to explain what happened. While Joey now held his baby brother, the nun reluctantly admitting saying, "Bu-bu-bu-bu-Biden." Mrs. Biden went face-to-face with her and said, "If you ever speak to my son like that again, I'll come back and rip that bonnet right off your head. Do you understand me?" She followed this up with: "Joey, get back to class" (Biden, 2007, pp. 10–11).

Biden wrote, "The one thing... mother could not stand was meanness" (Biden, 2007, p. 11). Jean Biden also instructed and even rewarded her sons to stand up for the rights of children being bullied. While Joey's father was quieter than his wife, he shared the same values. He would bring up big issues like "morality, justice, and equality" and even the Holocaust, saying that "We each had a personal responsibility to... speak out when we saw that kind of wrong" (Biden, 2007, p. 13). He lived the words he spoke. When at a holiday party with his wife, his boss demeaned his workers by throwing silver dollars on the dance floor for employees to scramble for, right then Joe Biden Sr. walked out on a good managerial job with the approval of his wife. As chair of the Senate Foreign Relations Committee, Biden sought to put these values into practice when faced with the atrocities in the Balkans and elsewhere.

Biden reports never being hit by his parents, who not only set a model of moral behavior but also listened when their son was struggling with trying to determine what the right thing to do was. In grade school, the boy was quite proud of having been given a shiny blue badge when he made a safety patrol lieutenant. However, his sister Val's misbehavior on the bus left him torn between reporting her or not living up to his responsibilities. After carefully listening to his son's dilemma, his father pointed out that he had a choice to make. The next day Joey turned in his badge (Biden, 2007, p. 13). This decision was a significant step in his moral development. Joe Biden sits down and listens, as his namesake did with him, rather than jumping into action before having heard the different sides of an issue. In his politics, Biden is known for his loyalty. The Bidens were raised with the belief that their word was their bond. It is no accident that both of his autobiographical books contain the word "promise."

As a young boy, Joey Biden was a daredevil, a fine athlete, and leader of the neighborhood boys despite being mocked as "Stutterhead," "Dash" (as in the dot dash of Morse Code), and "Bye Bye Biden" in the schoolyard. He inclined to stutter when called upon in school. His mom told Joey that he stuttered because he was so bright that he just couldn't get the words out fast enough (Biden, 2007, p. 5). With careful planning and great determination, he found ways to work around his stutter by memorizing work and figuring out when he would be called upon in class so that he could be prepared. The habit of planning ahead would subsequently be an important asset when he assumed leadership roles. In retrospect, he writes, "I wouldn't wish away the darkest days of the stutter.... [It] ended up being a godsend for me... made me a better person" (Biden, 2007, p. 4). By his sophomore year of high school, he was able to address the student assembly without stuttering. He proceeded to excel at student politics being elected class president in his junior and senior years.

Throughout his entire life, Joe loved to connect with people, including those of different generations. Because of economic necessity, the Bidens moved into the crowded intergenerational home of his mother where he listened to his grandfather and uncles talk politics. They were Truman Democrats. Biden surrounds himself with people to the point that he even took a younger boy along with his date to his senior prom.

Love, Loss, and Politics in the Life of Joe Biden

Joe Biden has been tested by loss to an unusual degree, which was all the more painful as a result of his deep devotion to his loved ones. He accepted his mother's teaching that "there is no one in the world you are closer to than your brother and sister. You have to be able to count on each other"

(Biden, 2017, p. 153). Siblings Jimmy and Val, "my best friend," were there for their brother's political activities. The "Biden code" of loyalty to your family had been stressed by their father and Joe would speak of it. He also took young sons Beau and Hunter on his political campaigns.

While they were still in college, Joe and Neilia Hunter fell passionately in love. They overcame her family's concern regarding his Catholicism, married while he was in law school, and had three children at a young age so they would be able to enjoy the middle years of their life with each other without the burden of raising children. The Bidens worked well as a team, and Neilia played an important role in Joe's budding political career. However, tragedy struck even before Biden was old enough to be sworn into the Senate after an upset victory. Their baby daughter and Neilia were killed in a traffic accident that left their two sons in critical condition. Devastated, Biden reports that "suicide, wasn't just an option to him, but a rational option." It was only the needs of his three and four-year-old boys that kept him alive and he struggled to put aside his rage at his crushing losses while his life "collapsed into their needs" (Biden, 2007, p. 80).

The Bidens rallied around Joe with his sister Val even going as far as to move in with him and stay for three years starting when one of the boys was well enough to come home while Joe stayed with the other in the hospital. He lost all interest in the Senate, although he was talked into taking his seat on a six-month trial basis and took his oath in a cloakroom of his son's hospital. Filled with rage at his unbearable loss, he suffered from insomnia except when he agreed to travel to campaign for other candidates. Sometimes, his brother Jimmy traveled with him because the family feared what he would do if he came back to an empty hotel room. "Finally," he reported, "I began to make my peace with God or with myself …. I just got tired of wallowing in grief" (Biden, 2007, p. 96). His attachment to his three- and four-year-old sons was such that when they awakened in the morning, he was there for them and back from his Amtrack train commute in time to eat dinner while they had their dessert. He took the boys' phone calls regardless of who he was with and brought them to Washington to "Daddy's Work" whenever they requested.

The close attachment between father and sons continued into adulthood. Beau (Joseph Biden III) followed his father into politics and was elected attorney general of Delaware, with plans to run for governor and then the White House. Biden wrote that Beau was:

a rising star in Democratic politics.... [And] was generally regarded as the most popular politician in the state, more popular than even his father. Delawareans saw in him what I did. Beau Biden at age forty-five was Joe Biden 2.0. He had all the best of me, but with all the bugs and flaws engineered out.... I was pretty sure Beau would run for president one day, and with his brother's help, he would win.

(Biden, 2017, p. 14)

Joe Biden has had two very close, successful marriages. About two years after the tragic loss of Neilia and his daughter that brought him to the verge of suicide, his brother gave 32-year-old Biden the name of a 24-year-old college student who he was immediately smitten by. Although Jill Jacobs liked him and his sons, the problem was that she was enjoying living on her own after marrying young, separating, and being in the process of divorcing. Dating was all she was interested in at the time. Finally, she accepted the Senator's fifth marriage proposal after facing the choice of ending the relationship or going to the altar. Both boys played an active role in the ceremony. Later, a daughter was born. Both husband and wife wrote their own books (in contrast to Trump and so many politicians). Jill's *When the Light Enters: Building a Family, Discovering Myself* (2019) is a revealing and direct account of her life together with Joe and her own career. Earning degrees and becoming a college professor at a community college was made possible by her determination and a supportive husband. He is proud of his wife earning her credentials and continuing her career while he served as vice president and she plans to do the same during his presidency. Her book focuses on building family rituals, love, the devastating loss of Beau to brain cancer, mutual support, and especially her need to find her own voice. The sense of real love among the Bidens is apparent.

There was a role reversal within the family with Biden writing, "I am not sure when it happened, but somewhere along the way I had begun to look up to my own sons" (Biden, 2017, pp. 14, 54). His dream of becoming president, which started at age 12, was dashed in the 1988 and 2008 campaigns and transferred to his eldest son.

Beau Biden's death was a devastating blow to the family, especially Joe who wrote a book about his namesake's long struggle with brain cancer. *Promise Me, Dad: A Year of Hope, Hardship, and Purpose* (2017) is Joe's recount of his son's heroic struggle for life and desire that his father should run for president once again. Biden believes that his sons had saved his life 40 years earlier, and now he was losing the son he felt most attached to. Amidst all this, he was serving as vice president with Obama delegating enormous responsibility to him including responsibility for the Recovery Act of 2009, budget negotiations with Mitch McConnell, and working for democracy in Ukraine. His greatest focus was on his son and dealing with his own grief. In 2016, he was just too close to Beau's death to run for president, but he kept his son's advice in mind: "Don't let them see your pain, Dad." In 2017, when President Trump said that there were "very fine people on both sides" in the white supremacist Charlottesville rally at which a young anti-racist woman was killed, Joe Biden was so outraged that he began his third and ultimately successful campaign for the Oval Office.

Learning from Failures of Leadership

Below I will discuss some of the leadership failures that Joseph Biden, Donald Trump, and I experienced. There is no leading without followers. Certainly, I've had my share of failures. For example, when coming to Ramapo, I saw myself as organizing extensive faculty symposia. However, my colleagues were too busy creating a new college and struggling with the realities and anxieties involved. They were simply too preoccupied elsewhere and I was busy devoting 70–80 hours a week to create my ideal student-centered interdisciplinary institution. Consequently, based on a lack of sustained interest, I let these seminars drop, eventually using the History Club to contribute to the intellectual life of the college.

An experiment in group process analysis led to frustration and failure. As an enthusiastic scholar/clinician, I have presented at all 43 annual conferences of the International Psychohistorical Association and served in almost all the offices of the organization, which I still contribute to as a member of the leadership committee. Group process analysis was one of the most exciting innovations of this group. The theory, based in part on the research of Wilfred Bion, was that we would be a self-analytic group able to avoid the self-destructive pitfalls that groups often fall into. An hour at the end of each three-day conference was devoted to sitting in a large circle and speaking about feelings. Initially, I wholeheartedly embraced this idea, only to be horrified by some of the reality. There was little regard for confidentiality and colleagues with no analysis whatsoever mixed with seasoned psychoanalysts and theoreticians, telling the group process participants what they were allegedly feeling. So much depended on the quality of the leaders in the group—some sessions drove promising newcomers away.

One year, after training at the Leadership Education Institute of Rutgers University, I assumed the role of group process analyst and attempted to merge certain principles of leadership with listening to the attendees. In this endeavor, I was an abysmal failure as the group seemed to not hear me and carried on with the usual mixture of the variety of agendas colleagues brought to these meetings and insufficient concern for the newcomers. As usual, it was a combination of some concern for the feelings of those present and the continuation of previous differences that left newcomers feeling like outsiders. I identified strongly with these first-time attendees who had often come from across the country and world only to often feel ignored when they should have had an ideal opportunity to be heard. In hindsight, my identification with these newcomers had much to do with my feeling like an outsider who identified with my immigrant parents' experience of being outsiders. As a psychoanalytic historian, I was never made to feel completely at home with my history colleagues, which relates to my feelings of being apart from the other kids in growing up. In frustration, I went as far as to stop attending these group process meetings for several years. When my unrealistic dream of an almost perfect self-analytic group ended, I found that most of the sessions were helpful to group solidarity.

Another arena of my mixed success and failure is as the editor of Clio's Psyche: Understanding the 'Why' of Culture, Current Events, History, and Society (1994-present). Many of my Call for Papers (CFPs) for special issues are based on the concerns of colleagues or current events. A few CFPs have been abject failures. For example, neither our usual authors nor the 10 African American psychoanalysts I approached expressed any interest in writing about the Black Lives Matter movement. I have been unable to get authors for symposia or special issues on the psychoanalysis of screens (as opposed to movies), music, and some other issues. Most distressingly, fewer colleagues have been willing to do the time-consuming and laborious work of finding the sources for the family backgrounds, childhood identity formation, personalities, and leadership development of historical personages.

My ideal of *Clio's Psyche* being a mostly psychoanalytic-based historical journal has not been achieved. Of course, failure is an important part of the learning process, so I have dissected mine and sought to avoid future ones.

Moving away from the scholarly field and into the presidential one, Donald John Trump has failed numerous times as a businessman; however, his fear of being labeled a "loser" keeps him from acknowledging failure and therefore learning as much as he should from it. After being bailed out by his family and banks (who considered him too big to fail) from his disastrous Atlantic City casino failures, he increasingly relied on using his name as a brand. For example, he got paid one million dollars to put "Trump" on the facade of buildings in Korea and elsewhere. As a husband he failed two marriages, relying on prenuptial agreements to lessen his monetary losses, and then in choosing a third model as a wife followed his own advice of finding a "low-maintenance" one. As president, he has failed the nation by denying its severity and not establishing a consistent national policy in combating the Coronavirus. This and so many other of his failures are related to his lack of empathy for others and surrounding himself with "yes men" rather than confronting unpleasant facts. Following his longstanding practice of blaming others for his failures, Trump after being soundly defeated by seven million votes still insists that the election was "stolen." When contradicted by his cybersecurity chief, he fired the man for doing his job rather than acknowledging reality. Trump's refusal to acknowledge reality is part of a lifelong pattern.

Joe Biden has had his share of failures during his long political career. As a cocky young senator running for the presidency in 1987, he erroneously and foolishly claimed that he had graduated in the top half of his law class (76 out of 85) and went as far as to tell an annoying newsman that he had a higher IQ than the reporter. In remembering these instances, he calls this behavior "stupid" (Biden, 2007). Biden is also known for talking too much at times and making gaffes, some of which are simply saying what people in his circle are thinking Biden has an observing ego and therefore learns from his mistakes.

Conclusion

My journey as a leader of applied psychoanalysis in the safety of the US has led me to adventures so different from those of my idealized father, who grew up amidst World War I and the Russian Revolution. He escaped to America to avoid being shot for showing the losing army a river crossing; I struggled to know myself and fought intellectual battles in the name of expanding our knowledge. He led a small family business while I have had the opportunity to teach young people for over half a century and help to develop a psychoanalytically based field of psychohistory with the co-operation of fellow historians and psychoanalysts.

Exploring the family backgrounds, childhoods, defense mechanisms, personalities, leadership, and successes as well as failures of numerous American presidents and candidates for the Oval Office has been and continues to be a fascinating adventure. The year 2020 has been an especially compelling one for presidential research as Biden and Trump's conflict continues even after the election. The childhoods of these two men helped shape them, for better or worse, into the leaders they are, as my childhood shaped me into the particular type of leader I am today. In relating my personal history to the leaders of our country, I hope to demonstrate the importance of listening to our leaders, who by being attuned to and listening to their followers are in the end the most effective.

References

Biden, J. (2007). *Promises to keep: On life and politics*. Random House.

Biden, J. (2017). *Promise me, dad: A year of hope, hardship, and purpose*. Flatiron Books.

Biden, J. (2019). *When the Light Enters: Building a Family, Discovering Myself*. Flatiron Books.

Blair, G. (2001). *The Trumps: Three generations of builders and a presidential candidate*. Simon & Schuster.

Carter, J. (1975). *Why Not the Best?* Broadman Press.

D'Antonio, M. (2015). *Never Enough: Donald Trump and the pursuit of success*. Thomas Dunne Books, p. 39.

Elovitz, P. (1977). Three days in Plains. In L. deMause & H. Ebel (Eds.), *Jimmy Carter and American Fantasy* (pp. 33–57). Two Continents, (Original work published in *Journal of Psychohistory*).

Elovitz, P. (March 1997). My motivation: Patterns and secrets of an immigrant family. *Clio's Psyche*, 3(4), 104–108. http://cliospsyche.org/wp-content/uploads/2017/03/Clios-Psyche-3-4-Mar-1997.pdf

Elovitz, P. (2007). Presidential responses to national trauma: Case studies of G. W. Bush, Carter, and Nixon. *Journal of Psychohistory, 36*(1), 36–58.

Elovitz, P. (2016). A presidential psychobiographer's countertransference to Trump. *Clio's Psyche, 23*(1), 1–8. http://cliospsyche.org/wp-content/uploads/2018/03/201688-14-June-Issue-7-17-16.pdf

Elovitz, P. (Spring 2018). The jailing and disillusionment of Red Rose. *Clio's Psyche, 24*(3), 346–355. https://cliospsyche.org/wp-content/uploads/2019/02/2018_93-7-Spring-Issue-4-8-18-1.pdf

Elovitz, P. (2020). Probing Trump's disruptive, narcissistic personality. In M. Maccoby & K. Fuchsman (Eds.), *Psychoanalytic and Historical Perspectives on Donald Trump's Leadership: Narcissism and Marketing in an Age of Anxiety and Distrust* (pp. 43–57). Routledge.

Elovitz, P. (2020a). Exploring my impulses for service. *Clio's Psyche, 26*(3), 265–273. https://cliospsyche.org/wp-content/uploads/2021/05/CleanCopySpring-2020-11.pdf

Elovitz, P. (2020b). Trump profiteering, racism, and Biden's gaffes. *Psychohistory News.* https://sway.office.com/QG4kuITGi3Njg52T?ref=Link

Elovitz, P., & Jeansonne, G. (1991). George Bush: From wimp to president. In J. Zuckerberg (Ed.), *Politics and Psychology: Contemporary Psychodynamic Approaches* (pp. 99–116). Plenum Press.

Elovitz, P., & Shalaan, M. (1991). Presidents Carter and Sadat: The repudiation of the peacemakers. In J. Zuckerberg (Ed.), *Politics and Psychology: Contemporary Psychodynamic Approaches* (pp. 143–173). Plenum Press.

Hurt, H., III (1993). *Lost tycoon: The many lives of Donald J. Trump.* W. W. Norton.

O'Brien, T. L. (2005). *TrumpNation: The art of being the Donald.* Open Road Media.

Obama, B. (2004). *Barack Obama's keynote address at the 2004 democratic national convention.* [Speech transcript]. PBS NewsHour. https://www.pbs.org/newshour/show/barack-obamas-keynote-address-at-the-2004-democratic-national-convention

Renshon, S. A. (1996). *The psychological assessment of presidential candidates.* New York University Press.

Trump, D. (1987). *The art of the deal.* Random House.

Trump, D. (2004). *Trump: Think like a billionaire: Everything you need to know about success, real estate, and life*. Ballantine Books.

Trump, M. (2020). *Too much and never enough: How my family created the world's most dangerous man*. Simon & Schuster.

Ullman, M., & Zimmerman, N. (2019). *Working with dreams*. Routledge. (Original work published 1972).

EPILOGUE, LEADERSHIP, PSYCHOANALYSIS, AND SOCIETY

Michael Maccoby and Mauricio Cortina

Now that the dynamics of leader-follower relationships and the personality of leaders have been addressed, two critical questions need to be answered. The first, how can we keep toxic leaders from gaining power? The second, how can we develop effective and, in Jon Stokes' term, inspiring leaders who promote progressive human development rather than division, oppression, and regression?

Recognizing toxic narcissists before they gain power can be difficult. Some of them, like Napoleon Bonaparte, start out as innovators and liberators and only become toxic later. In contrast, some narcissists, like Steve Jobs, start out as exploitative and abusive, but learn to partner with others and accept coaching.

The men who designed the American Constitution believed, like Alexander Hamilton, that "it is not safe to trust to the virtue of any people." Hamilton added, "we must take man as we find him" (Ricks, 2020, p. 206). This includes potentialities for virtue, but also for all the deadly sins. Hamilton and James Madison, writing in *The Federalist Papers* argued that while people might follow a toxic leader, protections were needed to limit their power.

They and the other founders designed a constitution with built-in protections against a leader who threatened individual liberty. These protections—the separation of powers, the law-making Congress, and Courts—limiting presidential authority, were tested when Donald Trump tried to annul the election that ended his presidency and was stopped by the courts.

But as Mauricio Cortina writes, although creating and expanding democratic institutions has been a major accomplishment, there is no guarantee they will survive. Right wing, illiberal, authoritarian leaders have gained the support of millions throughout the world. Democratic institutions are based not only on structures but also intangibles, involving internalized social norms, what Alexis de Tocqueville termed "habits of the heart."

The human vulnerability to toxic leaders calls for structural safeguards against them, not only in government but also in organizations. There are few business leaders who create a culture of respect, much less caring. Progressive labor unions protect workers' rights to fair compensation, due process and voice, but they have been losing power.

There is another human vulnerability that creates fertile ground for toxic leaders to emerge. The great fourteenth-century Muslim historian Ibn Khaldun (1958) studied rich agricultural societies on the northern coast of Africa. He documented case after case in which the leaders and elites of these rich societies exploited the lower classes. Despite having much larger armies and fortified cities, these rich societies, lacking social solidarity, became vulnerable to a successful invasion by the fierce and highly cohesive nomadic tribes of the desert.

Something like this could happen to us. Social inequalities created by economic policies have increased the gap between the rich and super rich and everybody else (Pikkety, 2020), and struggles over power and ideology have made politics a zero-sum game pitting political parties and their followers against each other. Toxic leaders provoke these tribal animosities and cripple the ability of society to address urgent existential threats such as pandemics, climate change, racism, and social inequalities. Building social solidarity, cooperation, and trust at all levels of society and between nations are powerful antidotes to avoid becoming vulnerable to toxic leaders. This requires exceptional leadership. Where will it come from?

Jeffrey Pfeffer points out that most executives who rise to the top of organizations are Machiavellian narcissists. As a professor at an elite business school, he is critical of leadership training that doesn't prepare would-be leaders to survive and prosper in organizational jungles. He writes that despite an enormous leadership industry teaching—and preaching—leaders to be modest, authentic, truthful, and to care for others, among other virtues, such behavior is extremely rare. Does this contradict descriptions by Heckscher and Duckles of effective leaders who develop collaboration? The difference is context. These people-oriented leaders don't get promoted to the C-suite. The people who get to the top of companies show extreme confidence, the ability to bluff and deceive in negotiations, and the ability to charm others. Particularly people like themselves. Pfeffer proposes that teaching students when, why, and how such behaviors are effective might help them gain power. While they may help business school students and corporate climbers get ahead, such teaching is not enough to develop the progressive leaders we need. To do so, leadership education should include understanding people, how to develop trust and as Bob Duckles writes, to bring out the best in people. Would-be leaders should learn how to craft a progressive leadership philosophy including purpose, practical values, and methods of measuring results that reinforce positive values.

The country also may benefit from more leaders, like those described by Charles Heckscher, who organized dialogues in local communities where people with different ideologies found common views in addressing divisive but essential issues.

We conclude with an observation by the founder of psychoanalysis. While Freud was skeptical of socialist utopias, he wrote that a civilization that leaves many of its participants dissatisfied "neither has nor deserves the prospect of a lasting existence" (Freud, 1927, p. 12).

Whether our society becomes more equitable and united or whether large numbers of participants feel alienated and dissatisfied will depend on the leaders we develop and follow and their success at building social solidarity at all levels of society.

References

Freud, S. (1927). 'The future of an illusion' in *The standard edition of the complete psychological works of Sigmund Freud, Volume XXI (1927–1931)* (pp. 5–56). The Hogarth Press, 1961.

Khaldun, I. (1958). *The Muqaddimah. An introduction to history*. Translated form the Arabic by Franz Rosenthal. Pantheon Books.

Pikkety, T. (2020). *Capital and ideology*. Harvard University Press.

Ricks, T. E. (2020). *The first principles, what America's founders learned from the Greeks and Romans and how that shaped our country*. Harper Collins.

INDEX